Africa's Development Challenges and the World Bank

Africa's Development Challenges and the World Bank

HARD QUESTIONS, COSTLY CHOICES

edited by
Stephen K. Commins

Lynne Rienner Publishers ◆ Boulder/London

Published in the United States of America in 1988 by
Lynne Rienner Publishers, Inc.
948 North Street, Boulder, Colorado 80302

and in the United Kingdom by
Lynne Rienner Publishers, Inc.
3 Henrietta Street, Covent Garden, London WC2E 8LU

©1988 by Lynne Rienner Publishers, Inc. All rights reserved

Library of Congress Cataloging-in-Publication Data
Africa's development challenges and the World Bank: hard questions, costly choices / Stephen K. Commins, ed.
"Originated at a conference ('Africa's Development Challenge and the World Bank Response') held at UCLA in November 1986 ... co-sponsored and co-funded by the World Bank, UCLA's African Studies Center, and the Center's Development Institute"--Acknowledgments.
Includes bibliographies and index.
ISBN 1-555-87116-X
1. Africa—Economic policy--Congresses. 2. Africa—Economic conditions--1960--Congresses. I. Commins, Stephen K. II. International Bank for Reconstruction and Development. III. University of California, Los Angeles, African Studies Center. IV. University of California, Los Angeles. African Studies Center. Development Institute.
HC800.A5724 1988
338.96--dc19   88-14875
                                                      CIP

British Library Cataloguing in Publication Data
A Cataloguing in Publication record for this book
is available from the British Library

Printed and bound in the United States of America

The paper used in this publication meets
the requirements of the American National
Standard for Permanence of Paper for
Printed Library Materials Z39.48-1984. ∞

Contents

Acknowledgments — vii

Contributors — ix

1 Africa's Development Challenge   *Stephen K. Commins* — 1

Part I THE WORLD BANK IN AFRICA

2 What Can Be Done in Africa? The World Bank's Response
  Edward Jaycox — 19

3 Policy Reforms for Economic Development in Tanzania
  Nguyuru Lipumba — 53

4 Impact of the World Bank-Supported Agricultural Development Project on Rural Women in Zambia
  Monica Munachonga — 73

Part II DONOR POLICY: THE CHALLENGES OF REFORM

5 Issues of Political Economy in Formulating Donor Policy Toward Sub-Saharan Africa   *Robert Christiansen, Cheryl Christensen, and Beatrice Edwards* — 91

6 The Political Basis for Agricultural Policy Reform
  Robert Bates — 115

7 Food Aid and Policy-Based Lending to Africa:
      Dilemmas for States and Donors   *Raymond Hopkins*   133

Part III PROBLEMS OF POLITICAL ECONOMY

8 Political Economy and Policy Reform in Sub-Saharan
      Africa   *Carol Lancaster*   159

9 Bureaucratic Growth and Economic Stagnation in
      Sub-Saharan Africa   *David Abernethy*   179

10 Structural Adjustment in the Longer Run:
      Some Uncomfortable Questions   *Charles Elliott*   215

    Index   235

    About the Book   243

Acknowledgments

This book originated at a conference ("Africa's Development Challenge and the World Bank Response") held at UCLA in November 1986. The conference was co-sponsored and co-funded by the World Bank, UCLA's African Studies Center, and the center's Development Institute. Credit for the success of the conference belongs to many people, especially Jamie Monson and Margaret Ngau, who were the primary administrators for conference logistics and procedures. The strong interest of the World Bank, especially of Dunstan Wai; and the active participation of Edward Jaycox, helped make the conference a unique opportunity for exchange and discussion.

Editing the papers could not have been completed without assistance from Alice Nnaabalalmba and Jean Moncrief at the African Studies Center.

Michael Lofchie, director of the African Studies Center, gave encouragement and support during the editing and revising of this volume.

Contributors

Stephen K. Commins is coordinator of the Development Institute at the UCLA African Studies Center.

David Abernethy is professor of Political Science at Stanford University.
Robert Bates is professor of Political Science at Duke University.
Cheryl Christensen is deputy director of the Resources and Technology Division, Economic Research Service, U.S. Department of Agriculture.
Robert Christiansen is an economist with the Agricultural Trade Analysis Division, Economic Research Service, U.S. Department of Agriculture.
Beatrice Edwards is a senior manpower specialist with the Organization of American States.
Charles Elliot is a fellow at the Overseas Development Institute, London.
Raymond Hopkins is professor of Political Science at Swarthmore College.
Edward Jaycox is vice president for Africa at the World Bank.
Carol Lancaster is professor of Political Science at Georgetown University.
Nguyuru Lipumba is senior lecturer in the Department of Economics at the University of Dar es Salaam.
Monica Munachonga is professor of Social Development Studies at the University of Zambia.

CHAPTER 1

Facing Africa's Development Challenges

Stephen K. Commins

Recitations of Africa's economic woes and political failings have become truisms. The high hopes of independence have been shattered in most sub-Saharan African countries through such painful realities as economic stagnation, political instability, civil strife, famine, and failed development strategies. Recurrent food shortages have underscored the vulnerability of many countries to the threat of famine, and the inability of some states to protect their citizens' lives. Precisely because droughts alone do not create famines, the political and economic weaknesses of African states are underlined by the miseries of the recent famine years.

The abrupt public visibility of the famine years should not obscure the evidence of stagnation or decline that existed prior to the 1984-1985 period. Indeed, a set of new priorities for African development was clearly proclaimed as early as 1981 through the so-called Berg Report (World Bank 1981), the first of four Bank documents that have dealt with the economic malaise afflicting the continent. The Berg Report sharply criticized the policies of the majority of African states as having undermined agricultural production and thus economic growth. Though this document was highly "internalist" in its assessment of the causes of economic stagnation, its interpretations were given powerful impetus by several factors that increased the squeeze on African economies.

The first half of the 1980s saw a persistent series of economic difficulties that affected most African countries. The oil price increases after 1979 were coupled with declining commodity earnings and the tightening of international markets. Per capita food production and overall export crop production stagnated or declined in most countries. The indebtedness of African countries increased steadily into the 1980s, with decreased resources available for the repayment of these debts. High interest rates and the strength of the dollar (through 1986) added to the difficulties facing small and relatively weak economies. These difficulties, along with other shifts, led the World Bank and the International Monetary Fund (IMF) to prescribe policies aimed first at fiscal stabilization (IMF) and then economic structural adjustment (World Bank).

By 1986 the focus on internal African government policies as primarily responsible for the continent's decline, which had been at least implicitly rejected by African heads of state (Organization of Africa Unity [OAU] Lagos Plan), was openly accepted by a number of African leaders at the UN Special Session on Africa. However, the willingness of African states to swallow stabilization and structural adjustment policies has never been simple in practice. The ongoing negotiations and shifts in agreements between such countries as Tanzania, Nigeria, and Zambia with the Fund or Bank are indicative of the conflict engendered domestically by abrupt fiscal and monetary changes, or the broader implications of structural adjustment packages.

New interpretations of development, economic growth, and the role of African states helped to provide the impetus for significant changes in development strategies and national economic policies. What has occurred in part is a major shift in the perception of the role of the state in national economies. Earlier policies by African governments were often based on the presupposition that state intervention in the economy through such avenues as pricing policies, marketing boards, and state ownership of certain industries was necessary because of inherent problems of market failues (e.g., social problems of capitalism, inequality, poverty, exploitation, etc.). Economic power had already accrued during the colonial period to marketing boards, licensing agencies, and other state bodies. Newly independent leaders saw that state as the one instrument capable of achieving national development strategies, overcoming the divisions with newly formed states, and providing an alternative to the existing colonially imposed economic linkages within and between states.

Since the late 1970s, the emphasis on the accepted central economic role of the state has been fundamentally challenged. Indeed there is a significant new emphasis on state failures and the potential role of markets in alleviating economic obstacles and creating new impetus for growth (*IDS Bulletin* 1987). It is essential to understand, however, that the reforms advocated by the World Bank and bilateral donors through such processes as structural adjustment lending are not simplistic cries of "free the market." As will be seen in the chapter by Edward Jaycox, the Bank does advocate a significant role for the

African state. What has changed fundamentally is that it is to be different from roles that were accepted in the past two decades. The various strategies for African development do not question the involvement of the state. The capacity of the state for accomplishing particular tasks and its efficiency in its work is as important as the size of the job.

As one observer has noted recently:

> Public sectors are incapable of maintaining most of the conditions which foster economic growth; they are overwhelmed by their own incoherence, indiscipline and shrinking fiscal base. (Sandbrook 1985, p.38)

This book will explore certain aspects of Africa's development problems and the various approaches suggested by the World Bank and other donors. The role of the state in economic development and the political nature of state decisionmaking will be featured in the discussions that follow. The advice given by donors contains complex messages that require African governments to strengthen the capacity of states to accomplish certain goals, even as they reduce the role of the state in direct market-related activities. The restructuring of states cannot be done in a theoretical policy vacuum. Political and economic relations shape state relations and will continue to affect how states design and implement economic policies. The particular configurations of economic and political realities that result in policies cannot be isolated from the choices made by donors. The essays in this book center on the dilemmas facing donors in their relation to African states, and the constraints facing African states as they examine their economic problems.

In the recent attempts to address economic stagnation in a large number of African countries, the World Bank has been a leading actor in determining the nature and form of structural adjustment. The role of the IMF in short-term stabilization lending, and the impact of bilateral donors, are also essential parts of the present policy landscape in sub-Saharan Africa. This book is built around three essays on the World Bank that offer diverse perspectives on the role and impact of Bank policies. The centrality of the Bank is that it is the most visible of the donor agencies operating in sub-Saharan Africa, and it is often required to coordinate donor policies for longer-term adjustment decisions in relations between African states and donors. The discussion therefore begins with the Bank's view, and is followed by two African perspectives, one looking at the Bank and an African state on the national level, the other looking at the Bank as its development policies are implemented at the community level.

The second and third parts of the book build upon the initial difficulties described in this introductory chapter and in Part 1. The chapters in Part 2 move beyond the focus on the World Bank to look at some of the challenges facing donors in general. The discussions in Part 3 move further into overall questions of politics and economics by attempting to picture the existing state and political relations in Africa and how they have evolved. In many of the chapters, an emphasis on agriculture or agricultural policy will be apparent. Although agricultural policies are only one part of the policy framework, they form a fundamental foundation for economic choices facing African states. As one observer has commented, the

> economic crisis is fed by and feeds on a political crisis in the developmental role of the African state . . . [the] inherent political nature of policy making and delivery, the fact that policies are shaped by flows of power and clashes of interest within the state itself and in society at large. (White 1986)

Policies cannot be created and delivered in a political or historical vacuum. The political and organizational factors that shape the capacity of states to implement development goals or policy reforms are issues for both African states and for donors. How these factors are addressed will be as important as the decisions about specific policy changes. The economic difficulties hampering African economies are rooted in a variety of causes that are closely linked to the political and economic structures within and encompassing African countries today.

AFRICA'S DEVELOPMENT CHALLENGES

The rethinking of economic strategies has occurred because previous development approaches have lost their intellectual appeal or have been seen as practical failures. The decay of many African economies can be seen in deteriorating infrastructures, increasing debt burdens, stagnating agricultural production, and worsening external trade balances. In addition, the accepted mechanisms for delivering assistance through bilateral and multilateral aid programs have been increasingly questioned. Growing disillusionment with present development strategies makes it important to briefly consider some aspects of the problems of the past two decades.

Underlying the surface image of famine are a number of deeply rooted food and cash crop production problems that have thwarted the development hopes of many African states. These problems are especially apparent in the food production sector, where a majority of

African countries have seen per capita food production stagnate or drop over the past fifteen years. The agricultural problems that have become increasingly visible in the mid-1980s were already apparent at the beginning of the decade (USDA 1981; World Bank 1981; Lofchie and Commins 1982). The apparent decline of the agricultural sector was one of the first warnings taken up by donor agencies.

Even before the sudden visibility of the "crisis" of the early 1980s, many African economies were in a precarious situation. General decline or stagnation in per capita food production meant an increasing dependence on external food sources, either through purchased food imports or food aid from the United States and countries of the European Economic Community (EEC). During the 1970s this rising dependence upon external food supplies moved African countries to launch numerous food self-sufficiency efforts. These efforts were generally stymied by overall economic weaknesses, poor government policies, political instability, external economic constraints, and ineffective aid programs. The agrarian and food crises of the 1980s are the most visible and painful results of long-term difficulties, rather than the sudden failure of the continent's agricultural sector.

A number of factors contributed to the stagnation or decline of national economies. The global recession following 1979 meant that both demand and prices for raw commodities declined over the next few years (USDA 1984; World Bank 1984). High interest rates in the 1980s exacerbated indebtedness, as did the strength of the dollar (into 1986), which also increased the relative cost of oil. Rising import costs for fuel and fertilizers also pushed up the costs of agricultural production and reduced the amounts of inputs available to commercial farmers. Whatever their internal market structures or prevailing ideology, African states have, with few exceptions, been unable to improve their countries' food security or economic prognosis in the 1980s. It is the long-term decline in per capita agricultural and food production, encompassed by an overall international economic recession, that offers both a partial foundation for national economic crises as well as a symptom of more general national and international political-economic failures.

A widespread reliance upon two or three primary commodities for export earnings has meant that African economies are especially vulnerable to instability in world commodity markets. Despite periods of good return for individual commodities, the fluctuations in prices has made those commodities unstable as consistent revenue producers for national economies. During much of the 1960s, a period of expansion and growth for industrial countries, commodity prices tended to be high in comparison to manufactured goods. The 1970s were a more disruptive and uneven period, as recession in the mid-1970s among the industrial states cut markets and prices for many commodities.

Since 1979, most African countries have experienced declining revenues and worsening terms of trade. The second oil price hikes of 1979 hit African countries harder over the long term, than had the price hikes of 1973. Squeezed by declining or uneven earnings and by the cost of imports, African states found themselves increasingly unable to service their debts in the early 1980s. Total indebtedness and the size of national debts when compared to economic resources are two more indications of the malaise affecting the region. Countries as diverse as Zambia, Zaire, Ghana, Tanzania, and Liberia were all forced to accept IMF-structured conditionality programs in return for loans from the IMF, World Bank, and Western governments. These countries often lacked the internal economic resources to quickly recover from their debt burdens. They were also hampered by their inability to invest adequately in the reconstruction of their economies.

Another troubling question facing both African states and donor agencies is the role of foreign aid. For many countries, neither agricultural development in particular nor overall national development growth in general appeared to have benefited from aid at expected levels of return. The debt squeeze meant that future assistance in forms of loans could worsen national economic stability. Critical attention to the role of states as developmental actors and to the potential for aid reform has become a fundamental part of policy reforms.

African governments often accepted aid both as a means of building national economies and as a tool for securing power for the states and the primary distributor of resources. African states were generally uncritical recipients of aid flows because the funds and projects enhanced the power of state agencies. Both bilateral and multilateral donors worked through state organizations, whatever their ideological preferences. This has meant that criticism of assistance programs was generally directed at individual failures, rather than at the system as a whole. The shift from a project to a program or policy reform emphasis is thus a radical change in the way that aid has been understood. Project aid continues, but the broader framework of policy reform has become central for the donors.

Part of the reason for the shift can be seen in the criticism directed against many African states for their policies that apparently undercut domestic food production. Critics of African governments have argued that their development priorities were skewed against efficient agricultural growth, through offering low prices to farmers and overvaluing exchange rates that hurt cash crop exporters. Furthermore, national fiscal policies and many marketing operations were seen as being counterproductive to agricultural growth. This has been especially noted for pricing and marketing policies (World Bank 1981; DeWilde 1984). The seemingly irrational nature of such agricultural policies can only make sense when, in Charles Elliott's terms (Chapter 10), the inherent "disequilibrium" of African economies is the result of political forces seeking balance.

The preceding discussion makes clear the reasons for disillusionment with the role of African states. Shifting state responsibilities through strengthening yet limiting states is a difficult challenge. The interwoven relationship between African political forces, the nature of African states, and economic stagnation make the task facing the World Bank and other donors that much more daunting. In looking at the Bank's policy reform emphasis, it is important to understand how the Bank's own perspective has continued to change as the development challenges in Africa keep unfolding.

THE WORLD BANK AND AFRICAN DEVELOPMENT

During the 1970s, the World Bank placed a major emphasis on development strategies that were designed to reach the "poorest of the poor." The Bank was harshly criticized by those on the Left who believed that the Bank was in fact attempting to capture peasant producers for international capital. The Bank was criticized from the Right by those who believed that the Bank had gone "soft" and was entering into realms outside its competence.

When the Bank shifted its focus in the early 1980s, however, it did so for two pressing reasons. One was that the world recession of 1979-1982 and the growing debt crisis in Latin America and Africa convinced the Bank that there was a dire need for better policies. The other reason was that the new orthodoxy in the West by 1981 was focused predominantly on reducing the role of the state and freeing up market mechanisms. Furthermore, the Bank was painfully aware, from its experiences of the 1970s, that many projects were wasted because of inappropriate national policies.

The emphasis of the first Bank report in 1981 (*Accelerated Development in Sub-Saharan Africa*) was both internal to African domestic policies and also heavily focused on agricultural development. The 1981 report noted that Africa's economic crisis was especially visible in the agricultural sector of most countries. Both the export production sector and food crop sector were stagnant or declining in a majority of countries. Despite obvious data problems on agricultural production reports from many sub-Saharan African countries, the general consensus by the beginning of the decade was that African agricultural production was, in general, disappointing.

The lack of growth in the agricultural sector was leading to broader economic problems. Increasing numbers of short-term balance of payments crises threatened the economic stability of African states. The Bank report argued that greater emphasis must be placed on production growth and market efficiency. Since the majority of most African countries' work forces still worked in agriculture, this sector had to be a foundation of renewed growth in the 1980s. Reforms were needed to improve market efficiency and price incentives in such areas as exchange rates, trade policies, and the allocation and utilization of resources overall in the public sector.

This report targeted agriculture as an important area for donor support in the years ahead and emphasized "smallholder" agriculture as the key for sustained development. The report did not in fact break from the poverty emphasis of the 1970s. Instead, it placed the focus on smallholder agriculture within the framework of what it deemed absolutely essential policy reforms. The smallholder framework included a number of priorities that were external to the farm site, such as better prices for small farmers, more competitive marketing systems, and greater access to farm inputs.

The authors noted that "policy related factors receive priority in this Report, because—for many of the countries involved—the prospects for more rapid and sustained economic growth are slight without appropriate adjustments" (World Bank 1981).

The so-called Berg report (after its primary author) generated great heat (and some light) over its analysis and recommendations. Some of the harshest criticisms focused on its "internalist" emphasis. That is, the burden of reform and change was laid upon African states and their policies, not upon international economic relations or donor policies. Critics pointed to a host of external factors—recession, U.S. inflation, oil prices, aid priorities—as being equally or more important in undermining African economies. They further noted that the Bank seemed to be moving away from a poverty focus towards a reliance on market mechanisms alone.

For a variety of reasons, the next three Bank reports on Africa (*Sub-Saharan Africa: Progress Report on Development Prospects and Programs,* 1983; *Towards Sustained Development in Sub-Saharan Africa,* 1984; *Financing Adjustment with Growth in Sub-Saharan Africa,* 1986) moved towards a more "balanced" view of the origins and solutions to Africa's economic difficulties. These reports took more account of the external factors that had a negative impact on African economies. The 1983 report noted that the weaknesses of African economies were exacerbated due to "deteriorating global trading and financial circumstances." In 1984 the Bank noted that the reforms being undertaken by African states could not succeed without greater assistance from donors. The report commented that "reform is critical but cannot be effective without external assistance." The most recent major report, in 1986, argued that African governments were in many cases making major structural reforms. The problem now was as much the lack of adequate donor support as internal policies. The Bank argued strongly that without increased financial resources from donors, structural reforms could not lead to sustained economic growth.

From these four reports it can be seen that the Bank took an increasingly broad perspective on the framework for internal policy change in sub-Saharan Africa. As many African states wrestled with the problems of achieving structural adjustment, the Bank and other observers were aware of the inadequate resource flow from donor agencies, as well as the continuing poor conditions of the world economy for many African economies. This left a number of African states in a more precarious position than before undertaking reforms. Because of the political risk involved in attempting major policy reforms, the Bank recognized the need for cushions through financial flows from donors.

The Bank's position on structural adjustment and the need for external financial support from donors to support such reforms, leads to two major areas for exploration: the nature of donor policy and the ability of African states to implement reforms. The essays in this book attempt to assess both the choices facing donors and the political structures and relations within African states that shape the setting for economic change.

ASKING HARD QUESTIONS

This book addresses the question of the World Bank and Africa's development challenge through an expanding perspective, beginning with the perspectives of the World Bank, as presented by Edward Jaycox. Part 1 offers an analysis from a representative of the Bank and two African country studies. Part 2 expands the focus of the study beyond the role of the Bank itself to donor policies. Part 3 presents larger questions of political and economic relations within which the

Bank and other donor organizations must act. It also raises larger issues regarding the nature of African states and the ways in which policy reforms are likely to take actual form.

The chapters that make up this book offer a focus that tends to place agricultural policies at the center of the analysis. There are clearly many other essential questions facing African states and donors that are outside the agricultural sector. Nevertheless, the core of donor policies and state reforms in relation to agriculture are paramount to the extent that agriculture provides the basis for food security, for essential exports, and for the ability of countries to generate the surplus for industrial development.

The first chapter in Part 1, by Jaycox, provides a succinct introduction to the analysis of the World Bank in relation to Africa's development problems. Jaycox notes that because of the deterioration of living standards and declining per capita food production, sub-Saharan Africa has become a priority region for the World Bank. Policy-based lending has emerged for the Bank as a critical tool for reshaping the context within which economic growth can take place. The Bank, according to Jaycox, is in the business of development, and its priorities for African countries are designed to make sustained development possible. This chapter makes it apparent that external shocks are partly responsible for present economic difficulties, but it focuses on the potential for reform of domestic policy deficiencies. The inherent argument here is that African states can protect their economies somewhat from external shocks with more appropriate policies. Jaycox's focus on policy reforms does not negate the Bank's concern with poverty, as he points out the need for growth to be linked with the alleviation of poverty.

The essays by Nguyuru Lipumba and Monica Munachonga approach the issue of the World Bank's policies from quite different perspectives. Lipumba offers a reflection on Tanzania's experience of policy reforms in relation to its national economy. After presenting a perspective on IMF and World Bank adjustment and stabilization policies, he points out some of the difficulties involved in determining appropriate goals for particular countries and the complications of negotiations and implementation. The struggle over an agreement between donors and Tanzania is illustrative of the hard choices faced by the Tanzanian state and the costs borne through adjustment decisions. The political and economic arrangements that helped to contribute to Tanzania's economic problems also present obstacles to effective policy reforms.

Even as the priorities for donors have shifted away from project lending towards policy reforms, a significant percentage of development assistance is still funneled through large projects. Given the impact of these projects on local communities, and the emphasis in the last decade on project reform, it is valuable to consider the difficulties faced by states and donors in implementing new project emphases. Munachonga's essay provides a critique of a World Bank-funded agricultural development project in Zambia. She points out that despite new rhetoric for participation and women's involvement in project benefits, the results did not achieve what might have been expected. Munachonga's essay is an important part of the book, as it is a reminder of the particular obstacles facing donors in achieving sustained agricultural growth at the village level. It also points out the continued gap between the reform of goals and the reform of practice, whether for project- or policy-based lending.

The chapters by Lipumba and Munachonga represent two different foci, yet both point out the need to carefully rethink donor policies. Part 2 begins with a chapter that attempts to provide this perspective on policy options. The authors of "Issues of Political Economy" offer a wide-ranging discussion of issues facing donors. (This chapter is in some ways parallel to the first chapters of Parts 1 and 3. Jaycox presents the Bank's overview of the problems in Africa—while Chapter 5 looks at the setting facing donors in general—and Carol Lancaster begins Part 3 by providing an introduction to the political-economic questions that are being debated about development and about the nature of African states.)

In "Issues of Political Economy," the difficulties facing donors seeking to support policy reforms are described, with some suggested options indicated. The authors note that donors face a number of complications that call for less than perfect solutions. Beginning by explaining the peculiar factors that affect African states and the politics of decisionmaking, they note the need to realign existing political relations and interests within African countries (see Nelson 1986). The authors offer a number of suggestions for adjusting various donor policies in order to improve donor efficiency in agricultural programs. Such changes are important in terms of enhancing the success of structural adjustment. It is also noted that even though an export-oriented strategy has serious problems, there are no easily available alternatives. The chapter finally provides a reminder that short-term agricultural growth can lead to other problems, such as land tenure shifts and the commercialization of agriculture. These are structural problems that will continue to bedevil policy choices.

Robert Bates in Chapter 6 presents an analysis of why African states choose particular agricultural policies. His discussion on "political origins" of economic failures points out policies that are often seen as harmful to sustained economic growth. He argues that the nature of African states and the composition of African elites makes reform of policies difficult. It is much easier to identify the necessary policy reforms than to implement them. In offering suggestions for specific policy changes, Bates moves beyond an internalist focus to note that there are important contributions that donors can make to help leverage policy reforms. In presenting some specific policy choices for states and donors, Bates links up the factors contributing to existing processes for political decisionmaking with reforms that could shift how initial policy choices are made.

In Chapter 7, Raymond Hopkins picks up one specific donor resource and seeks to show that it can be used as an effective mechanism for encouraging or strengthening policy reforms. Food aid has become a highly contentious issue in development debates. Its critics are well armed with arguments that food aid is a disincentive for peasant producers and for governments alike. The surplus, donor-driven nature of food aid makes it more a tool of disposal than development. Hopkins does not deny the potentially negative impact of food aid, but he argues that food aid can still be utilized effectively as targeted support for policy reforms. He sees food aid as providing a potential cushion for adjustment programs. It would be useful for ameliorating the impact of structural adjustment on vulnerable groups in different African countries. Hopkins presents some of the potential weaknesses in utilizing food aid, and then offers some ways for using it more effectively within adjustment strategies.

In introducing some of the issues faced in Part 3, Lancaster in Chapter 8 takes the discussion about Africa's development problems into a broader theoretical framework. She provides a survey of major approaches to development policies over the past twenty-five years and looks at what policy reformers can learn from political economists about the workings of African governments and institutions. She notes that there are important implications in the work of political economists, such as the problems of implementation and sustainability of policy reforms, and the particular role of foreign donors.

African states have been understood and interpreted in different ways, depending upon the viewpoint of the analysis. Modernization and dependency theories implied either autonomous or subservient states. Lancaster points out that recent studies of African states seek to understand a more complex dynamic of domestic pressures, foreign interests, and the interests of elite groups. All of these factors point to the question of how particular combinations impact policy decisions. In turn, she notes, the experiences of policy reformers need to be understood and incorporated by political economists.

David Abernethy in Chapter 9 takes up one aspect of African states, the internal logic of bureaucratic growth and change. He points out that a critical review of the effect of public sectors on national economies should include the patterns of expenditure as well as specific policies. In reviewing the seemingly inexorable nature of state expansion, Abernethy presents a number of factors that contribute to bureaucratic growth: state structures and administrative patterns from the colonial era; African nationalist antipathy to markets; demands for jobs in the public sector; and the economic imperatives to grow quickly after independence.

Abernethy argues that ideological preferences have been marginal in the expansion of African states. If one looks at parastatals in such countries as Ivory Coast, Malawi, and Kenya, it is clear that "market-" oriented states have also taken on major economic roles. Abernethy's conclusions are pointedly tough for those seeking to reduce the role of states with a concomitant shift to the private sector. The reduction of state expenditures will not be easy. More important, Abernethy argues that shifting resources to the private sector will not gurantee growth and efficiency.

Many of the arguments in this book note the difficulty facing both donors and governments in making fundamental shifts in economic policies. Charles Elliott in the final chapter provides a valuable conclusion to the issues raised in the preceding essays. Elliott argues that the historical factors that have shaped African states account for a particular "disequilibrium" that becomes an accepted norm. These disequilibria may be irrational from an economic point of view, but they are rational in terms of the survival of political leadership. What this means is that adjustment of economic variables to eliminate disequilibria is often unrealistic.

Elliott's chapter brings the reader back to the basic questions that underlie the book's major themes. The complex dynamics that have shaped and continue to shape African state policies need to be better understood in the planning of policy reforms. Otherwise, these reforms may create short-term adjustments without affecting political structures or internal economic relations. Elliott offers a warning that there are no quick or easy fixes to Africa's economic dilemmas.

This book has as its subtitle "Hard Questions, Costly Choices" because I believe that any simple "consensus" on Africa's development problems is likely to be both damaging and misleading. The past three decades of development and economic policies in Africa are more than series of failures or peculiar experiments: they are the stories of millions of aspirations for material improvement and securing of basic needs. All too often, in many African countries, misery or disillusionment have replaced the promises of independence or liberation.

The essays in this book cannot provide silver bullets or magical elixirs for the hard choices facing policymakers. They do offer both short-term suggestions and longer-term questions that need to be seriously considered. Again, the failures that underline such a dramatic "event" as the famines of 1984-1985 (and beyond) are written not merely in abstract numbers, but in the cost of broken hopes and shattered lives.

In his September 1987 address to the Board of Governors of the World Bank, Barber Conable stated:

> In Sub-Saharan Africa our goals are to help meet the current crisis by organizing major programs in the severely debt-distressed countries, to see the productive capacity of African economies rebuilt, and to help ensure that the welfare and food security of Africa's millions of poor people are protected in the process of adjustment and recovery.

The stated good intentions of the World Bank, Western donors, and African states remain to be tested in the rough waters of policy choices and constantly shifting political-economic relations that are explored in this book.

REFERENCES

Colclough, Christopher. 1985. "Competing Paradigms—and Lack of Evidence—in the Analysis of African Development." In Tore Rose, ed., *Crisis and Recovery in Sub-Saharan Africa.* Paris: OECD.

DeWilde, John. 1984. *Agriculture Marketing and Pricing in Sub-Saharan Africa.* Los Angeles: African Studies Center.

Gephart, Martha. "African States and Agriculture: Issues for Research." *IDS Bulletin* 17 No. 1.

Green, Reginald. 1986. "Sub-Saharan Africa: Poverty of Development, Development of Poverty." IDS Discussion Paper, 218.

Harris, Lawrence. 1986. "Conceptions of the IMF's Role in Africa." In Peter Lawrence, ed., *World Recession and the Food Crisis in Africa.* London: James Currey.

IDS Bulletin. 1987. "Retreat of the State?" Vol. 18, No. 3.

Lofchie, Michael and Stephen Commins. 1982. "Food Deficits and Agricultural Policies in Tropical Africa." *Journal of Modern African Studies* Vol. 20, No. 1.

Nelson, Joan. 1986. "The Diplomacy of Policy-Based Lending." In Richard Feinberg, ed., *Between Two Worlds: The World Bank's Next Decade.* Washington: Overseas Development Council.

Sandbrook, Richard. 1985. *The Politics of Africa's Economic Stagnation.* London: Cambridge University Press.

United States Department of Agriculture. 1981. *Food Prospects and Problems in Sub-Saharan Africa.* Washington: USDA.

———. 1984. *Sub-Saharan Africa: Outlook and Report.* Washington: Economic Research Service, USDA.

White, Gordon. 1986. "Developmental States and African Agriculture." *IDS Bulletin* 17 (No. 1).

World Bank. 1981. *Accelerated Development in Sub-Saharan Africa: An Agenda for Action.* Washington, D.C.: World Bank.

———. 1983. *Sub-Saharan Africa: Progress Report on Development Prospects and Programs.* Washington, D.C.: World Bank.

———. 1984. *Toward Sustained Development in Sub-Saharan Africa: A Joint Program of Action.* Washington, D.C.: World Bank.

———. 1986. *Financing Adjustment with Growth in Sub-Saharan Africa, 1986-90.* Washington, D.C.: World Bank.

PART I

The World Bank in Africa

CHAPTER 2

What Can be Done in Africa? The World Bank's Response

Edward Jaycox

Since its creation four decades ago, the World Bank has become the leading international development institution both in volume of lending and range of activities. The Bank's rise in stature has, however, sometimes led to misunderstanding and confusion about the power and influence it has acquired among its member countries, and worldwide. It is therefore important that we understand the main purposes for which the Bank was created before we assess its response to the development challenge in sub-Saharan Africa.

The World Bank was established for several purposes. The three main ones stated in the Articles of Agreement establishing the Bank are the reconstruction and development of the territories of member governments, the promotion of foreign investment and the promotion of the long-range balanced growth of international trade. In order to carry out these objectives the Bank has the following primary functions. First, the Bank raises money. The money the Bank lends comes from paid-in capital, retained earnings, and borrowing, which is by far the largest source. The Bank borrows through tapping the bond markets, and through special placements with Central Banks and governments. Second, the Bank lends money to developing countries following a careful process of analysis and dialogue, fitting each operation to the specific needs and potentials of the recipient. Third, the Bank provides advice on aspects of development. Fourth, the Bank carries out research on important issues such as debt and capital flows, pricing policies and trade liberalization. Fifth, it serves as a catalyst to stimulate financial flows from other sources.

These five activities of the World Bank are mutually reinforcing. The Bank has become a proficient development institution by being actively engaged in conceiving and financing development projects, analyzing constraints and opportunities, and advising about development policies. The advice of the Bank is sought because of its wide experience, and its advice is taken seriously because it is prepared to put money behind it. The Bank's catalytic role is made possible by its own lending and its experience with the practicalities of project financing and broader development issues. Its ability to raise money on favorable terms results from its excellent lending record, its substantial reserves, the quality of its pledged non-paid capital, and its impeccable record of collection. The Bank has never had a default on any of its loans. Moreover, the vast majority of projects it has financed have achieved their major objectives.

The Bank's main goal as a development institution is to assist a country both to accelerate its economic growth and reduce domestic poverty by increasing the productivity of the poor.[1] It is this important role of the Bank that led to its partnership in the development effort in sub-Saharan Africa. The Bank has been participating in the design and financing of projects, particularly in agriculture, transport, industry, urban development, power, and education. It has also offered economic advice to its member countries in Africa. In short, the Bank has been a party to the struggle against poverty in the region. In recent years, however, there has been a broad recognition, by the Bank—as well as by everyone else involved in development—that the magnitude of the problems facing Africa is greater than was anticipated. Consequently, the Bank has now made Africa its priority region and has readjusted its approach to meet the African challenge. But what is the nature of this development challenge in sub-Saharan Africa?

THE SUB-SAHARAN AFRICA DEVELOPMENT CHALLENGE

First, we must note the circumstances in Africa to which the World Bank is responding. By and large, it is now agreed that the results of the first twenty-five years of independence in sub-Saharan Africa have belied the optimism of the decolonization period and of the early years of independence. Of all the developing regions of the world, sub-Saharan Africa today faces the most serious development crisis.[2] The devastating drought of 1983-1984 brought Africa to everyone's attention. But for those in the development field, the unfolding tragedy is not of recent origin. Its causes are more deep-seated, structural, and have little to do with fluctuations in climate. Sub-Saharan Africa has the largest concentration of very low per capita incomes, Africa has grown more slowly than any region for nearly a quarter century. In fact, in the last decade, per capita income declined so much that it is now below its 1970 level. Moreover, we face the prospect that Africa will continue to experience a generation of declining per capita income.

Over the past two decades, Africa's food situation has deteriorated rapidly. The decline in per capita food production accelerated from 1 percent per annum in the 1960s to 2 percent in the 1970s. As a consequence, food imports have risen from an annual level of 4 million tons to 24 million tons. And yet, 60 percent of Africa's population is chronically malnourished. The decline in production, however, is not confined to agriculture. Mining output in 1982 was 68 percent of its 1979 level; in many countries industries are operating at 20-40 percent of capacity largely because of the extreme scarcity of imported parts and components.

The lack of real output growth has resulted in a steady decline in living standards. Per capita consumption is lower today than it was in 1970. Africa's endemic poverty is also evident in high infant mortality rates, low life expectancy and widespread disease. For example, half of all the rural children in Gambia die by age five; life expectancy is forty-nine years compared with seventy-five in the industrial countries. Less than 25 percent of the population in Africa has access to safe drinking water; and let us not forget that most diseases are waterborne.

Africa has been particularly hard hit by a series of devastating shocks. In addition to wars and two prolonged periods of drought, Africa has experienced, over the past decade, a fivefold increase in the price of grain, a sevenfold increase in the price of oil, inflation and recession in the industrial countries, high and volatile interest and exchange rates, and an unprecedented collapse in commodity prices.

It is true that these adverse events have confronted all developing countries; but the capacity to adjust has not been uniform. In general, those countries in Asia that have more flexible production structures and a longer experience with sound economic management have weathered these difficulties better than others. In the case of Africa, these shocks confronted economies with rigid production structures, an inadequate base of technical and managerial skills, a low margin of maneuverability and limited creditworthiness for commercial borrowing. These economies also suffered from weak institutions, overblown bureaucracies, and governments' commitments to expenditure programs that could no longer be supported. Many governments resorted to deficit financing, which fueled inflation and created further hardships. They often borrowed from overseas to maintain consumption; consequently many countries today are saddled with unserviceable debt burdens.

There is a growing realization that domestic policy deficiencies have also been key factors in Africa's slow growth. In general, inadequate attention has been paid to the efficiency of resource use. Policies have not provided producers with incentives for efficiency; they have eroded incentives for agriculture; they have encouraged inefficient and import-dependent industry; they have made exporting much less profitable than producing for the protected domestic market; they have allowed public enterprises to grow regardless of their ability to manage effectively or make good use of scarce resources; and public expenditure programs have been allowed to grow too large and investments have been poorly screened and monitored. Maintenance has been neglected and there has been a reluctance to stimulate traditional community activities (small farming and trade) and the private sector. But the principal policy failure, and one which has been dramatically illustrated by the drought, was Africa's failure to provide incentives in its agricultural sector.

The explanation for this sobering outlook in Africa lies in the basic constraints to development that the region has been subjected to for many years. First, when sub-Saharan African countries became independent about twenty-five years ago, they had a weak human resource base as a result of the lack of technical, managerial, and entrepreneurial skills. This was due to neglect of education during colonial times and the fact that most executive and technical jobs were held by expatriates at that time. Throughout the region, trade and industry were almost entirely owned and managed by foreigners. Zaire was an extreme example but it gives one a flavor of the situation: at the time of independence, there was not one African doctor, lawyer, or engineer.

Second, political fragility resulting from the newness of independence, diverse cultures and languages, and a lack of national integration has been a drawback to economic development. Besides, institutions inherited from the colonial era have not been restructured to respond to the demands imposed upon them.

Third, most African countries suffer from a heritage of uneven, dualistic development, weak infrastructure, and subsistence agriculture. At the time of independence roads, railroads, ports, and communications systems were scant. There was little in the way of private foreign investment, and no local resources were available for investment. But the other point to emphasize here is that Africa's physical terrain and scattered populations created special problems for developing transportation. Fourteen of the sub-Saharan African countries are landlocked. Transportation for people, goods, industrial and agricultural inputs, and exports require huge investments in road construction with long truck routes and extensive feeder networks.

Fourth, the interaction of climate and geography is such that most African soils are delicate, deficient in organic materials, and only moderately fertile. Only about one-quarter of the region is well-watered; the rest experiences inadequate and erratic rainfall—too little or too much most of the time. Recurrent severe drought is part of this environmental picture. There is growing evidence that African drought and desertification is not caused solely by a failure of nature. Where domestic animals have been allowed to overgraze and marginal land and forest areas have been cleared for subsistence agriculture or to provide fuel, changes in the rate of evaporation and rainfall patterns have been observed. The Worldwatch Institute, among others, argues that the loss of tree cover triggers a cascading decline of biological and economic productivity.[3] For example, as trees disappear firewood becomes scarce, and villagers begin to burn crop residues and cow dung. This in turn reduces soil fertility, leading to yield declines. As soil deteriorates and vegetation diminishes, soil erosion accelerates and runoff increases. Less moisture remains to evaporate, and eventually rainfall begins to decline.

Fifth, and closely related to the ecological dangers, Africa has an extremely rapid population growth, indeed, more than any other region at any time in human history.[4] Population growth accelerated from 2.3 percent per year in 1960 to 3.0 percent today. In 1985, sub-Saharan Africa's population was about 460 million—about twice that of the United States. By the year 2015, about thirty years from now, Africa will face a population of 1.0 billion. The impact of such a rapid population growth on forests, on desertification, on water supply, on urban growth, and on agricultural production will be staggering, as will the impact on poverty. Children under fifteen already constitute almost 50 percent of the total population, placing tremendous pressures on education facilities and future employment creation. This young age structure has a built-in population dynamic, which will mean relatively rapid population growth for years to come.

In the face of these problems, African governments have, by and large, failed to adjust their economies; therefore, they have been overwhelmed by difficulties of halting the decline. The policy failures have been discussed in many analyses—including three World Bank reports on sub-Saharan Africa—and are well recognized. Policy statements by heads of government, particularly at the twenty-first Organization of Africa Unity (OAU) summit (July 1985) indicate that most African governments now attach high priority to undertaking needed structural reform.

Again, this was evidenced in the UN *Program of Action for African Economic Recovery (1980-90)* adopted by the UN special session on Africa in 1986. During that session, African leaders acknowledged that, first and foremost, it was their responsibility to help themselves find the solutions to their problems. This recognition that they were prepared to face the harsh realities inherent in their predicament was heartening. But the pertinent question for this discussion is: what has been the Bank's response to the unfolding situation in sub-Saharan Africa?

THE WORLD BANK'S RESPONSE

The World Bank's partnership in development with sub-Saharan Africa dates back to the early 1960s when the first loan was granted to Ethiopia and the first International Development Association (IDA) credit to the Sudan in 1961. Since then, the World Bank Group, including IDA and IFC, has committed over $21 billion for priority development projects in the region.[5]

Evolution of the Bank's Lending Strategy

Basic infrastructure is the most important area for IDA investment in sub-Saharan Africa. Between 1966-1986, infrastructure accounted for 31 percent of all IDA commitments; 22 percent of these funds were for transport projects. Since sub-Saharan Africa has the least developed transportation system in the Third World, IDA and IBRD have spent more on this sector in Africa than on similar systems in other parts of the world. The second priority sector in Africa has been agriculture and rural development. From 1966-1986, about 28 percent of IDA and IBRD commitments were to this sector. The major objectives are to help develop food crops, to generate significant export earnings from cash crops to pay for needed imports, to create new jobs, and to increase family income. The major focus for IDA and IBRD lending to Africa has been human resource development. The Bank has also undertaken significant lending to other segments of the economy in Africa. These include small-scale enterprises, water supply systems, and urban projects (7 percent), and health care and nutrition projects (1 percent). In addition, the Bank has focused on industrial development through intermediary development finance corporations (10 percent of total lending to Africa) and through IFC joint ventures with the private sector.

Bank loans and IDA credits have had a direct beneficial impact on sub-Saharan Africa economies. The Bank has enabled many recipient countries to build highways and feeder roads, improve and expand their ports, fund their agriculture and rural development, and build secondary schools. The Bank's focus on issues of employment and poverty gained momentum via the financing of integrated rural development projects aimed at reaching the majority of rural people in designated areas; these projects involved the provision of credit, inputs, extension services, and marketing facilities, as well as needed infrastructure (e.g., feeder roads) and essential social services.

While the Bank's partnership with African countries has yielded many successes, it must also be acknowledged that there have been shortcomings and mistakes. This has been recognized by the Bank.

> It may be true that Africa has limited absorptive capacity and that the preconditions for a rapid growth in agriculture are not there. But then that is our challenge. We, I think it is fair to say, among all of our achievements, have failed in Africa, along with everybody else. We have not fully understood the problems. We have not identified the priorities. We have not always designed our projects to fit the agro-climatic conditions of Africa and the social, cultural and political frameworks of African countries. This is evidenced by the percentage of poorly performing projects in the agricultural portfolio and by the fact that we, and everybody else, are still unclear about what can be done in agriculture in Africa. While I don't have the solutions, some of the elements are clear. We need to do very much more to support research. We need to help build up more institutions in the agriculture sector. We need to work very much more at the simple approaches to extension. The designs of agricultural projects in Africa must be made more consistent with the implementation capacity of many of those countries.[6]

This failure of donors—and of African governments—to meet successfully the challenge of the region has led to a proliferation of assessments by the donor community itself as well as by African regional institutions and governments. The Bank has concluded that, in order to stem the decline and bring about a recovery in output growth and living standards in Africa, it has to adopt a more comprehensive approach.[7] Put simply, this approach focuses on policy reform (both on the demand and supply sides) and on critical sectors.

In its response to the daunting development challenge in sub-Saharan Africa, the Bank has diversified its lending instruments through shifts in sectoral allocations and types of projects, intensified its catalytic role in mobilizing resources through increasing cooperation with other donor agencies and with the International Monetary Fund

(IMF); and, most importantly, through a more systematic exchange with governments on policy issues. Of course, in these undertakings the Bank has to capitalize on its past experience (both successes and failures). This flexible and comprehensive approach emerged in 1984 when the Bank outlined a Joint Program of Action for sub-Saharan Africa. This program called for a collaborative effort by African governments and the international community. The essential thrust of the Joint Program is widely shared. The objective was to get Africa back on the growth path, and there are three main elements to the agreed-upon approach:[8]

1. The countries should undertake policy reforms that will provide a framework for sound economic growth—that is, policy reforms that will stress efficiency of investment, greater reliance on market forces, and reductions in the bureaucratic controls that have stifled development.
2. The quality of public and private investment expenditure must be improved in the short term. This will require the rehabilitation and maintenance of infrastructure, services, and enterprises. In the longer term, this will facilitate development in education, training, research, environmental protection and conservation, family planning, and institution building.
3. There is a need to assist governments to increase rapidly their capacity to manage their own economies through developing both human resources and institutions.

The diversified lending instruments that the Bank used in response to the changing needs of borrowers and their adjustment efforts fall under five main categories: specific investment loans; sector operations (sector involvement and maintenance loans, financial intermediary loans, and sector adjustment loans); structural adjustment loans and program loans; technical assistance loans; and emergency reconstruction loans. Sub-Saharan Africa has received loans or credits under all of these categories. A brief discussion of structural adjustment lending as an example of the policy-based operations will indicate the Bank's flexibility in readjusting to changing economic situations in member developing countries.

Policy-Based Lending

To help countries adjust their economies to the changing demands of the early 1980s, the World Bank instituted the structural adjustment loan (SAL). SAL is nonproject lending to support programs of policy and institutional change necessary to modify the structure of an economy so that it can maintain both its growth rate and the viability of its balance of payments in the medium and long term. There are three main distinguishing features of SAL: (1) SALs are used as fundamental instruments for the dialogue between the Bank and member countries on various aspects of development policy and the nature and scope of change to be supported; (2) SALs are expected to provide finance over a number of years in direct support of specific policy reforms; and (3) SALs are meant to quickly disburse foreign exchange to finance imports not linked in advance to specific investment programs.

A SAL program usually involves a reassessment of a country's medium-term investment program to bring it in line with available resources and to emphasize investments that would yield quick results. Among the issues usually addressed are: diversification of exports by means of new incentives, infrastructure, and marketing efforts; reductions in levels of import protection to make domestic industries more internationally competitive; measures to improve the policy formulation and implementation of the government; and issues of domestic resource mobilization, price incentives, or the efficiency of resource use.[9] Structural adjustment lending programs differ from IMF-supported stability programs in type, scope, maturity, and the time frame in which the impact of the adjustment policies take effect. The technique for preparing SAL programs involves prior agreement between the Bank and the government on the objectives to be achieved through steps or measures to be implemented and the criteria for monitoring their success or failure. The Bank's experience so far reveals that the introduction of SALs increased the comprehensiveness, depth, and impact of the Bank's economic policy discussions in most countries.

In Kenya, for example, SAL operations were supported and strengthened by related economic and sector work; they were further supported by project lending to help address the basic constraints of a rapidly increasing population, low levels of education and training, the need for improved production in agriculture, environmental hazards, and the rehabilitation and maintenance of infrastructure.[10] The performance of the SAL program in Kenya, however, has been mixed. Urgent short-term problems, such as foreign exchange shortage in 1982 and drought in 1984, to some extent distracted the government's attention from the long-term issues. The timetable for import liberalization was disrupted by foreign exchange problems. Little was done to promote exports or decelerate population growth. The grain marketing system was not reformed. On the positive side, however, the government did set agricultural and energy prices at broadly appropriate levels, and—with Bank assistance—prepared a public investment program for the first time ever. Under successive IMF programs, the government reduced its budget deficit, raised interest rates, and adjusted the exchange rate. These measures resulted in declining financial imbalances and rates of inflation. Kenya has so far avoided liquidity difficulties. It has successfully completed two standby arrangements in a row and, because of an improved balance of payments situation, it does not require another arrangement at the present time.

Although there were shortcomings in the implementation of SAL II in Kenya, Malawi has successfully implemented structural reforms under three Bank-financed SAL operations (approved respectively in June 1981, December 1983, and December 1985). The implementation of the structural adjustment program in Malawi has been successful in achieving most of its objectives, including: increased smallholder export production following an increase in price incentives; increased industrial production and investment incentives resulting from a program of price decontrols; increased domestic energy production; strengthening of the financial position of key public and private enterprises; and a reduction in the budgetary and balance of payments deficit. Although efforts to improve the control and allocation of public expenditures and to reduce the overall size of government have been slow, significant steps in the right direction have been taken. However, complacency must not be allowed to set in. While the economy has grown well in the last three years, prospects are for continued economic difficulties—hence the need for continued adjustment to balance of payments as well as fiscal and transport constraints.

Fear of the social implications of macroeconomic reforms has often retarded the adjustment process. It is therefore important that more attention should be given to the social implications of adjustment. Besides, structural adjustment should not be viewed as displacing project or sector lending. The SAL should be treated as an important means of assisting a country intellectually and financially in reorienting its development strategies, and as a critically important complement to project and sector lending. Indeed, policy reforms associated with adjustment operations should lead to improvements in the performance of other projects in the portfolio. So far, this has been particularly evident in agriculture. In some countries, exchange rate adjustments have led to improved performance in export-oriented agriculture projects, and domestic pricing and marketing reforms are stimulating crop production and enhancing the efficiency of the sector.

Such linkages between policy adjustment operations and regular projects are being anticipated and exploited to the fullest.

SALs require as a precondition that a short-term financial stabilization program such as those supported by the IMF be in place. While IMF programs focus on demand management and act on such policy instruments as interest rates, taxes, subsidies, exchange rates, and incentives, the SALs focus on medium-term issues of reforms in policies, institutions, procedures, and structure of investment and the efficiency of resource use. The relationship between the two respective programs of the Fund and the Bank is that the Fund cannot be totally indifferent to the medium-term impact of its programs, neither can the Bank overlook the short-term constraints or external resource availability. Hence, collaboration between the Bank and the Fund is essential for achieving broad objectives of adjustment programs.

The collaboration between the IMF and the World Bank on adjustment-related matters has become more structured during the last year. A Structural Adjustment Facility (SAF) was established by the Fund in March 1986 to provide additional balance of payments assistance to those IDA-eligible countries (India and China are excluded) that are pursuing structural adjustment programs. The eligible countries are expected to develop a policy framework indicating their medium-term objectives and the main outlines of the policies to be followed in pursuing these objectives. The relevant feature of this initiative is that these medium-term strategy papers will be developed jointly by the staffs of the Bank and the Fund and be approved by the boards of both institutions. Such medium-term strategy papers have already been prepared for a number of countries.

With these initiatives, the line between the areas of interest of the Bank and the Fund is not as distinct as it used to be. Both institutions try to approach the adjustment process in its entirety, not making a clear distinction between the demand and supply orientation. The staffs of both institutions need to, and do, interact in a substantial manner. This does not mean that agreement on these matters has always been easy. But the opportunity for the policymakers of the countries, the Bank, and the Fund to discuss a medium-term strategy framework provides a unique basis for improved policy designs for structural adjustment.

The other category of quick-disbursing instrument used by the Bank is the sector adjustment loan. Its conditionalities include the same type of reforms as required by SALs except that they are narrowed in scope to the issues of a particular sector. For example, a fertilizer loan would require reforms in the fertilizer subsector such as reductions in subsidies, commercialization of fertilizer retail channels, and improvements in procurement and marketing methods.

The Bank has learned several lessons from its policy-based lending. First, the preparation of these operations requires large amounts of policy-focused economic and sector work, and continuous exchanges with the government concerned from the earliest stages. Such procedures are applied to ensure mutual understanding, prevent false starts, and avoid exaggerated expectations. Second, it is essential to focus on selective and feasible reforms. Third, time needed to effect policy changes, especially institutional reforms, is much longer than often anticipated. It is also preferable to tackle problems before they reach crisis level.

In 1986, the Bank initiated "medium-term economic and financial policy frameworks." The objective of these papers is to strengthen our understanding and analysis of issues related to medium- and long-term economic development in individual countries. These papers describe the nature of problems confronting the country, the government's objectives of macroeconomic and structural adjustment policies to be pursued in the medium term, and the priorities in addressing the problems. The financing requirements and likely sources of financing are also identified. We expect that the medium-term economic and financial policy framework papers will improve the basis on which structural and sector adjustment lending operations are based, and help mobilize additional resources from the international donor community to support the adjustment effort.

The Bank's policy-based lending operations are aimed at creating a policy environment conducive to successful project financing. They are not substitutes for the Bank's traditional project financing. In sub-Saharan Africa, the Bank will continue to support the key sectors as part of its contribution to putting the region back on the growth path. A brief description of the main elements of the approach in a few of these sectors will help clarify the general thrust of the Bank's development strategy in the region.

Raising Agricultural Productivity and Environmental Protection

The World Bank's strategy in sub-Saharan Africa involves a focus on agriculture, not only for project lending, but also for helping governments to reform their policies and institutions that affect farming. The Bank will continue to focus on agriculture[11] because of its central importance, economically and socially, and because of the imminent dangers to the fragile environment inherent in the combination of traditional agriculture and increasing population density. In discussing the Bank's approach to raising agricultural productivity, we must keep in mind a number of points.

First, the weather has adversely affected agriculture in Africa. Average rainfall over the past fifteen years has been substantially lower than the fifteen-year averages in the first seventy years of the century. It is, however, worth noting that droughts and famine are not sudden or natural disasters, nor are they simply caused by lack of rainfall. They are the end result of mistakes and mismanagement by man; for instance, uncontrolled tree cutting and grazing have produced soil erosion on a large scale.

Second, since the 1960s, the share of agriculture in total investment has been less than 10 percent and little has been spent on research and extension. There has been inadequate and insufficient field-oriented research efforts, particularly for food crops other than the major grain crops. (Relatively neglected crops for food crops include pulses, oilseeds, bananas, roots, and tubers.)

Third, agricultural production has been hampered by low producer prices, overvalued exchange rates, taxes on agricultural exports, and inefficient parastatal agencies for the processing and marketing of agricultural products. Thus, food and agricultural policy are the crucial areas of needed policy reform. The World Bank's philosophy is that farmers are rational decisionmakers who, if given adequate opportunity, would increase their returns. The policies affecting agriculture must, therefore, be supportive of that philosophy. Agricultural growth is also hampered by the absence of technological packages adaptable to local resources, setting conditions that limit the use of ox-drawn cultivation equipment, and inadequate or unreliable rainfall.

Fourth, it must be remembered that less than 5 percent of the arable land in sub-Saharan Africa is irrigated. Fertilizer use in the region is the lowest in the developing world; the principal agricultural implement is the short-handle hoe, and the principal source of energy is human muscle. Given this environment, it is hardly surprising that yields on traditional agriculture are very low.

Fifth, an unstable political environment has affected production in a number of sub-Saharan African countries (e.g., Uganda, Ethiopia, Sudan, and Mozambique). Rural-urban migration has not, however, significantly affected agricultural production, at least not in eastern and southern Africa.

It is clear, therefore, that despite the agricultural potential in sub-Saharan Africa, several constraints have limited agricultural development. For example, in the case of Zambia,[12] inadequate planning and lack of a clear agricultural development strategy have led to the creation of many ill-conceived new programs and organizations. The government-controlled monopoly parastatals and cooperatives have had negative margins to cover even purchase costs of crops, let alone recoup their marketing costs. These organizations have thus constituted a permanent drain on their own and on the government's financial resources. Since marketing institutions do not have adequate financial resources, they rely almost exclusively on expensive commercial credit to cover their working capital needs. This situation has inevitably led to late input deliveries, inefficient marketing arrangements, and frequent delays in crop payments. Such conditions, together with cumbersome credit procedures, have discouraged many farmers from starting cash cropping with purchased inputs. Pricing policies in Zambia in the past have also induced inefficient patterns of crop production and resource allocation by subsidizing transport costs and encouraging consumption of imported wheat and rice and the major staple, maize, instead of such traditional food crops as cassava, finger millet, and sorgum. Agricultural productivity, both per unit of labor and of land, is low, partially as a result of inadequate technical packages for smallholders and partially because of managerial and labor constraints. In addition, the sector has been consistently accorded low priority in the allocation of financial resources: capital and recurrent budgets in agriculture between 1970 and 1980 averaged only around 3 percent of total annual government expenditures, and declined by 1.3 percent per annum in real terms. The situation deteriorated still further during 1980-1984.

The Bank's priority in raising agricultural productivity in Zambia is to remove disincentives to production. These include exchange rate adjustment, liberalization of marketing, adjustment of specific export taxes, and the elimination of subsidies (for example, fertilizer and food subsidies). As regards long-term objectives, these would include diffusion of improved technologies where they exist, and their creation through applied research where they do not. They also include measures to arrest resource degradation, through land terracing, agroforestry, and better-balanced use of livestock within the farming system. The Bank also recognizes that institution building forms a key area of agricultural development. The Bank is therefore focusing on building an efficient extension service, commercial credit systems, and input supply through commercial channels. Direct government expenditure should, in the Bank's view, be concentrated in the areas of research, resource conservation, and extension, and should not be used to subsidize credit, production, or marketing.

The World Bank has also been advising sub-Saharan African countries on the importance of agro-industrial linkages, particularly in view of the poor world market prospects in primary commodities. The areas to be developed would include efficient domestic textile industries, leather goods, oilseed processing (soap, oil, animal fodder, etc.), furniture, and simple food processing. But these can be successfully developed only if policy measures are focused on the development of commercial credit facilities, the reduction of regional tariff barriers and administrative controls on foreign capital and ownership, and on measures to encourage the training of skilled manual workers (preferably by private apprentice schemes). Land tenure reforms are being studied in a number of countries with a view to converting traditional tenure systems into long-term leaseholds and ensuring better use of these lands.

With regard to extension, the Bank's experience has been mixed. There have been some very effective commodity-based extension efforts, for example, by the Kenya Tea Development Authority in Kenya. Training and Visit (T&V) extension is showing good results on a pilot scale in Ethiopia, as are ongoing extension projects in Kenya and Zimbabwe. The Bank has found that the success of T&V depends on a research organization that is effective and responsive. There must be an effective chain of authority over extension workers, with regular programs designed for them, sufficient funds to ensure their mobility, and reliable input supply.

The Bank attaches great importance to environmental protection in sub-Saharan Africa. Several borrowers, such as Ethiopia, Sudan, and Uganda, need urgent action to reverse the process of deforestation and soil erosion. In Ethiopia, some 50 million hectares of forest have been lost in the past eighty years, through clearing of agricultural land and cutting of wood for fuel. The Ethiopian landscape today is largely wasteland and open savannah, with only about 3 million hectares of dense forest remaining. In its new forestry project, the Bank is supporting the establishment and upgrading of both large state plantations and small fuelwood plots managed by peasant associations. Equally important, the Ethiopian government has agreed to increase the producer price and liberalize the marketing arrangements for fuelwood, which will improve the incentives for people to grow and manage trees properly.

The importance of agricultural research is closely related to the problem of environmental protection, because ways must be found to intensify production on existing farm land, instead of constantly expanding the area under cultivation. Technologies for arid and semi-arid areas are urgently needed, and a renewed effort will also be made to improve the technical options to farmers. The Bank sponsors and chairs the Consultative Group on International Agricultural Research

(CGIAR), an association of countries and organizations that support a worldwide network of thirteen research centers in developing countries. CGIAR will give greater emphasis to raising the productivity of smallholder agriculture in Africa. Many of the technologies developed at the CGIAR centers are already making their way into farmers' fields. The International Crops Research Institute for the Semi-Arid Tropics (ICRISAT), for example, has been developing new high-yielding grains that can raise the standard of living of millions of people in drought-prone areas. The Bank also has recently sponsored a new initiative on agricultural research—the establishment of the Special Program of African Agricultural Research (SPAAR). The program's objective is to improve the effectiveness of the substantial sums of money being invested by African governments and donor organizations on agricultural research. It will coordinate donors' activities, disseminate information on promising technologies, and help national and regional research programs.

The Bank will provide support to African governments that are prepared to give priority to the agricultural sector by raising incentives, relaxing controls on the sector, and increasing services available to farmers. It is the Bank's view that these changes will show early and positive results.

Promoting Industrialization

At independence, most sub-Saharan African economies were small, highly dependent on mineral or agricultural exports, and had a very small manufacturing sector. Colonial policies had in general discouraged manufacturing. In 1960, manufacturing in sub-Saharan Africa accounted for less than 7 percent of GDP, as compared with 12 percent in low-income economies. Newly independent nations saw industrialization as a means of achieving rapid economic growth and reducing dependence on imported manufactures in exchange for primary exports. This strategy was supported by the perception that industrial production must expand to avoid falling terms of trade for primary exports. Industrialization was also expected to provide productive employment opportunities to the new countries' growing populations. Impatient with the pace of earlier industrial development, which had been largely in foreign private hands, governments tried to speed up the process of industrialization through direct government investment in the sector and through a policy environment geared towards increasing the profitability of industrial investment at the expense of agriculture and mining.

Most of sub-Saharan Africa adopted similar policies to accelerate industrial production, although there were differences in emphasis and timing. Local industries received high levels of protection against competing imports through import tariffs or quantitative restrictions on imports. They were granted duty-free imports of capital equipment, raw materials, and intermediate goods. During the 1970s, as inflation accelerated and the terms of trade for many sub-Saharan African countries deteriorated, the real exchange rate was often allowed to appreciate in an attempt to keep down the price of imported raw materials and other industrial imports. Price controls on agricultural products were adopted to keep the urban cost of living—and hence industrial wages—under control. Interest rates were also kept low (in many cases negative in real terms) to keep down capital costs. The combined effect of government interventions to stimulate industrial growth resulted in a strong bias towards import substitution of consumer goods and discouraged the development of industrial exports. At the macroeconomic level, it also discouraged agricultural output and exports. The distortions in prices provided the wrong signals to producers and permitted profits even in assembly-type industries where, occasionally, the foreign exchange costs of the inputs exceeded the international value of the output. Also, by reducing the cost of capital, the incentive structure favored large-scale, capital-intensive operations. This tendency was reinforced by a relatively high wage structure among urban workers that resulted from their growing political weight. In summary, the incentive systems adopted by most sub-Saharan African countries was conducive to the creation of industries divorced from these countries' comparative advantages and factor endowments, and may have contributed to the deterioration of agricultural output.

The high level of protection given to import-substituting industries, together with price controls on agricultural products and higher-than-average taxation of agriculture resulted in direct and indirect resource transfers from agriculture to industry and reduced production of agricultural raw materials as well as agricultural exports. Lower agricultural production and exports, in turn, limited the growth of rural incomes and hence the demand for manufactured goods (both consumer and capital) outside urban areas. Although there have been some instances of good backward linkages (processing of agricultural goods), the large majority of industrial enterprises have continued to depend heavily on imported inputs.

The strong emphasis on industrialization of the newly independent sub-Saharan African countries was partly in response to the perceived need to reduce their dependence on imported manufactures in exchange for primary products. The import-substitution strategy followed by most sub-Saharan African countries did succeed in reducing their dependency on imported consumer goods, but increased their reliance on imported inputs and spare parts. They did not raise greatly their ability to export the final products. This had a strong negative impact on manufacturing (and GDP) growth when the importation of industrial inputs had to be cut back sharply in most sub-Saharan African countries after the mid-1970s (as a result of the balance of payments crisis precipitated by the oil price increases, declining agricultural exports, increased food imports and the record-high interest rates in the late 1970s and early 1980s). On the other hand, high production costs due to inefficiency and the overvalued exchange rate prevented the development of industrial exports.

The industrialization strategy adopted seemed to be successful during the prosperous 1960s and early 1970s. During the 1960s manufacturing output in sub-Saharan African countries grew faster than other sectors and industry increased its share of GDP from 6.8 percent in 1960 to 8.6 percent in 1970. The underlying problems with the industrialization model followed by most sub-Saharan African countries became increasingly apparent, however, as a result of the external shocks in the mid-1970s. During the 1970s, manufacturing output grew at half the growth rate of the previous decade (with negative growth for low-income countries), and the sector's share of total GDP decreased to 8.2 percent. Furthermore, with industrial sectors unable to compete in export markets, the sub-Saharan African countries' share of total manufactured exports fell from 1.1 percent in 1970/71 to 0.6 percent in 1975/76, whereas that of other developing countries grew.

An increasing number of sub-Saharan African countries are now beginning to recognize the failures of their past industrial strategy. Many governments are introducing policy reforms and are adopting policies that stress pragmatism and a growing commitment to increased efficiency and greater reliance on market mechanisms. Several African countries now see the exchange rate for the powerful macroeconomic variable that it is. They understand that following a realistic exchange-rate policy can help promote exports, encourage efficient use of resources, and restore external equilibrium. Ghana, Nigeria, Zaire, Zambia, Guinea, and Mauritius are examples of countries that have made a courageous break with past exchange-rate policies and which have now either achieved, or are moving towards, exchange rates that accurately reflect the scarcity of foreign exchange in their economies. Several sub-Saharan African countries are moving towards tariff regimes that will promote more efficient, export-oriented industrial development by means of a reduction in protection levels. These include, in addition to the above, Ivory Coast and Madagascar. Many

African countries have also come to the realization that government ownership of industrial enterprises is overextended. This has been due to a pragmatic reassessment of past performance in which it was concluded that the states' managerial resources—limited to begin with—were not commensurate with the demands put upon them by the *dirigiste* role that many countries had been following.

Public sector industries have in general proved disappointing in their economic and financial performance. Many of them have been a net drain on public finances. The main problems are: overstaffing, price controls, political interference in day-to-day operations, underutilization of capacity, and lack of working capital. Unable to generate investible resources, and given the financial crises affecting many countries in sub-Saharan Africa, public sector investment has become increasingly dependent on availability of foreign exchange through bilateral and multilateral assistance. In recent years, many sub-Saharan African governments have initiated actions to improve the efficiency of public industrial enterprises, including in some cases full or partial privatization of the enterprises.

Both the circumstances and the nature of Bank industrial lending to sub-Saharan Africa have changed significantly since the post-independence period. Much of the early assistance to industrial development was indirect, through infrastructure projects. The emphasis in the 1960s and 1970s was on supporting specific investments, especially for new capacity in mining and resource-based heavy industry. Many of these projects have not met performance expectations because of difficulties in project implementation, weak markets, overcapacity and insufficient management and labor skills. During the 1970s increased attention was given to efficiency improvements and rehabilitation in the mining sector and to developing financial institutions that could support the growth of industrial investment, especially in small- and medium-scale private enterprises. These lines of credit, too, have run into some difficulties, sometimes because of institutional weaknesses within the intermediaries, but more often they are related to general economic problems, past policy distortions and, more recently, problems encountered by firms in adjusting to major changes in the policy and economic environment. These problems, together with limited entrepreneurial, management, and human resources, have made it more difficult for the Bank to achieve its institution-building objectives. While Bank support to small and medium enterprises (SME) has also exhibited only mixed results, it appears that more needs to be done in this sector, both by the governments and by the Bank Group. SME development is an important aspect of the "new" industrial development strategy for sub-Saharan African countries in that it would provide a major contribution to entrepreneurship development and can reduce the capital and import dependence of manufacturing in the region.

In recent years, the emphasis of bank operations has shifted towards an integrated approach to industrial development issues that focus on: (1) policy improvements at the macroeconomic and sectoral levels; (2) rehabilitation of existing large—often publicly-owned—industrial enterprises looking at technical, managerial, financial, and economic aspects, and including in some cases support to the new privatization policies of some governments; (3) continued support to medium-scale, mostly private, enterprises through lines of credit, using a growing variety of financial institutions; (4) increased emphasis on small-scale enterprise (SSE) development as a source of employment and entrepreneurial talent; and (5) policy and institutional improvements in the financial sector as a major facilitator of industrial development. To achieve this multilevel, integrated set of objectives, the Bank Group has evolved a growing "bag of tools" that contains several types of lending operations supported by an expanded analytical effort in macroeconomic and sector work.

The main instruments used to support policy improvements at the macroeconomic and industrial sector level are the Structural Adjustment Loans and Credits (SALs) and the Industrial Sector Adjustment Operations (ISALs). These operations, which have been growing in volume in both absolute and relative (to total lending) terms, have assisted governments in their efforts to improve exchange-rate policies, initiate the liberalization of the external trade regime, liberalize pricing policies, improve fiscal and other incentives to private investment, streamline the preparation and evaluation of public investment programs, and address the complex issues of parastatal reform and, in some cases, privatization. The policy and institutional reforms have been facilitated by providing technical assistance and quick-disbursing foreign exchange resources both to accelerate the supply response from the productive sectors of the economy and to ease the short-term social and economic costs of the adjustment process. The growing importance given by the Bank to these operations and to the adjustment programs they support indicates our perception that the macroeconomic and sectoral policy improvements are necessary prerequisites for the remaining objectives mentioned above.

The rehabilitation of large industrial enterprises is another major objective of the Bank Group operations, supported by specific operations directed to individual firms (e.g., in the fertilizer, steel, mining, and oil refining sectors) as well as in the context of SALs and

ISALs and operations focusing on the entire category of public enterprises. All these operations share the governments' concern with the financial and economic profitability of public enterprises and, in a growing number of cases, with the managerial demands that they place on the governments' limited capital resources. The Bank is also supporting the attempts by a number of governments to divest their industrial firms to the private sector.

The new types of operations in support of sub-Saharan Africa's efficient industrial development have not replaced, but have been added to, the Bank's more traditional operations in support of medium- and small-scale industrial firms. In fact, credit lines for development of medium-size enterprises and special projects focusing on SSEs are being expanded by using a growing number of financial intermediaries in addition to the development finance institutions (DFIs) used in the 1970s. The main focus of the Bank operations in this area is to expand the number and strengthen the quality of local financial intermediaries providing term financial resources to the industrial sector and SSEs. This is particularly important in the case of SSE financing where we are supporting the participation of commercial banks and of less formal financial institutions (e.g., savings and credit cooperatives). The financial intermediation operations are also supporting the DFIs' efforts to cope with the serious portfolio problems they face in the wake of their countries' economic difficulties and the crisis in the industrial sectors.

Last, but not least, the greater attention paid to a variety of financial intermediaries has led to a growing concern with the role of the financial sector in facilitating industrial and general economic development. In particular, we are focusing on the issues of resource mobilization, competitiveness and efficiency of financial intermediaries (and the impact on the cost of resources), the role of interest rates in mobilizing savings and resource allocation, and the legal and institutional framework under which financial institutions operate. The increased attention paid to the financial sector is reflected in all types of operations, as summarized earlier. In addition, the Bank is now in the process of preparing a new type of sectoral adjustment operation (similar in many ways to those discussed earlier) specifically addressing the financial sector issues.

A final point in this general area refers to the amount of resources (both human and financial) that the Bank Group has been devoting to industrialization issues in sub-Saharan Africa. Is it worthwhile to spend so much time, money, and effort on the sector that produces such a small (and in the past decade declining) share of GDP? The answer is yes and the reasons are several. For one thing, the industrial sectors of many countries in the region use a proportion of scarce foreign exchange for inputs, capital, and spare parts that is far larger than their contribution to output. Thus, efficiency improvements in this area will lead to very high payoffs. Equally or more important is the overall role that industry will play in the general economic development of the region in the late 1980s or 1990s. If this role is to change from the slowing-down effects it has had in the past (by using a large volume of resources in an inefficient way) into a dynamic element providing growing employment, new skills and technological development, and a positive contribution to the balance of payments, it is imperative that the policy, institutional, financial and technical issues facing the sector be addressed decisively and urgently. More and more governments in the region are beginning to do so and the Bank Group intends to continue supporting their efforts with the full variety of instruments at its disposal.

Institution Building

Over the years, the Bank has found that one of the main factors contributing to project failure, particularly in sub-Saharan Africa, is the limited institutional and administrative capacity of borrowers. To correct this weakness, the Bank is committed to strengthening the indigenous capacity of borrower institutions to perform their functions on a sustainable basis. The Bank's objectives in institution building in sub-Saharan Africa are applied to four major areas:[13]

1. Public management at national level, in particular aimed at improvements in the management of economic policies and in the performance of the public service: Effective policy management requires an institutional structure capable of designing, implementing, and monitoring a minimum set of economic and administrative activities.
2. Public enterprise reform: Public enterprise deficits and inefficiencies are major constraints to growth; African governments therefore need to redefine the role of the public enterprises and provide them with a clear framework for operation.
3. Strengthening and redesign of institutional structure at the sector level: These structures are often ineffective, overlapping and confused, in part because of proliferation of multisectoral programs and agencies beyond countries' administrative capacities, streamlining these structures is an important aspect of sectoral adjustment programs.

4. Strengthening of delivery systems at the local level, in areas such as agricultural extension and health delivery services: Improving the effectiveness of service delivery, especially in rural areas, is essential for achieving objectives of poverty alleviation, increased agricultural production, reduction in the rate of population growth, and improved health standards.

As regards reform in public enterprises, a brief background to the problems they pose is in order. It is worth noting that African countries on the threshold of independence were receptive to ideas of state control because they lacked capital and were opposed to foreign control. Once foreign influences were excluded, modernization and development devolved on the state. And since private enterprise was minimal, its place had to be taken either by ownership or by governmental investment in partnership with private capital. Widespread nationalization was thus seen as a means of Africanizing control of a foreign-dominated economy. There were pragmatic reasons for the expansion of the state sector. Politicians found public enterprises to be excellent means of rewarding supporters with jobs and of forestalling urban discontent. International donors have also often insisted on the creation of public enterprises as semi-independent bodies to work through. Now the tendency in the development community is to view public enterprises as hopelessly incompetent, fit only for privatization. Indeed, it is true that many have not fulfilled the objectives that were set for them, and have in fact been great brakes on the development process. We should, however, recognize that in Africa the period of state expansion was to a great extent a necessary phase—a phase of political establishment and consolidation.

As regards the response of the World Bank, it has throughout its history dealt with hundreds of public enterprises in different countries, focusing on them individually (or on small groups of them), and helping to design programs to improve their performance and reduce losses. It has become increasingly evident, however, that often only a small proportion of the factors determining the performance of a public enterprise is directly under the control of the enterprise's management. Another quite important proportion is in the hands of the central agencies that define the framework under which those enterprises operate. Since about 1983, the Bank has therefore been giving increasing emphasis to reforming government/public enterprise relations. The objective of this effort is to help define an appropriate framework, or "rules of the game," for the operation of the public enterprise sector whereby it could operate on a competitive and cost-effective basis, free from day-to-day intervention, and phase out activities for which it is ill-equipped.

Not less than twenty countries in sub-Saharan Africa have embarked on a program of parastatal reform with Bank support. Typically, this involves a restructuring of the government's relations with its parastatals including legal and institutional changes; changes in pricing, trade, investment, and borrowing policies affecting parastatals; financial and physical rehabilitation of potentially viable state enterprises; and the liquidation, sale, merger, or reabsorption into the government of selected parastatals. Privatization of public enterprises can be achieved in at least two ways: it can be accomplished through changes in ownership—selling shares of stock to private parties, either individuals or corporations—or it can be carried out through changes in management, financing, and production of service delivery arrangements. As one Bank report recently pointed out: "Management of public sector-owned assets can be made more private by leases or management contracts. The financing of publicly provided goods and services can be shifted to consumers and away from taxpayers by wider application of user fees. Service delivery can be privatized, either by contracting-out, or by load shedding (withdrawing from some lines of activity), sometimes by removing regulations restricting private competition with public agencies."[14]

Sound investment and the capacity to manage the development process lie at the heart of the development process and are woefully lacking in sub-Saharan Africa. Here, the Bank is working with the United Nations Development Program (UNDP) and other donors to examine the effectiveness of technical assistance, and its past efforts at institution building, and to develop with each country strategies for human resource development. This is necessary not only because no one agency or donor has the required resources to be effective alone, but also because coordination of purpose and discipline on the donor side of the equation is absolutely essential to avoid waste and confusion.

Resource Mobilization and Aid Coordination

There have been severe constraints on resources available for sub-Saharan Africa. The reasons for this are several: deteriorating terms of trade, declining absorptive capacity in traditional investment areas, and a high debt service burden.[15] The downturn in external resource flows to the region appears also to reflect the overall decline in official lending to Africa (aid fatigue). It also reflects the increasing tendency of donors to tie aid and provide it on a parallel basis. But,

> in order to meet Africa's growing foreign exchange requirements, resource flows from external sources will need to increase during

1986-90, but the recent trend has been just the opposite. In 1984, gross capital inflows to low-income Africa from all sources were about 15 percent lower in current prices than in 1980-82. This was due to a decline in nonconcessional flows in particularly private capital flows. . . . Nonconcessional capital flows were more than 25 percent of total gross capital in 1980-82: however, with increasing debt service difficulties, they have been declining steadily. The decline was particularly marked for private commercial flows which dropped from about $1.6 billion a year during 1980-82 to about $0.4 billion in 1984. Nonconcessional flows from official sources (bilateral and multilateral) have also declined, though not so sharply.[16]

The Bank has sought to overcome some of the problems that have contributed to the inadequate external resource flows to sub-Saharan Africa through a number of approaches:

- Through economic reporting, the Bank has sought to disseminate to donors information on development priorities and economic absorptive capacity.
- Through sectoral reports, special reports, and public dissemination of the Bank's investment decisions, the Bank has provided guidance to other donors.
- The Bank's procurement procedures encourage borrowers and other donors to open up projects to least-cost international competitive bidding, and also encourage borrowers to look at a variety of technologies and competing products.
- Use of co-financing has enabled the Bank to develop close relations with a number of donors, and facilitates an exchange of expertise on a sector and country basis.
- Donor coordination through a variety of mechanisms, most prominent of which is the Consultative Group, encourages donors to share their expertise in a country and concentrate their programs of assistance in support of agreed-upon public investment programs.

The pressing need for external resource support for Africa suggests to us that the Bank has to use its lending program to examine co-financing as part of the Bank's resource mobilizing strategy. In sub-Saharan Africa, co-financing normally means the association of other multilateral or bilateral funds in projects we appraise. However, for the Bank as a whole, co-financing includes the association of export credits and commercial bank funds in the financing of its lending operations. Such financing, because of its relatively high cost and generally harder terms, is normally not appropriate in sub-Saharan Africa. The main objective of co-financing is, therefore, to increase the flow of capital and technology that can be used to accelerate growth and development. The advantages of co-financing are threefold: it permits larger projects to be undertaken as economies of scale are exploited, it promotes international cooperation by bringing together institutions specializing in development, and it facilitates activities undertaken by newly created development agencies, thus raising the amount of capital devoted to development projects.

The Bank sees co-financing as serving its objective of mobilizing additional funds and thus directing scarce resources to the development priorities of member countries. In order to attract such co-financing the Bank often designs projects on the basis of relatively large sectoral programs. This is increasingly true in transport, energy, and agriculture, because of the great need for rehabilitation in Africa. This approach allows us to offer co-lenders packages that are attractive to their own national programs of assistance. Additionally, the approach of identifying and seeking co-financing of large, often multifaceted projects, allows the Bank to share expertise and knowledge with other agencies, reduces the risk that the Bank and other donors will work at cross purposes by financing redundant or competing investments, and ensures a better selection of projects for all concerned.[17]

Co-financing can be broken down into three broad categories according to the source of funds: official aid, including both governmental and multilateral; exports credits, that is, government-guaranteed commercial credits for the export of specific goods and equipment; and commercial lending carried out in association with a Bank loan. It is evident that most of the co-financing with the World Bank in Africa has been "official" co-financing. The number of projects that have benefited from exports credits and commercial bank lending has averaged no more than two Bank Group operations per year in Africa. And the total resources mobilized by such operations have averaged only $50 million per year.

Official co-financing has been included in more than half of Bank-funded projects in the past ten years and has accounted on average for almost $700 million in resources per year (not counting the Special Facility for Africa). Furthermore, co-lenders, and we have had seventy-four different co-lenders, have provided an amount approximately equal to that provided by the Bank Group in all co-financed projects. The sectors that have attracted the greatest amount of co-financing are agriculture, energy, and transportation, which account for about two-thirds of all co-financing. A survey of co-lenders indicates that those that provided $350 million or more during this period included the Caisse Centrale Coopération Economique and the African Development

Bank for about $750 million each, followed by the European Development Fund, the Saudi Fund, and the International Fund for Agricultural Development, all of which were in the range of $350 to $450 million in co-financings with the World Bank. All of them exceeded twenty co-financed operations with the Bank, with one co-lender participating in seventy-five operations.

There are two principal co-financing mechanisms: joint and parallel financing. The former refers to a scheme in which the various lenders share, on an agreed proportion, the financing of a common list of goods and services required for the project. In parallel financing the co-lenders finance the procurement, and distinct packages are primarily resorted to in cases where the funds are tied. The selection between the two types of financing depends upon the nature of the project, the mandate, and the operational style of technology and equipment. Joint financing has some advantages for the recipient country in that it ensures uniform procedures with respect to project appraisal, international bidding, contract conditions, terms, and facilitation of disbursement. Normally, the Bank Group's procurement rules requiring international competitive bidding are applied in our joint financing operations.

In addition to the above mechanisms, another form of official co-financing is increasingly being used. It involves funds entrusted to the Bank's administration for use in or in association with Bank projects. In such cases the funds are deposited in an account on which the Bank can draw to meet agreed-upon project costs. The use of the funds allows in some cases for untied procurement, but the Bank has accepted to administer tied funds provided competitive bidding procedures are employed. Normally the Bank receives some remuneration for its services. In eastern and southern Africa several donors made use of this mechanism, for example, the Netherlands, Belgium, and Italy.

Our experience in co-financing in Africa shows that it is not without risks. First, problems lining up donor contributions and satisfying their lending requirements routinely cause delays in effectiveness. Second, differing philosophies and management styles can lead to friction with donors who, like the Bank, wish to supervise co-financed projects actively. Third, and increasingly serious, is the problem the Bank encounters when African States default on their debt to a co-financer. As a result of arrears to the main Arab funds (which do not accept rescheduling), we have had to redesign and scale down a number of projects to allow for a withdrawal of Arab funding. In ongoing projects, suspension of Arab disbursements is causing damaging component delays. The external debt situation in the region leads one to believe that such events may become more commonplace.

Given the failure of IDA-VII to grow in line with sub-Saharan Africa needs, the Bank organized a Special Facility for sub-Saharan Africa (SFA) in which donors were invited to participate. An initial group of sixteen donors agreed to contribute a fund of about $1.3 billion, which subsequently grew to $1.7 billion and twenty donors, to assist IDA-eligible countries in sub-Saharan Africa. For a period of three years (through the end of 1987), SFA funds were available to IDA-eligible countries that had programs of adjustment and economic reforms accepted by the Bank (and a country had to have an IMF stabilization program). The programs supported by the SFA include both major sectors, particularly in agriculture, industry, and transport, and macroeconomic reforms.

The Bank's tendency to concentrate available resources on a limited number of better performances creates a need to provide strong policy guidance to capitalize on countries' willingness to promote economic reform and to assist them in mobilizing the external resources needed to support their adjustment programs and promote their growth. In order to mobilize resources and ensure their effective use the Bank is emphasizing increased aid coordination both through Consultative Groups, UNDP-sponsored Round Tables, sector investment meetings, and local aid coordination meetings. To make these consultations effective for all concerned, the Bank presents to the participants viable medium-term financial scenarios, based on a coherent and feasible policy framework, including well articulated public investment programs that can be monitored through field-level aid coordination. Increasingly, the Bank sees aid coordination as a vital complement to the more policy-oriented Consultative Group or Round Table meetings, since the need for monitoring policy and investment performance is making itself keenly felt.

The shortage of resources for Africa's development means also that resources mobilization for African countries must include improving their savings rates and attracting investment capital from foreign private investors. The Bank has therefore, as part of its resource mobilization, put increased emphasis on the role of private enterprise in African economies and has supported their efforts to become more outward looking. In this effort, the Bank took the initiative to establish the Multilateral Investment Guarantee Agency (MIGA). The central purpose of MIGA is to increase the flow of private investment to productive projects in developing countries by providing guarantees to investors against noncommercial risks such as expropriation, currency inconvertibility, and armed conflict. Private direct investment in manufacturing facilities is likely to be the main beneficiary of MIGA.

CONCLUSION: LEADERSHIP FOR SUSTAINED DEVELOPMENT

The magnitude of the development challenge in sub-Saharan Africa requires no emphasis. I have tried to provide an overview of the Bank's response. The question of what can be done is not fully answered, nor can I pretend to be able to do so within the confines of these pages. It is, however, clear that the Bank has given sub-Saharan Africa highest priority and has therefore put its institutional credibility on the line. It recognizes that the gravity of the current crisis requires an extraordinary response both from the international donor community and from the African governments. The situation also demands more sustained commitments from the donors than have been exhibited in the past. With its technical and financial skills, the Bank has accepted a leadership role to assist sub-Saharan African nations in undertaking effective growth programs and to enhance multilateral economic coordination. But the emerging consensus on the nature of the development problems in the region must be followed with adequate resource support.

In 1986 and 1987 a number of the poorest African countries embarked on courageous domestic policy reform initiatives: realigning exchange rates, cutting back on subsidies and introducing realistic pricing structures, restructuring parastatal companies, and encouraging the privatization process. These major structural reforms undertaken by many African countries have not yet been matched by adequate external support. Indeed, the World Bank estimates that, at the very least, there will be an annual gap of $2.5 billion in the resource needs of sub-Saharan Africa between 1986 and 1990. That gap must be closed, for in the absence of adequate financial support, structural reforms cannot be achieved with growth. And let there be no mistake about it: adjustment through further economic contraction is simply not an alternative for countries that have already effectively "lost" twenty-five years of progress in their economic development.

The Special Facility for sub-Saharan Africa, which made commitments of $782 million in its first year of operation, is playing an important role. But it is a one-time, five-year operation. So an IDA-VIII of sufficiently large size will be needed if African prospects over the next few years are to improve. Reflows from the IMF's trust fund account will certainly provide additional and welcome assistance. But while Africa's leaders must continue to exercise the political will to ensure that both domestic and foreign resources are used as efficiently as possible, so too Africa's donors and creditors must think seriously about how the level of concessional resources can be increased and how the debt burdens of the world's poorest countries can be reduced.

During the 1986 special session of the United Nations General Assembly on the critical situation in Africa, the African nations indicated that they were prepared to face the hard realities inherent in their predicament. But the "Program of Action for African Recovery and Development, 1986-90," which was approved at that special session, also underlines that the African development crisis is "not an exclusive African problem but one that concerns mankind as a whole. . . . A stagnant and perpetually economically backward Africa is not in the interest of the world community."

The Bank's role will be of crucial importance to the success of sub-Saharan African countries in achieving sustained noninflationary growth in the years ahead. First, the Bank must strengthen its ability to play a leading role in support of programs aimed at medium-term adjustment and growth in the region. Over the past several years, the Bank has been positioning itself to play this role. It has made greater use of various lending instruments, especially structural and sectoral adjustment loans; it has speeded up and increased its disbursements; and, in a number of cases, it has worked with African countries to design and implement medium-term adjustment programs. The lessons learned from this experience indicate that the essential ingredients for effective growth-oriented adjustment programs are realistic, mutually agreed-upon objectives; adequate timeframes in which to achieve objectives; and high-quality implementation and monitoring of the programs. Now is the time for the Bank to maximize the comparative advantage it has gained in this area. Through a greatly increased operational emphasis on "country assistance management," the Bank's traditional project investments will be viewed in the larger context of the borrower's overall medium-term development needs and strategy. This will allow the Bank to be more flexible and responsive in identifying the policy and institutional impediments to a country's chosen development objectives and in assisting the country to deal with them.

The second area in which the Bank should increase its emphasis is in extending its catalytic and coordinating role in mobilizing increased levels of private and official resources to support sub-Saharan African countries. Again, the Bank has already taken some significant steps in this direction. It has expanded its co-financing activities in general; it has taken a stronger part in aid coordination efforts; and, more recently, it has initiated the Multilateral Investment Guarantee Agency as part of its drive to promote increased investment in the developing countries. At the same time, the Bank's affiliate, the International Finance Corporation, with its capital base recently doubled, is also playing an important innovative and catalytic role in helping to attract investment to the private sectors of the developing countries and particularly those in sub-Saharan Africa.

We all recognize that whatever the Bank's resources might be, they will cover only a small proportion of the external capital needs of the developing countries. This fact makes the Bank's catalytic role even more crucial. For the Bank must use its leverage to ensure that the borrowing countries maximize the resources available to them. At the same time, the Bank must use its leverage to encourage more quality lending by the commercial Banks and from bilateral sources.

Third, it must be remembered that the Bank's catalytic role is not just financial. The intellectual leverage of the Bank must also be maximized in advising both borrowers and lenders on the right policies to pursue. The World Development Report 1986, which highlights the interdependence of domestic agricultural policies throughout the world and the large potential gains to be made from more liberal trade in agriculture, is a good example of the Bank's leadership role in the marketplace ideas. That role is needed now more than ever in response to the African situation.

Fourth, there should be an expansion in the Bank's lending program to help sub-Saharan African countries meet the challenge of adjustment with growth. The Bank's lending program increased to $2.8 billion in FY86. It is possible that the demand for Bank lending beyond FY87 might exceed the level that can be sustained with the capital now available to it. This underlines the need for a capital increase. If the Bank is to play the expanded role in the adjustment-with-growth process that is expected of it by its African member countries, it must not be constrained by a lack of resources. An IDA replenishment of adequate size is also imperative. Given IDA's importance to these countries, it is essential to ensure that the Association is adequately replenished.

Meeting the objective of economic adjustment with growth will require the commitment of the African countries to policy reform, and the commitment of the industrial countries to keep their markets open and to keep the financial resources flowing. The IMF, the World Bank, the African Development Bank, and the other multilateral institutions will be key players as counselors, catalysts, and coordinators in the process. In particular, Bank/Fund collaboration, which has grown substantially in recent years, will become even more crucial in the future. Macroeconomic stabilization and structural adjustment must be pursued simultaneously and together must lead to growth. I think it is now agreed that the support provided by the IMF and the Bank should be—within the two institutions' respective mandates—mutually supportive and appropriately coordinated. The two Bretton Woods institutions are expected to be creative and flexible, and to play a leadership role in engaging in constructive dialogue with their African countries and in coming up with durable solutions to the problems which those countries face.

It is now clear that one of the major constraints to the development effort in sub-Saharan Africa has been political instability. Hence, the African countries should establish systems of government that are hospitable to economic development. Without political stability, no economic growth will ever take place.

While the donor agencies need to do more in sub-Saharan Africa, they also need to do things differently. They need to look at Africa's problems comprehensively, and existing aid should be utilized much more efficiently. Development institutions must be willing to try new approaches. The peculiarity of the African situation requires flexible, adaptable, and responsive instruments. This is why the Bank instituted quick-disbursing loans and credits for structural and sector adjustment programs.

To put the African countries on the growth path, it is important that African governments and bilateral and multilateral organizations should recognize the overriding importance of the development of indigenous managerial, executive, research, and innovative capability; creation of an honest, dedicated, and loyal body of managers and entrepreneurs; development of appropriate technology, appropriate prices, and adequate control over public enterprises; and the need for their economies to be flexible and to shift resources from one activity to another.

Donors should avoid proposing prescriptive policy packages that are not politically feasible. It is important to take into account real political fears and carry out detailed analysis of implementation problems to avoid undesirable income distribution and power distribution effects. In other words, donor agencies must propose step-by-step implementation sequences with buttressing and buffering measures to make them less painful or dangerous.

The Bank assesses continuously the direction and efficiency of its assistance to Africa. It will constantly examine the appropriateness of its policy content prescription and determine the likelihood of its real impact on the countries. The Bank places greatest importance on poverty alleviation and will keep it as a central objective in the design of its program and project lending in Africa. Above all, the Bank believes no external agency can succeed in sub-Saharan Africa without seeking the full cooperation of the African countries.

Although the development challenge in sub-Saharan Africa is

daunting, it is not without hope. If we look back several decades to the problems that then beset Asia, and compare the accomplishments that have resulted there from hard work and donor assistance, we can hope for a similar measure of success for Africa. It will take time, resources, and patience, and there will be false steps. We have no chance, however, but to join in partnership with these countries which have so far to go, to ensure their effective entry into the modern world.

And what will be the World Bank's role in all of this? The Bank's new president, Barber Conable, has already articulated it clearly:

> The central challenge to the World Bank is the central concern of our world. It is the same as in 1946: to mobilize the will and the resources of the affluent and of the afflicted alike in the global battle against poverty.
>
> We have made real progress in that fight. We have much still to do.
>
> We have done well. We must, we can do better.[18]

For the Bank to achieve its objectives in Africa and elsewhere, it need not take a new road or a fundamentally new direction; rather, it needs only a renewed drive and reinvigorated dedication to its original and enduring purpose. That purpose is development. And the Bank's role—and its response to the African challenge—will be to promote resolute leadership for sustained development.

NOTES

1. The World Bank comprises three different but closely related institutions: the parent organization, whose official title is the International Bank for Reconstruction and Development (IBRD), founded in 1944; the International Development Association (IDA), established in 1960 to provide assistance to the poorest countries on concessional terms; and the International Finance Corporation (IFC), established in 1956 to promote and assist development of the private sector. The Bank has also established an autonomous center for the settlement of investment disputes (ICS), and is in the process of creating an affiliate known as the Multilateral Investment Guaranty Agency (MIGA) to promote private investment through the provision of guarantees against noncommercial risks.

2. On the request of the African Governors of the World Bank, the Bank prepared a comprehensive diagnosis of the nature of the African crisis. See *Accelerated Development in Sub-Saharan Africa, An Agenda for Action*, Washington, D.C.: World Bank, 1981.

3. Lester R. Brown and Edward C. Wolf, "Reversing Africa's Decline," World Watch Paper 65, World Watch Institute, Washington, D.C.: June 1985.

4. *Population Growth and Policies in Sub-Saharan Africa, A World Bank Policy Study*, Washington, D.C.: World Bank, 1986.

5. Most sub-Saharan Africa countries are eligible only for IDA credits. IFC joint ventures in the region are not discussed in this paper.

6. Ernest Stern, "The Evolving Role of the Bank in the 1980s," speech to the Fourth Agriculture Sector Symposium, January 1984. *The Bank's World* 3:2, February 1984, p.15.

7. See *Toward Sustained Development in Sub-Saharan Africa: A Joint Program of Action*, Washington, D.C.: World Bank, 1984.

8. Ibid.

9. "Structural Adjustment Lending—A First Review of Experience," report of the Operational Evaluation Department, Washington, D.C.: World Bank, 1986.

10. Ibid.

11. See note 7.

12. "Zambia—Agriculture Sector," internal World Bank document, 1986.

13. For details, see *Institutional Development in Africa: A Review of World Bank Project Experience*, vols. 1, 2 Washington, D.C.: World Bank, 1984.

14. *Institutional Development in Sub-Saharan Africa*, Washington, D.C.: World Bank, 1986.

15. See Edward V.K. Jaycox, et al., "The Nature of the Debt Problem in Eastern and Southern Africa," in Carol Lancanster and John Williamson eds. *African Debt Financing*, Institute for International Economics Special Reports, No. 5 (May 1986), pp. 47-62. Also see Chandra Hardy, *Africa's Debt Crisis*, a background paper for the Committee on African Development Strategies, Overseas Development Council, 1985.

16. *Financing Adjustment with Growth in sub-Saharan Africa, 1986-90*, Washington, D.C.: World Bank, 1986, pp. 38.

17. Edward V.K. Jaycox, *Resource Mobilization for Sub-Saharan Africa*, Washington, D.C.: World Bank, 1986. I have drawn substantially from this paper written specially for the OECD.

18. See Barber Conable's presidential address, *The World Bank/IMF Annual Meetings*, Washington, D.C., 1986.

CHAPTER 3

Policy Reforms for Economic Development in Tanzania

Nguyuru Lipumba

Sub-Saharan Africa as a region has been facing an economic crisis since after the second oil price hike. However, this crisis has not been uniform. Famine, the most visible manifestation of political and economic breakdown, did not affect all of Africa and deaths from the famine were concentrated in a few countries. Other signs of economic decay were more subtle, more apparent in such areas as national accounts, trade balances, and investment failures. These imbalances are what have drawn the attention of donors, especially the mutlilateral agencies of the International Monetary Fund (IMF) and the World Bank.

Although sub-Saharan Africa has become a region of particular attention because of widespread economic problems, specific countries offer diverse economic experiences. In terms of addressing development strategies, national states are responsible for the design of economic policy. Even though African borders are porous, economic conditions vary drastically from one state to another. Thus, it is important that relevant evaluations of economic policies and recommendations should be concretely based on country studies. I present here an overview of policy reform debates in the context of the ongoing economic difficulties afflicting Tanzania.

As an introduction to a discussion of policy reforms, the first section describes IMF stabilization programs and World Bank lending, and their relevance to Africa. The second section analyzes the nature and causes of the crisis in Tanzania, and the third reviews government policy response to the crisis of 1979-1986. In the final section I summarize the discussion by looking at the Economic Recovery Program and prospects for its success.

THE IMF STABILIZATION PROGRAMS AND THE WORLD BANK STRUCTURAL ADJUSTMENT LENDING

The International Monetary Fund has been a prominent institution in African economies mainly because many countries have had unsustainable balance of payments deficits and have had to go to the IMF to negotiate funds for balance of payments support. The IMF conditionalities have been only reluctantly accepted by most African governments because they considered them too drastic and out of touch with the realities of African economies. The IMF prefers "shock treatment" stabilization programs that front-load adjustment policies. At one stroke previous overvaluation of the currency, as estimated by simple purchasing power parity adjusted for suppressed inflation and terms of trade deterioration, is to be removed. Nominal interest rates are to be sharply increased to attain positive real interest rates within a year. Growth of nominal credit, particularly government borrowing from the banking system, is to be drastically reduced. Economies that for a long period have been characterized by a plethora of administrative controls are supposed to immediately operate by the use of market signals.

The continuation of IMF balance of payments support is conditional on meeting quarterly performance tests in the form of aggregate credit ceilings. Production cycles in economies dependent on agriculture usually take a year. The size of agricultural harvest cannot be accurately predicted. Historical data show wide swings on the total output purchased from farmers. As a result, credit requirements for the purchase of agricultural produce cannot be accurately predetermined. Thus, passing or failing credit ceilings performance tests is not a good indicator of what is happening in the real economy. A bumper crop will require a larger credit to finance the purchase of crops from farmers. If the government insists on meeting quarterly performance tests, farmers will be unable to sell all the crops they have. Not meeting IMF performance tests and extending more credit to finance the purchase of the bumper crop will lead to a better real economic performance.

The IMF standby arrangements are designed for countries that have temporary balance of payment problems mainly caused by overly expansionary policies that increased domestic absorption relative to income. For countries that are facing fundamental problems of reversing economic decline and initiating a process of sustained economic growth, IMF stabilization programs are not adequate and they can actually prevent a process of economic recovery. The IMF attempted to address this problem by introducing an enlarged access policy where countries could negotiate an extended financing facility program that will provide balance of payments support for a period of two to three years. However, the conditionalities are similar to the standby arrangement. For practical purposes the extended fund facility is like having two or three back-to-back standby arrangements.

The inability of IMF stabilization programs to address structural problems that constrain growth in many less developed countries, and the limitation of project lending to deal with macroeconomic policies and institutional problems that inhibit growth led the World Bank to establish the Structural Adjustment Lending (SAL) facility. According to Yagci et al. (1985),

> the purpose of SAL has been to support the implementation of policies and institutional changes necessary to modify the structure of an economy so that it can maintain both its growth rate and the viability of balance of payments in the medium term.

Thus, while stabilization programs focus mainly on restoring balance of payments equilibrium, structural adjustment programs aim at simultaneously correcting balance of payments deficits, restoring economic growth, and preventing future balance of payment problems.

Given their objectives, structural adjustment programs involve detailed discussions of policy and institutional reforms. The development strategy that is considered by the World Bank as appropriate is an outward-looking development strategy that encourages the private sector to produce for export. Policy instruments recommended in structural adjustment programs are not different from those used in stabilization programs. To remove biases against export production and efficient import substitution, major devaluation is usually required. Where budgetary deficits are large, reductions in government expenditure and increases in tax revenue are considered necessary for both controlling inflation and balance of payments deficits. Predominance of state enterprises is usually considered a source of budgetary deficits and inefficient utilization of resources. Privatization of state-owned enterprises that are not producing "public goods" is a preferred policy.

However, many governments usually oppose privatization of state enterprises. Under those circumstances, streamlining public enterprises and letting them operate as commercial enterprises with clear commercial objectives and without central government interference is considered a second-best policy. Another policy favored by the World Bank is trade liberalization that reduces quantitative restrictions. This would require a move toward selective use of tariffs along with an overall general reduction of tariff barriers. In African countries, agriculture is rightly considered as the key sector. The focus of structural adjustment lending is usually on increasing real producer prices partly through exchange rate adjustment and partly by improving the efficiency of the marketing system through policies that allow the private sector to participate in marketing and in controlling the overheads of marketing boards.

Structural adjustment lending does not involve strict quantitative targets but is monitored by periodic evaluation of the implementation and outcome of policies. For governments convinced that an "outward-looking" development strategy is the best strategy, structural adjustment lending offers a more realistic approach to resolving development and structural problems. However, it seems that reaching an agreement with the IMF is a necessary requirement before a country can finalize a SAL with the World Bank. This has led to the delaying of adjustment programs in some African countries.

For countries that are not convinced of the development philosophy of the World Bank, structural adjustment lending involves more interference with domestic policies than IMF programs. This is usually recognized when an agreement with the IMF is finalized and the World Bank starts negotiating details of policy and institutional changes in the major sectors of the economy. Implementing structural adjustment programs in many African countries requires a critical mass of reformers in both the political wing of the government and the bureaucracy. It is absolutely necessary, though not sufficient, for the president to generally understand the requirements of the program and be committed to its implementation. Where programs are accepted primarily for an inflow of foreign exchange, the outcome is likely to be worse with than without the program.

THE ECONOMIC CRISIS IN TANZANIA: AN OVERVIEW

Since the end of 1978 Tanzania has experienced a persistently worsening economic crisis that is unprecedented both in its intensity and duration since the country achieved its independence twenty-five years ago. For the past nine years, per capita GDP has continuously declined because of low and sometimes negative growth rates. Per capita real monetary GDP in 1985 was less than 50 percent of the level attained in 1971. Moreover, the only sector that recorded high rates of growth is public administration and other services, which mainly indicates the wage bill of the government. Total agriculture output growth rate has not kept pace with population growth rates. Real output of commercial agriculture, particularly exports, drastically declined over the past decade. The manufacturing sector was the most hard hit. Persistent high negative growth rates have been recorded since 1978. The real value of output in 1984 is estimated to be only 37 percent of the 1978 output.

Inflation as measured by the percentage change in the National Consumer Price Indices (NCPI) accelerated from 12 percent in 1977 to 30 percent in 1984. The NCPI is likely to underestimate the price level because of the existence of widespread shortages of goods and official price control. The combined effect of decrease in production and increase in prices reduces real incomes of both rural and urban dwellers. The International Labor Organization (1985) estimates declines of 13.5 percent and 65 percent for rural incomes and nonagricultural wage incomes respectively, for the period 1979/80-1983/84.

It is generally agreed that both external and internal factors have contributed to the current economic crisis. Policymakers and their sympathizers tend to emphasize external factors (Nyerere 1982; Green 1983; International Labor Organization 1982). The external shocks include: (1) the first and the second rounds of oil price increases in 1973 and 1979; (2) the sharp fall in the terms of trade since the end of the coffee boom in 1977; (3) the breakdown of the East African Community, which necessitated large investment in infrastructure to provide services that were formerly offered by the community using facilities located in Kenya; (4) the Uganda war that was imposed on Tanzania by Amin; and (5) recurring poor climatic conditions.

Critics of Tanzanian development policy, such as Uma Lele (1984), have put more weight on internal causes, including: (1) a very poor performance of the monetized agricultural sector, particularly a fall in the production of export crops; (2) poor economic and financial performance of most parastatal enterprises, particularly, but not exclusively, those in agricultural marketing and domestic trade; (3) rapid increase in government expenditure financed by bank borrowing, and an increase in credit to parastatal enterprises causing a high growth of money supply that fueled inflation; (4) rapid expansion of a highly import-dependent industrial structure that increased demand for foreign exchange to purchase intermediate inputs; (5) an incentive and institutional structure that has discouraged individuals, including smallholder farmers, from efficiently utilizing resources to increase production.

The World Bank (1983) has estimated the cost of the external shocks to the economy. The terms of trade loss for 1973-1982 added up to $630 million; the total food import bill, including food aid, for 1973-1981 amounted to $413 million (this is assumed to be losses due to poor climatic conditions—output losses of export crops are not included); the direct cost of the Uganda war was $500 million; and the cost incurred because of the dissolution of the East African Community (EAC) was $200 million. Thus, the rough estimate of the total cost of external shocks during 1973-1982 was $1.7 billion. During the same period, total aid inflow amounted to $2.7 billion which more than "compensated" for the estimated value of the external shocks. It is certainly wrong to conclude that because of this "compensation" the adverse impact of the shocks on economic performance could have been completely removed. There is a time lag between external shocks and a flow of aid that ameliorates their impact on the economy. More importantly, aid is not necessarily fungible for utilization in those sectors with maximum impact on growth or balance of payments adjustment.

The economic crisis has been characterized by two major macroeconomic disequilibria: the balance of payments disequilibrium and its concomitant, an acute shortage of foreign exchange, and budgetary deficits financed through borrowing from the banking sector.

For the period 1976-1985, the trade balance deficit rose from $146 million in 1976, with a peak of $715 million in 1980, to $631 million in 1986. The trade balance deficit is likely to have been higher if foreign exchange to finance imports had been available. The inability to pay for imports caused the accumulation of import payment arrears since 1978. The cumulative import payment arrears may have reached $900 million by the end of 1984, which is more than twice the value of exports and net services of 1985. Thus, while the outstanding external debt of Tanzania is not large in absolute terms ($3.7 billion by June 1986), import payment arrears are a major constraint to resuming normal channels of financing imports.

From 1978 to 1986 export earnings financed less than 50 percent of imports. An increased dependence on external financing occurred despite a drastic decrease in the volume of imports—despite the fact that the average annual volume of imports for 1982-1984 was around 50 percent of the peak volume of imports for 1978. Excessive imports due to overexpansion of aggregate demand is not the fundamental cause of balance of payments disequilibrium in the foreign exchange control regime of Tanzania. The main cause is the decline in the aggregate purchasing power of exports.

Over the years 1970-1982, the trend in the annual decline of the purchasing power of exports was 7.2 percent for this period. Indications for 1983-1985 are that the aggregate purchasing power of exports continued to decrease. This decrease was mainly caused by the continuous fall in the volume of exports from its peak in 1972 and the deterioration in the commodity terms of trade since the end of the coffee boom in 1977. It is important to note that by 1977, a year of good weather, and before the beginning of severe foreign exchange shortages, the volume of exports was 40 percent below the 1972 peak. The volume of exports declined despite a general improvement in the commodity terms of trade during 1972-1977. The bottlenecks that hinder increase in the volume of exports because of lack of foreign exchange provide only a partial explanation. The basic problem in Tanzania is an incentive structure and institutional setup that has, over time, discouraged agricultural producers from increasing commercial agricultural production in general and export crops in particular.

The poor performance of the economy, particularly the decrease in commercial agricultural production and manufacturing, reduced the tax base. Government expenditures continued to increase causing persistent budget deficits. Before fiscal year 1978/79 the recurrent budget normally recorded a surplus. The Uganda war necessitated an increase in expenditure that could not be financed by taxes. But even after the war, recurrent budget deficits persisted, as government expenditures continued to increase faster than the increase in government revenues. The recurrent budget deficits and development expenditures were financed partly by external loans and grants and increasingly from bank borrowing. Government borrowing from the banking system, and the financing of financial losses of the major crop authorities through borrowing from the National Bank of Commerce, increased money supply that contributed to inflationary pressure in the economy.

Despite the increase in government expenditure, the quality of government services has deteriorated. Maintenance of existing capital stock has generally been neglected while investment expenditure continued to account for 20 percent of GDP.

The extensive shortages in the economy caused a significant growth of a "parallel" market where prices are much higher than the official prices. Rent-seeking activities have increased because private return from hawking scarce commodities is very high. People on fixed wages and salary earners literally cannot survive on their official wages and salaries and have to engage in other legal and illegal activities even when they are supposed to be at their formal jobs. Efficiency is badly impaired and performance of socioeconomic institutions have significantly deteriorated over the past eight years.

POLICY RESPONSES

The intensity and seriousness of the crisis was not adequately appreciated by policymakers in 1979-1980 mainly because since October 1978 the national effort had been directed towards the war with Uganda. The euphoria of the victory made economic problems look relatively simple and it was perceived that within eighteen months, the worst part of the crisis would be over and a period of normal economic conditions and growth would return. Consultation with the IMF to negotiate a standby arrangement loan in 1979 caused a major disagreement that led the president, in his 1980 New Year speech, to publicly denounce the IMF for taking advantage of Tanzania's economic problems to interfere in the domestic economic policies with the aim of changing the socialist orientation of the country. President Nyerere (1980) argued:

> Externally caused problems are obvious and so is our need for an injection of balance of payment support [but] Tanzania is not prepared to devalue its currency just because this is a traditional free market solution to everything and regardless of the merits of our position. It is not prepared to surrender its right to restrict imports by measures designed to ensure we import quinine rather than cosmetics, or buses rather than cars for the elite. . . . And above all we shall continue with our endeavors to build a socialist society.

Politically, a number of policy instruments that are common in a conventional stabilization program such as a major devaluation, reduction of government expenditure on social services, and removal of price controls were rejected, because their adoption could be interpreted as "giving in" to IMF pressure. This public political stand constrained policy decisions in future negotiations. Nyerere's attack on the IMF coincided with a period when the IMF relaxed its conditionality because many countries were avoiding the IMF and borrowing from commercial banks. Despite the disagreements, negotiations with the IMF continued and a two-year standby agreement was signed in August 1980.

The standby arrangement that was reached in 1980 was to provide $230 million over a two-year period. Unlike most IMF-sponsored programs, this standby did not front-load policy adjustments. The program had general objectives without clear policy instruments. The objectives of the program were

1. to establish a sound basis for more balanced growth of domestic output over the medium term by reversing the

declining trend in output of exports;
2. to reduce excess liquidity in the economy to ease pressure on prices;
3. to curb the external payment deficit while gradually liquidating payment arrears.

The shilling was not devalued but it was agreed that a joint in-depth study with the Fund would be carried out and an appropriate exchange rate agreed upon before June 30, 1981. The basic quantitative conditionalities included ceilings on total domestic credit and credit to the government. The credit ceilings for the initial nine months of the program were exceeded within the first three months. The standby arrangement was suspended in the first quarter and the government utilized only SDR (Special Drawing Rights) 25 million out of the SDR 179 million in the agreement. The control of government and parastatal expenditure was not taken very seriously, and no expenditure programs were eliminated after the agreement was signed. During the negotiations, credit requirements of the major crop marketing authorities were not computed in detail.

In 1981 the government launched the first National Economic Survival Program (NESP) that aimed at increasing food production to attain national food self-sufficiency, and increasing exports of both agricultural and manufactured goods. The program was long on targets but short on policy instruments to achieve those targets. It was mainly prepared by the Ministry of Development Planning and Economic Affairs but did not have concrete operational support in the sectoral ministries.

After the breakdown of the standby arrangement, negotiations for an extended facility loan of $400 million were initiated but reached a deadlock because of policy disagreement. According to Green (1983), the IMF "package" appears to have required a 66-75 percent devaluation, nominal interest rates of 35-40 percent, a freeze in nominal wages and salaries, dismantling of price controls and a 50-75 percent increase in producer prices of export crops, and a 25 percent increase in producer prices of staple grains. The government maintained that devaluation and increase in interest rates were irrelevant policy instruments for achieving balance of payment equilibrium. Imports were already reduced to very low levels and exports could only be increased when specific bottlenecks that related to a lack of imports were removed.

The Structural Adjustment Program

The World Bank, the leading source of funds for many development projects in Tanzania that have generally been unsuccessful, sponsored a sympathetic Advisory Group to analyze the economic situation and propose necessary policy measures that should be taken by Tanzania. It was anticipated that the advisory group would bridge policy differences between the government and the IMF, which would facilitate reaching an agreement on the extended facility loan and also enable the World Bank to extend a structural adjustment loan.

In preparing its report, the Tanzania Advisory Group incorporated views from a number of local economists and thus, at least at the technical level, the proposed Structural Adjustment Program (SAP) had local input and support. The program recognized four major imbalances in the economy: (1) budgetary imbalance and resulting monetary growth which fuel inflation; (2) external imbalances caused by terms of trade deterioration and sluggish export performance; (3) imbalance between productive and nonproductive activities; and (4) imbalance between official economy and parallel economy. The major objectives of SAP were to eliminate these imbalances over a three-to-five-year period by implementing policies that would increase output rather than decrease income without abandoning the provision of basic needs and the egalitarian income distribution objective of the government.

The core policy framework of SAP was centered on:

1. The restructuring of future economic activities through altering the incentive system, particularly by providing improved incentives to support export production. This would be achieved by offering higher producer prices, providing inputs, and improving the overall marketing system. The manufacturing sector was also expected to increase exports.
2. The rationalization of existing economic activities through increasing capacity utilization by switching resources from capacity expansion to provision of intermediate imports and maintenance of existing capital stock. In the government budget, development expenditure was to be reduced in favor of recurrent expenditure to provide adequate resources to properly run existing services and to maintain capital stock. The government was to negotiate with the major aid donors to switch from project aid to general import support.
3. Improved government planning and control systems. It was observed that there was lack of coordination in the investment programs of sectoral ministries and parastatal organization. There was neither adequate appraisal of investment projects nor uniform criteria for selecting projects. There was a strong need

to improve the technical capacity of the Ministry of Development Planning (Dev Plan) to enable it to coordinate investment programs and to take into consideration the recurrent budgetary consequences of these programs.

The "specific" SAP that was formulated by the Tanzania Advisory Group was based on the assumption that additional balance of payments support (over and above "normal" aid flows of $500 million) to the tune of $210 million a year for three years would be forthcoming, mainly from the World Bank and the IMF. The balance of payment support would be used to import intermediate inputs to reactivate the manufacturing sector, and spare parts and transport equipment to rehabilitate the transport sector that is central for the agricultural sector, and provide imported inputs to rehabilitate the agricultural export production.

Under the additional resource inflow scenario, the exchange rate was to be adjusted from Shs. 9.3 to Shs. 11.0-13.0 per dollar. A larger devaluation was considered to be potentially inflationary despite the existence of foreign exchange control regimes and significantly higher prices for imports than prices that would prevail if the official exchange rate were ineffective. The major export crop authorities were incurring large losses partly because of increases in producer prices they paid to farmers that were not matched by an exchange rate adjustment, and partly because of inefficient management. It was anticipated that this devaluation and an improvement in the financial management of the crop authorities would reduce their deficits.

The development expenditure budget was to be reduced by Shs. 1.0 billion. Projects financed by foreign aid worth $100 million were to be stopped and $80 million of project aid was to be switched to support local costs. Financing through bank borrowing was to be limited to Shs. 1.6 billion. Recurrent spending, particularly on defense, was to be drastically reduced and government revenue increased, particularly through presumptive tax assessments.

A major constraint to recovery according to the program plan was the severe shortage of foreign exchange. An injection of foreign exchange would increase capacity utilization in manufacturing and provide incentive goods and inputs to the agricultural sector that could lead to an increase in exports. Tax revenue would rise with the increase in the output of manufacturing sector, particularly through a higher sales tax. Without a foreign exchange injection, however, the breaking of the vicious spiral was seen to be almost impossible.

A three-year (1982/83-84/85) SAP adopted by the government assumed a scenario of additional foreign exchange inflow. The program could not be effectively implemented because of a lack of foreign exchange inflow, as there was no agreement with the IMF and the World Bank. The objective of restoring external balance was the worst failure of SAP. Export earnings in current dollars declined during the SAP period. Export earnings for the period were only 66 percent of SAP targets. Instead of the projected reduction of import payment arrears over the program period, there was an increase in import payment arrears of $650 million.

During the first two years of SAP, pricing policy was not actively used. The SAP target of increasing real producer prices by 5 percent annually was not attained, and real prices continued to fall. The decrease in real producer prices was caused by high rates of inflation and relatively moderate nominal price increases to producers. Nominal price increases were limited by budget deficit pressure. The exchange rate was only adjusted from Shs. 9.3 per dollar to Shs. 12.2 per dollar in June 1983, a devaluation of 20 percent that was recommended by the Advisory Group for March 1982. Increasing producer prices while maintaining f.o.b. prices at fixed exchange rates entailed absorbing growing losses of crop parastatals into the budgetary deficit and providing an increase in domestic credit. The increase in nominal producer prices of food crops, while maintaining subsidized consumer prices, raised National Milling Corporation (NMC) losses that were absorbed into the budget deficit and into the expansion of domestic credit.

The worsening of economic conditions, particularly the intensification of shortages of consumer goods, increase in the budget deficit and inflation, and the domestic debate on economic policy that called for a shift in economic policy towards a more flexible system and use of the market, influenced new policies that were adopted in the 1984/85 budget (Lipumba, Msambichaka, and Wangwe 1984). Significant and positive steps were taken to reduce price distortions.

Since 1980 the shilling has increasingly been overvalued because of the high domestic inflation rate relative to trading partners. While there is no generally accepted method of estimating a correct equilibrium exchange rate of a foreign trade regime with extensive exchange control, simple purchasing power parity computation can be used as a crude indicator of overvaluation. Given the existence of suppressed inflation, which is not captured in the official price index, estimates of exchange rate that will restore purchasing power parity still underestimate the "equilibrium" exchange rate.

The overvaluation of the shilling increased sharply beginning in 1980. The overvaluation of the shilling was reduced by a 26 percent devaluation in dollar terms in June 1984. Food subsidies to consumers and fertilizer and other inputs subsidies to producers were removed.

Nominal prices were increased to compensate for both the removal of input subsidies and the high rate of inflation. Real producer prices for predominant staples were increased by 24 percent and for export crops by 3 percent. Price control of domestically produced consumer goods was limited to sixty-nine specific commodities. Official restrictions on domestic trade of food grains were reduced. Exporters of non-traditional exports were allowed to retain 10 percent of their export earnings in foreign exchange to finance their import needs.

To surmount the severe shortage of consumer goods, import restrictions on goods, spare parts, and intermediate inputs financed by privately owned foreign exchange reserves were removed. The bulk of the imports under the liberalized scheme were allowed to be sold at market clearing prices. A major part of the parallel market was legalized and business confidence, at least in trading activities, was restored.

Policy Lessons

There are several lessons to be learned from the post-July 1984 adjustment effort and its aftermath. First, the immediate effect of lifting the lid on prices was to increase the officially measured rate of inflation. The rate of inflation increased from 27.3 percent in 1983 to 35.8 percent in 1984. This jump reflected mainly a movement from suppressed to open inflation and the capturing of parallel market prices in the official consumer price index. Subsequent effects of increased supplies of consumer goods, including food, caused the rate of inflation to decline to 24.5 percent in 1985 (September 1984- September 1985), the lowest inflation rates since 1980. This indicates that a program of recovery that combines reduction in price distortions and resource inflows that increase aggregate supplies, is likely to have a once-and-for-all increase in the officially measured inflation rate followed by a deceleration of inflation.

The second major lesson pertains to the effective rate of relative prices. Real producer price increases were higher for food crops than for export crops. This was partly caused by the smaller adjustment of the exchange rate combined with the objective of reducing losses of export crop marketing parastatals. As a result, while food production made a significant improvement, export crops did not, other things remaining the same. This would indicate that a larger adjustment of exchange rate would be necessary to allow for a greater increase in producer prices of export crops.

The third major lesson is the likely structure of imports resulting from complete liberalization of foreign exchange allocation. The 1984/85 shift in import composition indicates what might happen when a large injection of foreign resources is allocated under a completely competitive allocation system such as through auctioneering of foreign exchange. It was reasonably hypothesized that the change in the structure of imports was caused solely by the additional import capacity outside the official banking system. The share of consumer goods in non-oil imports increased from 29 percent in the first quarter of 1984 before liberalization to nearly 50 percent by the first quarter of 1985 after liberalization. This shift was caused by the relatively higher rents earned from consumer goods and luxuries that had a higher scarcity premium due to stricter import controls before liberalization. There is greater uncertainity in the realization of rents from imports of intermediate inputs. Even importers under export retention schemes import consumer goods that they can quickly sell, rather than intermediate input. In order to increase domestic production through providing import and infrastructural services to the agricultural sector, and to increase capacity utilization of the manufacturing sector, the composition of imports must favor intermediate inputs. Thus a policy instrument in an adjustment program must incorporate a category-guided allocation system with the possibility of competition within categories to allow the most efficient users to get access to inputs. Firms that are hopelessly inefficient and have negative value added at world prices should be identified and eliminated.

The fourth major lesson, which was obvious even before liberalization, is the ineffectiveness and negative impact of price control on even essential goods if supply cannot be increased. Market prices of essential goods such as cooking fat, clothes, etc., were two to five times the official prices of similar domestically produced goods. Local producers of essential goods, particularly parastatals, were unable to capture the scarcity rent that could enable them to effectively compete for any imported intermediate inputs and spare parts. Further relaxation of price controls for essential commodities is a sensible policy. Where there is adequate competition either from other domestic producers or imports, producing firms should be allowed to set their own prices.

The fifth major lesson is the need for sustained adjustment efforts to ensure sustained progress toward recovery and to prevent backsliding. The 1985/86 budget did not build on the 1983/84 budget. Producer prices of export crops were increased without any adjustment of the exchange rate and despite a high rate of inflation. This has contributed to an increase in losses of agricultural crop parastatals and a subsequent increase in budget deficit and growth in money supply.

The sixth major lesson is the existence of widespread capital flight. It was not clear how "liberalized" imports were financed. It was earlier believed that most imports were financed by relatives of residents who live abroad, particularly in the Gulf States and in Europe, and only a small part of the imports were financed by foreign exchange earned through illegal exports. It was expected that a large volume of imports financed by private transfers could not continue for a long period, particularly given the slump of the Gulf economies. However, since the liberalization of June 1984 the dollar value of the liberalized imports has increased quarter after quarter. In 1985, it is estimated that over $400 million worth of imports accounting for 40 percent of total imports were financed by foreign exchange owned by importers. The value of official exports was around $340 million, which is the lowest nominal value for the past decade. It is impossible to get good estimates of illegal exports but they are quite large.

The policies adopted in the 1984/85 budget were considered a significant move towards more realistic economic policies by major aid donors, including the World Bank. The IMF saw these policies as positive but still "too little and too late." They provide a basis for further consultations to prepare the ground for negotiating a standby arrangement. In the negotiations, the major area of contention was exchange rate adjustment. The IMF technical team insisted on using simple purchasing power parity estimates while Tanzania experts wanted to base exchange rate adjustment on producer prices and the finances of the state-owned export crop marketing companies. Specifically, government experts preferred an exchange rate adjustment that would allow these companies to break even.

In 1985, no agreement on exchange rate adjustment was reached. The policy measures advanced by the government were seen to be relevant only if an agreement with the IMF was reached. Once there was no agreement, those policies were not implemented. Exchange rate adjustment policies proposed by the government were mainly a reaction to the proposals of the IMF mission. An independently formulated and technically credible adjustment program was lacking.

A breakthrough in negotiation had to wait until after the October 1985 election. The new government initiated policy discussions with the IMF on the magnitude of exchange rate adjustment and other policy actions that would be necessary for Tanzania to have access to IMF resources. Aid donors were urging the government to implement major policy adjustments, particularly devaluation, increase in producer prices, and liberalization of the marketing system. The Netherlands, Canada, and the United Kingdom publicly indicated that unless major macroeconomic adjustments were taken and an agreement with the IMF reached, they would reduce their aid commitments.

The foreign exchange shortage worsened and acute shortage of fuel was common in the first quarter of 1986. The need for policy reforms, particularly exchange rate adjustment, was heatedly debated. Most local economists argued that the shilling was extremely overvalued. Ndulu and Lipumba (1986) suggested an immediate devaluation from Shs. 16.00 per U.S. dollar to Shs. 40.00 per dollar and an automatic periodic adjustment to correct for inflation differential with the basket currencies.

After full-scale negotiations in January 1986 and further consultations in April, the government, in close cooperation with the World Bank, prepared the Economic Recovery Program whose objectives were related to the Structural Adjustment Program. The government accepted the need to take drastic policy measures, particularly regarding devaluation, increase in producer prices, and credit control. The World Bank and other major donors considered the policy action the government intended to take as very significant, and thus worthy of donor support. The IMF did not consider the measures as adequate but acceded to the World Bank and other aid donors. The IMF and Tanzania were able to agree on an eighteen-month standby arrangement for SDR 64.2 million, which is only 60 percent of Tanzania's quota of SDR 107 million. This is a very small amount compared to the last standby arrangement in 1980 that authorized the Government of Tanzania to purchase up to SDR 186 million in two years.

In order to gain new donor support, several major changes were announced. The government adopted policies that included a more flexible exchange rate. The shilling has been periodically devalued from Shs. 16 per U.S. dollar to Shs. 40 per dollar in June 1986. The Bank of Tanzania expected to periodically adjust the exchange rate to remove overvaluation caused by high inflation in Tanzania relative to the major trading partners. Producer prices of agricultural commodities were significantly increased. The government committed itself "to set producer prices at a level equivalent to 60-70 percent of the FOB prices, or to increase them by 5 percent per annum in real terms whichever is higher." The effectiveness of the agreements and the policy changes remain to be seen.

THE ECONOMIC RECOVERY PROGRAM AND PROSPECTS FOR ITS SUCCESS

Conflict over policy goals and economic priorities continually marked the negotiations between Tanzania and donor agencies. Deeply engrained political arrangements and economic structures made it difficult for the Tanzanian government to accept the prescriptions offered by the IMF and World Bank. In this section I will briefly consider some key areas of agreed reform—agriculture, manufacturing, parastatals—between Tanzania and donors. I will show that ongoing tensions remain over policy reforms, as entrenched state interests will not disappear with the signing of an agreement.

The Economic Recovery Program (ERP) aims at increasing the growth rate of GDP at an annual rate of 4.5 percent between 1986 and 1991. It is projected that after five to seven years, a sustainable balance of payments position and a low rate of inflation will be achieved. The specific program adopted will run for three years. The objectives of the program are expected to be achieved through an increase in the production of food and export crops, and an increase in the capacity utilization of the existing industries from the current 20-30 percent to 60-70 percent in 1988/89. Foreign exchange earnings from exports are expected to increase by 11.6 percent in 1987, and 19 percent in both 1988 and 1989.

The ERP emphasizes maintenance and rehabilitation of the existing capital stock rather than new investments, and the provision of current inputs to reactivate the production sector. The main constraint to increasing production is seen as lack of adequate foreign exchange. The preparation of the program concentrated on estimating minimum import requirements. To finance the program the government is mobilizing additional external funding. During the Paris Consultative Group meeting in June 1986 a number of donors pledged their financial commitments to implementing the ERP. Supplementary pledges resulting from the Paris meeting amounted to $136 million.

Negotiation of funding from the World Bank was not yet completed and was dependent on agreement on a system of allocating foreign exchange. IMF funding hinged on whether the quarterly performance tests were met. Despite these complications, the ERP started during a good year because the weather was very favorable and food production was high. The short-term problem facing the agricultural sector is that the marketing system is still very inefficient. While producer prices for export crops are remunerative, payment delays are still common and timely distribution of inputs has not been achieved. The restoration of cooperatives was expected to improve efficiency in marketing. Most cooperatives do not have grassroot support and accountability, and they have started operations with high overheads. Unless there is an improvement in the marketing system, the objective of increasing export earnings is unlikely to be achieved.

Foreign exchange shortage is one of several problems facing the manufacturing sector. Past investments and choices of technology have led to the establishment of a high-cost import-intensive industrial sector. A World Bank mission surveyed the industrial sector in 1984 and concluded that apart from food and beverage industries and few others, many industries had negative value added at world prices. In many cases the problem is not simply poor management but structural. To economize foreign exchange some industries must be permanently closed. This is a politically difficult decision to make. However, if available foreign exchange is spread to operate each industrial establishment, the industrial sector will not recover.

At the present time, parastatal organizations continue to dominate the economy. Unfortunately many are run inefficiently and are therefore a burden to the national economy. A significant privatization policy has not been adopted and even if one were adopted, it would not solve the problem of inefficiency in the public sector. An efficient public sector is a necessary component of any successful economy. In Tanzania the government has overstretched itself and has taken responsibilities that exceed its administrative capacity by taking over commercial operations that could best be left to the private sector. Parastatal organizations are not facing competitive pressure that could spur cost reduction and efficiency performance. Inefficient public enterprises prevent the successful control of credit and monetary expansion that is necessary if inflation is to be contained. When the government monopolies incur financial losses, there is political and economic pressure to bail them out. If they are allowed to collapse, there are no alternatives to offer similar services. For example, Regional Cooperative Unions have monopolies in marketing major export crops. If they are inefficient and no credit is extended, crops will not be purchased and this will discourage production.

The problem facing structural adjustment and stabilization in Tanzania is such that the ERP is constrained by the ongoing reluctance of the state to change its public sector operations. The government has to choose whether to allow private competition or to cover the losses of public enterprises. If the public enterprises collapse without any private alternatives, the solution is likely to worsen existing economic problems. If this is the case, then the stringent credit controls necessary to meet the IMF and World Bank criteria may actually lead to production declines and drastic increases in prices.

REFERENCES

Amin, Samir. 1974. *Accumulation on a World Scale.* New York: Monthly Review Press.

Balassa, B. 1984. "Adjustment Policies and Development Strategies in Sub-

Saharan Africa 1973-78." In Moshe Syrquin, Lance Taylor, Larry E. Westphal, *Economic Structure and Performance.* New York: Academic Press.
Bank of Tanzania. 1984. *Economic and Operations Report.*
Dell, Sidney. 1982. "Stabilization: The Political Economy of Overkill." *World Development* 10 (No. 8).
Diaz-Alejandro, Carlos F. 1981. "Southern Cone Stabilization Plans." In W.R. Cline and S. Wietraub eds., *Economic Stabilization in Developing Countries.* Washington D.C.: The Brookings Institution.
Green, R.H. 1983. "Political-Economic Adjustment and IMF Conditionality: Tanzania, 1974-81." In John Williamson, ed., IMF Conditionality, Washington, D.C.: Institute for International Economics, pp. 348-379.
International Labor Organization (ILO). 1982. *Basic Needs in Danger: A Basic Need Oriented Development Strategy for Tanzania,* Addis Ababa.
International Labor Organization (ILO). 1985. "Distribution Aspects of Stabilization Programs in Tanzania," Geneva.
Killick, T. 1984. *The IMF and Stabilization: Developing Country Experiences.* London: Heinemann.
Krueger, Anne O. 1978. *Foreign Trade Regimes and Economic Development: Liberalization Attempts and Consequences.* Cambridge, Mass.: Ballinger.
Kruman, K.L. 1985. *The External Debt of Sub-Saharan Africa: Origins, Magnitude and Implications for Action.* World Bank Staff Working Papers, No. 741.
Lele, U. 1984. "Tanzania: Phoenix or Icarus." In Arnold C. Harberger, ed., *World Economic Growth.* San Francisco: Institute of Contemporary Studies, pp. 159-196.
Leys, Colin. 1982. "African Economic Development in Theory and Practice." *Daedalus* 3 (No. 2).
Lipumba, N.H.I., L. Msambichaka, and S.M. Wangwe. 1984. *Economic Stabilization Policies in Tanzania.* Dar es Salaam: University of Dar es Salaam.
Ndulu, B.J. and N.H.I. Lipumba. 1986. "Adjustment Processes and Effects: Toward Economic Recovery in Tanzania." Paper presented at the Economic Policy Workshop on Policies and Strategies for Economic Recovery, February 1986.
Nyerere, J.K. 1980. "No to IMF Meddling." *Development Dialogue,* pp.7-9.
———. 1982. *Five Years of CCM.* Dar es Salaam: East Africa Publishing House.
United Republic of Tanzania, Ministry of Agriculture, Marketing Development Bureau. 1984. *Price Policy Recommendations for the 1984 Agricultural Price Review: Summary,* Dar es Salaam.
———, Ministry of Finance, Planning and Economic Affairs, *Budget Speech 1986/87,* Dar es Salaam.
———, Ministry of Planning and Economic Affairs. 1984. *Hali ya Uchumi wa Taifa Katika Mwaka 1984,* Dar es Salaam.
———, Ministry of Planning and Economic Affairs. 1983. *Structural Adjustment Program,* Dar es Salaam.
UN Conference on Trade and Development (UNCTAD). 1983. *Handbook of International Trade Statistics.*
World Bank. 1981. *Accelerated Development in Sub-Saharan Africa.* New York: Oxford University Press.
———, 1982. *Tanzania Agricultural Sector Report,* Washington, D.C.: World Bank.

———. 1983. *Sub-Saharan Africa: A Progress Report on Development Prospects and Programs.* Washington, D.C.: World Bank.

———. 1984. *World Development Report.* 1984. New York: Oxford University Press.

Yagci, F., S. Kamin, and V. Rosenbaum. 1985. *Structural Adjustment Lending: An Evaluation of Program Design.* World Bank Staff Working Papers, No. 735.

CHAPTER 4

Impact of the World Bank-Supported Agricultural Development Project on Rural Women in Zambia

Monica Munachonga

Much of the literature on development in the Third World indicates that complex factors, both endogeneous and exogeneous, have contributed to the current economic problems facing those countries. Many accounts stress the problem of food shortages and poverty among the majority of the populations in the developing countries. Various efforts are being made by those countries, with help from governments of industrialized countries and international aid agencies, notably the World Bank and the International Monetary Fund (IMF). For instance, Zambia has introduced new measures or policies, such as decontrol of prices and auctioning of foreign exchange, in which the IMF has played a major role. Zambia introduced these measures to effect changes in the distribution of income sections of its rural and urban populations and to stimulate production in key sectors of the economy, which include the agricultural sector.[1] Increased production in agriculture is regarded as important not only because it will result in a reduction in the food import bill, but also because it constitutes a main means of raising the living standards of the majority of the rural population (see *Third National Development Plan*, 1979).

It is within the context of the serious economic problems of developing countries, government efforts to deal with those problems, and the role of aid agencies that this paper is placed. Using Zambia as a case study, I will examine and assess the impact on rural women of one of the ongoing development projects in Zambia supported by the International Development Association (IDA) of the World Bank. This project, the Agricultural Development Project, has been introduced in two of Zambia's traditionally agricultural provinces, Eastern and Southern Provinces. The project began in 1981 in Eastern Province where the total estimated cost is U.S. $29.1 million, and in 1983 in

Southern Province where the total estimated cost is $24.6 million (see Table 4.1). As Table 4.1 shows, the World Bank places considerable emphasis on agricultural and rural development in Zambia.

The Agricultural Development Project is fairly recent in Zambia, which may mean that previous evaluations of its achievements and/or constraints are likely to be few. Consequently, my assessment of the project's impact on women will emphasize its potential (based on its methods of identifying target groups and providing extension services) for providing meaningful participation by women. Since little empirical research has been carried out on the project, my discussion will be limited in terms of quantitative analysis as regards male and female rates of participation, which necessarily implies emphasis on a more qualitative assessment of the project's impact on rural women.

Many accounts of agricultural and rural development in Zambia stress that most, if not all, development projects in this sector of the economy have reflected male bias as regards identification of target groups and provision of extension services (see ZARD 1985, chap. 4). The crucial questions then are: To what extent has the Agricultural Development Project departed from the approach used by previous projects in selection of target groups and provision of extension? Has the project any potential for increasing direct participation by women in agriculture? It is my view that, given the predominance of women in the agricultural sector of the economy (see, for example, Chilivumbo

Table 4.1   Zambia—Ongoing Projects Financed by World Bank/IDA

Name of Project	Total Costs in US$ Million
1. Coffee Production Project- Credit No. 864ZA	8.3
2. Technical Assistance Project- Credit No. 873ZA	5.0
3. Southern Province Agricultural Development Project-Credit No. 1193ZA	24.6
4. Smallholder Dairy Development Project- Credit No. 1196ZA	11.6
5. Fifth Education Project- Credit No. 1251ZA	39.2
6. Coal Engineering Project- Credit No. 1333ZA	6.1
7. Rural Water Supply Project- Credit No. 1362ZA Special Fund-Credit No. SF2ZA	20.0
8. Industrial Forestry Development Project- Credit No. 1437ZA	67.5
9. Fisheries Development Project- Credit No. 1529ZA	10.6
10. Agricultural Rehabilitation Project- Credit No. 1545ZA	65.0
11. Third Highway Project- Loan No. 1566ZA -Credit No. 798ZA	26.7
12. Third Railway Project- Loan No. 1790ZA- Credit No. 973ZA	188.15
13. Fourth Railway Project	83.1
14. Second Development Bank of Zambia Project-Loan No. 1923ZA	15.0
15. Eastern Province Agricultural Development Project- Loan No. 2001ZA	29.1
16. Indeni Refinery Modification Project- Credit No. 2151ZA	5.8
17. Petroleum Exploration Promotion Project- Loan No. 2152ZA	8.1
18. Export Rehabilitation and Diversification Project- Loan No. 2391ZA	300.0
19. Industrial Reorientation Project	62.2
20. Tazama Pipeline Rehabilitation Engineering Project	3.1
21. Fertilizer Input Restructuring Project	10.0

and Kanyangwa 1985; Safilios-Rothschild 1985), any agricultural and rural development project that does not seek to involve women directly is not likely to reduce gender inequalities in favor of women, nor is it likely to be successful in terms of achieving the objective of increased agricultural and food production.

The problem of male bias has been stressed in studies of development and social change, in general. Reports show shifts in government policy in favor of equality of opportunity between the sexes in terms of access to scarce resources and contribution to national development. While the colonial administration sought to restrict women's access to resources and participation in the national economy, the post-independence government has sought to give women equal opportunities with men in all aspects of social life. However, there is also evidence that the egalitarian policies have not been effectively implemented. Women still lag behind men in terms of education, training, and employment (see Bardouille 1981, 1982; Hansen 1980; Munachonga 1986), and also in agriculture and rural development (Keller 1984a). In other words, available evidence indicates that certain colonial legacies persist in present-day Zambia, and that development and social change has been to the detriment of women. How is this so in agricultural development?

WOMEN'S ROLE IN AGRICULTURE AND FOOD PRODUCTION IN ZAMBIA

It should be mentioned here that the majority (nearly 60 percent) of the country's population are rural dwellers, earning their livelihoods mainly from farming (see Zambia 1985a, p.67). Traditionally in Zambia, women have played a major role in agricultural crop production. Massive empirical evidence indicates that women still provide most of the labor required in agricultural production, both for subsistence food needs and for the market (Chilivumbo and Kanyangwa 1985; Munachonga and Serpell 1986; Mwanwaja and Kuezi-nke 1986; ZARD 1985). Women participate in almost all agricultural activities—clearing fields; planting; tending standing crops; harvesting, collecting, and storing crops; shelling; and transporting crops for sale. Moreover, food processing at household levels is a predominantly female activity, just as water and firewood collection are also exclusively female activities (see, for example, Milimo 1984). This suggests that rural women's lack of access to labor-saving technology has important implications for changes in the sex-division of labor. It has been reported that developments that have taken place in the agricultural sector of the economy, as a consequence of the introduction of modern technology, have affected women adversely. The introduction of the money economy has, for instance, resulted in production not only for subsistence needs, but also for the market. Reports show that cash crop production has come to be monopolized or dominated by men, while women continue to be the main food crop producers (Chilivumbo and Kanyangwa 1985; Mwanwaja and Kuezi-nke 1986; see also Colson 1958).

As regards the usual household arrangements for agricultural production, a woman is allocated by the male head of household her own plot where she can grow crops such as groundnuts (traditionally a female crop), maize, millet, sorghum, beans, and cassava. Women work on their fields, in addition to their family plots, usually for the purpose of growing cash crops; all their work is under the control of the male head of the family. This practice favors men in terms of access to allocation and control within the family as well as disposal of family income from crop sales. It should be pointed out that although women have rights to sell surplus food crops from their fields, they are limited by the fact that the crops are usually used for household consumption. This means that rural women, in general, are financially dependent on the male heads of their households (i.e., husbands). However, available empirical evidence on financial relationships between husbands and wives in both rural and urban areas indicates that the amounts allocated to wives by husbands is at the discretion of the latter (Munachonga 1986; ZARD 1985). Thus, while the official view of income allocation within the household assumes that money that enters the household is equitably distributed among the members, a situation which has also been reported elsewhere in developing countries (see Pahl 1983; Whitehead 1981), in actual fact there are financial inequalities within households in favor of men.

Findings indicate that technological innovations in agriculture have not only led to changes in sex-division of labor and income distribution in favor of men, but also that the innovations have had the effect of increasing women's workload (Mbulo 1980). Expansion of farms, for example, means that women must spend more hours on weeding, planting, harvesting, etc. Mbulo (1980) found that women were also performing strenuous tasks (e.g., stumping, handling planters, ox-ploughs, cultivators), which were previously performed by men and which are still performed by women outside the Farm Settlements Schemes in the Southern Province. Increase in women's workload as a result of agricultural modernization and emphasis of production for the market has been demonstrated by previous researchers in terms of increases in the number of hours women spend in agriculture as compared to men. For example, Due and Mudenda (1984) found that during the farming season, women contributed 53 percent of total hours in agriculture compared with 47 percent by men (see also Mbulo 1980).

The importance of women's labor in agriculture is also demonstrated by the fact that, in some areas, it has increased the incidence of *polygyny* (Mabeza 1977; Mbulo 1980). Nevertheless, despite the important role that women play in both subsistence and cash-crop production, research findings indicate that women have not been integrated into agricultural development projects. That is, women are not benefiting equally with men from important projects of the Integrated Rural Development Programme (IRDP), such as Lima, which was initiated in the 1970s to increase the productivity, income, and standard of living of small-scale farmers. In terms of definition, a *lima* is a quarter of a hectare. The arrangement is that a farmer wishing to participate in Lima can obtain a small loan through a government credit agency for improved seeds, fertilizer, etc. However,

> at the time that 'Lima' was introduced, no attempt was made to ensure that female farmers, married and unmarried, would be able to participate. The 'Lima' message went through the established channels—from men to men. In peasant households of married couples, a new 'Lima' field intended for production of surplus for the market became the husband's field. (ZARD 1985, p. 113)

This may be explained, at least in part, by the general assumption that the allocation and control of money within households is done on an equal basis. On the contrary, empirical findings indicate that, in actual practice, men benefit more from cash-crop sales (see also Munachonga 1986, on the situation in towns). Field research findings show that although a relatively high proportion (about one-third) of all households in Zambia (see *Zambia 1985a*) are headed by women, the latter have largely been excluded from Lima cultivation (Safilios-Rothschild 1985). Thus, the important production-oriented Lima program has had little impact on women in, for example, North-Western Province (Geisler 1984). It appears that the selection of target groups for the Lima program has not taken into account sex ratios in the agricultural sector, which has placed women, particularly heads of households, in a vulnerable position.

The relative exclusion of women from agricultural and rural development programs and projects has worsened their economic position as compared to men. This exclusion has in turn increased the concern of outside donor agencies. Studies show the important role of donor agencies like Norwegian Overseas Aid (NORAD) and Swedish

International Development Agency (SIDA) in promoting and introducing agricultural projects specifically for women that will improve their productive skills and reduce their financial dependence on men (see Chilivumbo and Kanyangwa 1985; Munachonga and Serpell 1986). Until recently, emphasis has been on women's clubs that carried out mainly home economics activities. By contrast, women's agricultural projects sponsored by SIDA, for example, give loans, extension service, and training opportunities for women's Lima fields (not their family plots). However, research findings indicate that the idea of making women financially independent from husbands is not favored by members of the public, especially men (Munachonga and Serpell 1986). Thus, women's clubs supported by men are those that do not aim at equipping women with productive skills and that are not likely to improve their economic position.

Attitudes that favor the exclusion of women from the development process in general have been reflected in and reinforced by national development plans. For instance, both the First National Development Plan (1966-1970) and the Second National Development Plan (1972-1976) do not make reference to women as a section of the population that needs particular assistance in order to overcome their developmental problems. It should be pointed out that although the Third National Development Plan (1979-1983) includes a few lines on women under the Community Development section, this is in reference to "women's clubs" that stress improving women's performance as homemakers and mothers.

However, it is also important to note here that there is increasing awareness on the part of the government about women's development problems, partly as a consequence of Zambia's participation in the UN Decade for Women (1975-1985) and because of the influence of donor agencies. As a result, the government has decided to include a chapter on women in the Fourth National Development Plan based on a document reviewing the current situation of women, prepared at the National Commission for Development Planning (NCDP). Moreover, existing women's clubs are being encouraged to place less stress on the traditional role of women in favor of income-generating activities.

The foregoing discussion of the role and situation of rural women in development in Zambia leads us to consider the impact on women of the Agricultural Development Project supported by the World Bank. How has this project operated? To what extent does it have potential for women's participation and benefit? The method of identifying target groups is considered crucial, and it will be used here as one main means of determining possible increases in rates of participation by women. I shall now examine the implementation of the project in each of the two provinces involved, beginning with a description of the project in terms of its main objectives and methods of achieving those objectives.

THE AGRICULTURAL DEVELOPMENT PROJECT

According to the midterm reviews of the project from both provinces, one main objective is to increase production of agricultural crops, including maize, groundnuts, cotton, sunflower, beans, and soyabeans, by adopting improved technical packages (i.e., improved seeds, fertilizer, pesticides, and appropriate production practices by small farmers). In other words, the project aims at improving the nutritional and living standards of currently low-income rural producers. Other project inputs are improvements on the agricultural camps, construction of staff houses, renovation of staff houses, provision of the necessary equipment, vehicles, and cycles, and meeting of operational costs. The project also includes radical changes in the extension service system as well as attempts at the redistribution of income in favor of the rural poor. All this is in line with a broad government policy that seeks to raise the living standards of a large proportion of the rural population.

In order to improve extension services to the small farmers, a new extension service system, called Training and Visit (T&V), was introduced. This system has now been adopted as a national model. T&V is an extension methodology by which new farming techniques and practices are introduced by extension workers to farmers. In each of the provinces involved, there is a Team Leader, a Farm Management Specialist, and an Extension Specialist. These people train extension workers in various agricultural techniques, who in turn pass on the technical messages to farmers through various channels of communication: radio, training courses at Farmers' Training Centers, bulletins, theatre, and visits to villages. As will be shown later, several districts in each of the provinces have been selected as pilot areas. In general, the project has necessitated complete reorganization of the provincial extension service system. T&V appears to be a technically efficient approach to agricultural development. However, its technical efficiency and, more importantly, potential for improving the living standards of rural women in Zambia must be measured against its actual practice in terms of implementation and operation. The first question is: How are target groups identified, and by whom?

Identification of Target Groups for the Project

As already explained above, the project aims at increasing the production capacity of small peasant farmers, most of whom are women. A close examination of midterm evaluation reports reveals some slight differences as regards the definition of the project's principal target groups. There are also differences between the provinces in the procedures for selecting contact farmers. These will be illustrated later.

In general, each province is divided into agricultural blocks and camps staffed by the Block Supervisor and Camp Officer, respectively. In the T&V system each agricultural extension worker identifies seven units, (each consisting of eight to ten contact farmers). The extension worker is expected to visit each one of the seven groups once every two weeks, delivering whatever extension message is relevant at that particular time. The extension workers themselves also receive appropriate training through, for example, field days at research stations, and workshops.

The Eastern Province Agricultural Development Project

The Eastern Province Agricultural Development Project (EPADP) was introduced in 1981. The first three growing seasons were spent mainly on carrying out preliminary research on growing particular crops, and also on the necessary reorganization of the provincial extension service in order to establish the T&V model. Currently, five districts are involved in the project (see Table 4.2). As regards the question of who constituted the principle target group for the project, it is stated in the midterm review that the project in Eastern Province is aimed at *hoe cultivators*. The category includes a majority of women producers, since the general tendency in agricultural modernization is for the men to monopolize modern technology. It is from among hoe cultivators that contact farmers were to be selected. Procedures for selecting contact farmers are explained as follows:

> Contact farmers are meant to be selected because they represent the majority interest. This has not happened in all cases. In some villages they (i.e. contact farmers) have been selected by Camp Officers or Village Headman which has resulted in some contact farmers not being representative. . . . This is supported by [available] material which suggests that Contact Farmers are [those] more likely to use fertilizers, own oxen and receive credit. (Zambia 1986, p.6)

This shows that in actual practice, poor farmers appear to be

Table 4.2 Extension Service: Present Distribution of Staff and Camps

District	No. of Blocks	No. of Camps	T&V Units	New[a] Camps
Chipata South	4	24	24	3
Chipata North	4	15	23	4
Katete	4	14	16	3
Lundazi	5	29	37	13
Chandiza	4	15	19	2
Petauke	4	20	0	0
Nyimba	2	7	0	0
Chama	5	19	0	0
Mambwe	1	4	0	0
TOTALS:	33	137	119	25

Source: EPADP/IBRD/IFAD Mid-Term Evaluation, March, 1985, page 11.

Note: [a] = Being built

excluded from the project. What of the involvement of women as contact farmers? In this regard, the EPADP midterm evaluation report states:

> Staff are encouraged to include females as Contact Farmers. It is estimated that 30 percent of heads of households in the province are female. *Currently only 3% of contact farmers are female* [emphasis added]. (Zambia 1985b, p.13)

As regards actual figures on contact farmers, this is not made clear in the report. However, the percentage of female contact farmers stated above indicates that women are underrepresented in the project. In other words, the report suggests that the way the project has been implemented discriminates against women. Another problem relating to statistics is that the evaluation report does not provide information on the actual numbers or on the sex composition of extension workers. However, from national statistics in other research reports, where it is stated that only 7.3 percent of 1,956 extension workers in the country were women in 1984 (Keller et al. 1985), one may conclude that the number of female extension workers for the project is low. Moreover, the majority of female extension workers in Zambia are home economists rather than agricultural extension workers.

Major constraints of the EPADP. Among some of the major constraints mentioned in the EPADP midterm evaluation report are the following:

1. Lack of adequate funds to train Zambian staff for the project,

particularly at the postgraduate level (p.4). This implies continued reliance on expatriate personnel.
2. Shortage of extension staff (p.10).
3. Lack of adequate transport for the project. In this regard only 18 of the planned 26 four-wheel-drive vehicles have been allocated by the project; about 33 instead of 100 motorcycles have been purchased. However, more bicycles (210 instead of the planned 170) have been provided. Nevertheless, it is also reported that most of the bicycles are already out of use. It should also be explained that both motorcycles and pedalcycles are for purchase by extension workers with staff loans. It is suggested that few staff manage to buy these because prices of these items are high (pp.11-12).
4. Inadequate credit facilities (p.17).
5. Low motivation among field staff which, it is indicated, arises from the fact that they are not trained for the T&V system which "imposes a high degree of discipline and planning on staff" (p.13).
6. Problems of getting materials for communicating technical messages—e.g., difficulties in getting batteries for radios by farmers, inappropriate equipment for visual aids, etc.

The Southern Province Agricultural Development Project

Although the Southern Province Agricultural Development Project (SPADP) was initiated in 1983, staffing problems caused delays in its actual implementation; it was not implemented until January 1985. At that time, the project covered a total of seventy-four camps and 5,200 contact farmers (see Table 4.3). Southern Province has a total of seven districts, each with two farming blocks. As in the Eastern Province, extension service has been reorganized in order to establish the T&V system and to increase production by *smallholders*. In other words, the target group for the project was those with lower standards of living.

Table 4.3 T&V Expansion Program

Year	No. of Blocks		No. of Camps		No. of Contact Farmers	
	Appraisal	Actual	Appraisal	Actual	Appraisal	Actual
1983	—	—	—	—	—	—
1984	—	—	40	—	9,600	—
1985	—	14	84	74	20,160	5,200
1986	—	14	139	74	31,920	5,200
1987	—	21	187	110	44,880	7,700
1988	—	33	197	200	47,280	14,000
1989	—	33	197	200	47,280	14,000

Source: SPADP Mid-Term Evaluation Report, September 1985, p. 15.

Selection of contact farmers. The evaluation report explains that the current 5,200 contact farmers were *selected by the farmers themselves* with assistance from extension workers. The report is silent as regards the sex composition of the contact farmers. However, field research findings suggest that the rate of participation by women is very low.[2] In terms of actual selection of contact farmers, it is explained:

> Special attention was paid so that the contact farmers belonged to the different socio-economic groups of the area, they are practising farmers and willing to adopt relevant recommendations, they are dispersed throughout the group area and represent major crop and livestock enterprises. (Zambia 1985c, p.3)

This implies that even the already progressive farmers can be selected as contact farmers. Moreover, a willingness to adopt relevant recommendations in agriculture is likely to be expressed by those who can afford it financially and who understand the advantages of changing their farming practices in favor of modernization. Do the majority of women producers fall into this category? The argument here is that emphasis on farmers' willingness to adopt extension workers' recommendations may provide an excuse for staff not to try to include women whose husbands are unlikely to approve their participation. Research findings indicate that women's participation in development projects tends to be determined more by their husbands' or male guardians' approval than by their own choosing (Munachonga and Serpell 1986, Report 2, p. 44).[3] Research findings also indicate that women lack access to extension services (Serpell 1980).

As regards the participation of women as extension workers, no statistics are provided on extension staff positions.

Constraints to implementation of SPADP. Among the main factors identified as constraints affecting the operation of the new extension service system are (see Zambia 1985c, Working Paper 1, pp.10-11):

1. Transportation problems, which are said to have adversely affected communication of information on technical packages by Camp Officers (i.e., Village Extension Workers), to farmers, and the attendance of Provincial Specialists and district staff at training courses conducted by Agricultural Block Supervisors for Camp Officers
2. Delays in release of funds for purchase of needed materials
3. Inadequate funds for necessary materials
4. Shortage of specialist staff

5. Low participation rate of specialists due, it is argued, to unclear definition of their roles in the project, and also possibly to lack of transport
6. Lack of understanding of the project due to inadequate discussion during initial stages
7. Overloading of extension staff with data collection, writing of quarterly reports, and retraining for the T&V system at the same time that the project is being implemented
8. Small farmers' lack of access to credit facilities: "At present the small holders in the Province do not have access to medium-term credit either from Agricultural Finance Company (AFC) or the commercial banks." (Zambia 1985c, Working Paper 5, p.7)

CONCLUSION: IMPACT OF THE AGRICULTURAL DEVELOPMENT PROJECT ON RURAL ZAMBIAN WOMEN

The preceding examination of the operation of the Agricultural Development Project supported by the World Bank has revealed that women in both provinces have not benefited from the project. It has been demonstrated that women have not had equal access with men to the "technical packages" aimed at improving the productive capacities and living standards of small agricultural producers, most of whom, available information shows, are women.

The way that the T&V system has been implementated has discriminated against poor women farmers. This is despite the 1985 policy directive that field staff should work with male and female contact farmers (Keller et al. 1985). As we have seen, male extension staff in the Eastern Province appear to have ignored pleas for them to "encourage" women to be contact farmers. It has also been reported that women's Lima groups have not been involved in the T&V extension system, which has led to the conclusion that *the T&V model is a good example of a technically efficient approach to agricultural development which excludes women* (see ZARD 1985, p. 114). Taking into account the above observations about operation of the project as it has been implemented in Zambia, it is not unreasonable to suggest that lack of participation by women is largely due to the fact that the extension service is still dominated by men. As we have seen, only a tiny minority of extension workers are women and these are largely home economists rather than agricultural extension workers. Research findings show that home economists are assigned lower status than agricultural extension workers in the Department of Agriculture, which tends to lower their morale and commitment to women's development (see Munachonga and Serpell 1986).

It should, however, be pointed out that the exclusion of women from agricultural development and modernization is not characteristic of or unique to the T&V model. We have seen that many other development projects in the country—for example, such agricultural programs as the 'Lima' program (an important production-oriented program) and the Integrated Rural Development Programme—have not included women as a special target group. This adversely affects the economic position of rural women, female household heads in particular. In general, although women are expected to contribute (and actually do contribute) their labor in both subsistence and cash-crop production, they do not have access to productive resources and to income realised from the sale of crops. Therefore, agricultural and rural development continues to benefit the male population of Zambia's rural society.

Gender inequalities in rural development can be reduced only when women, who are also the main food and agricultural producers, are given access to factors of production. The need for radical changes in the provision of extension services to favor women farmers can be achieved by identifying women as target groups. This argument is based on the fact that many previous agricultural and rural development projects directed at men by virtue of their status as traditional heads of households have not succeeded.[4] All this implies the retraining of extension staff to make them more sensitive to women's developmental problems—problems that have been stressed in most of the available literature.

Changes in policies for agricultural development and extension services should be based on needs assessment surveys, an important means of finding out and understanding the prevailing patterns of female/male relationships, sex-division of labor and, in particular, the agricultural activities of the food producers (i.e., women). Needs assessment surveys may be useful to development agents and governments in providing political education to the rural population about the importance of giving women direct access to factors of production. The general public must be helped to understand that women's access to factors of production is mainly to benefit their families and the nation at large.

NOTES

1. I have analyzed in another study the economic hardships urban poor women are experiencing, and the survival strategies they have had to adopt as a consequence of the new economic measures that have led to the sharp

increases in prices of essential commodities. (For details, see Munachonga 1986b.)

2. For example, only one female in Gwembe and none in Namwala was reported to be a contact farmer among the women we interviewed in the areas. See Munachonga and Serpell 1986.

3. In general, Zambian traditional norms require wives to seek their husbands' approval in order to be engaged in activities ouside the home. This implies that husbands can withhold such approval if they consider the activity in question to be in conflict with their own interests.

4. One good example of such projects is the water project in the Western Province, introduced by NORAD in 1977. It has been reported that this project has failed mainly because experts at the time of introduction decided to consult men rather than women, the main collectors and users of water. Thus, the wells and boreholes were sunk where they were not actually needed. For more details, see Milimo 1984.

REFERENCES

Bardouille, R. 1981. "University of Zambia Students' Career Expectations." In Manpower Research Report, No. 9. Institute for African Social Research, University of Zambia.

———. 1982. "Men and Women's Work Opportunities in the Informal Sector." Manpower Research Report, No. 10. Institute for African Social Research, University of Zambia.

Blake, J. 1984. An analysis of IRDP/Northern Province: Development Strategy for Rural Women. Kasama: Integrated Rural Development Programme.

Chilivumbo, A. and J. Kanyangwa. 1985. "Women's Participation in Rural Development Programmes: The case of the SIDA Lima Programme." Occasional Papers, No. 22. Rural Development Studies Bureau, University of Zambia.

Colson, E. 1958. *Marriage and the Family among the Plateau Tonga of Northern Rhodesia.* Manchester: Manchester University Press.

Due, J., T. Mudenda, and P. Miller. 1984. "How Do Rural Women Perceive Development? A Case Study in Zambia." WID Working Paper, No. 63. Michigan State University.

Geisler, G. 1984. "Possible Women's Programmes in the IRDP Project Area of North-Western Province, Zambia." Lusaka: GTZ/IRDP North-Western Province.

Hansen, K.T. 1980. "When Sex Becomes a Critical Variable: Married Women's Extra-Domestic Work in Lusaka, Zambia." *African Social Research* (No. 30). Institute for African Studies, University of Zambia.

Keller, B.B. 1984a. "The Integration of Zambian Women in Development." Lusaka: NORAD.

———. 1984b. "Women in Agriculture." Paper prepared for Women's Affairs Planning Committee for the Women's Chapter, for the Fourth National Development Plan. National Commission for Development Planning.

Keller, B.B. et al. 1985. "Women in Agriculture." Paper prepared for the Food and Agriculture Organization (FAO). Human Resources, Institutions and Agrarian Reform Division, Rome.

Mabeza, R.M. 1977. "The Changing Role of Women in Development." M.A.

Thesis. Clark University, Worcester, Massachusetts.

Milimo, M.C. 1984. "Women and Water: The Involvement of Women in Rural Water Supply Projects in the Western Province of Zambia, Part 1: the Mongu Area." Consultancy Report for NORAD.

Mbulo, M.P. 1980. "The Effects of Cash Crop Production on Men's and Women's and Children's Participation in Agricultural Production: A Case Study of the Magoye Settlements in Mazabuka District." Report of a research project. Lusaka: University of Zambia, Institute for African Studies.

Munachonga, M.L. 1986a. "Conjugal Relations in Urban Zambia." Master's thesis, University of Sussex.

———. 1986b. *Impact of Economic Adjustments on Women in Zambia*. Lusaka: National Technical Cooperation Assessments and Programmes (NatCap).

Munachonga, M.L. and N. Serpell. 1986. "Needs Assessment Survey of Rural Women in the Gwembe and Namwala Districts of Southern Province, Zambia." Reports 1 and 2. Consultancy Reports for Ministry of Agriculture and Water Development (Home Economics Section) and Swedish International Development Agency (July).

Mwanwaja, V.D. and J.V. Kuezi-nke. 1986. "Women in Agriculture and Food Production in Zambia." Background Paper for National Technical Cooperation Assessments and Programmes (NatCap) in Zambia (April).

Pahl, J. 1983. "The Allocation of Money and the Structuring of Inequality Within Marriage." *The Sociological Review Monograph* 30, pp. 237-262.

Safilios-Rothschild, C. 1985. "Policy Implications of the Roles of Women in Agriculture in Zambia." Lusaka: Planning Division Special Studies, No. 20.

Schuster, I. 1979. *New Women of Lusaka*. Palo Alto, Calif.: Manyfield Publishing Co.

Serpell, N. 1980. "Women in Zambia: An Analysis of Services in Rural Areas." Lusaka: UNICEF. (Mimeo)

Whitehead, A. 1981. "I'm Hungry Mum: The Politics of Domestic Budgeting." In K. Young et al., eds., *Of Marriage and the Market*. London: CSE Brooks.

Zambia. 1966. *First National Development Plan, 1966-1970*.

———. 1972. *Second National Development Plan, 1972-1976*.

———. 1979. *Third National Development Plan, 1979-1983*.

———. 1985a. Central Statistics Office. *1980 Population and Housing Census of Zambia (Analytical Report, Vol. 2)*.

———. 1985b. Ministry of Agriculture and Water Development, *Eastern Province Agricultural Development Project (EPADP) Mid-Term Evaluation*. Chipata, Eastern Province (March).

———. 1985c. Ministry of Agriculture and Water Development. *Southern Province Agricultural Development Project (SPADP), Mid-Term Evaluation Report*. Livingstone, Southern Province (September).

———. 1986. EPADP. A study of the Communication Needs of the Extension Service in Eastern Province (August).

ZARD (Zambia Association for Research and Development). 1985. *An Annotated Bibliography of Research on Zambia Women*. Lusaka: ZARD.

PART II

Donor Policy: The Challenges of Reform

CHAPTER 5

Issues of Political Economy in Formulating Donor Policy Toward Sub-Saharan Africa

Robert Christiansen, Cheryl Christensen, and Beatrice Edwards

There can be little question about the severity of the economic crisis that plagues Africa. For-thirty nine sub-Saharan countries with a combined population of 400 million, the average per capita gross domestic product (GDP) declined 2.4 percent per year between 1980 and 1985, to $410 (USDA/ERS, 1986, p.14). Population growth rates averaged nearly 3 percent and reached a high of 4 percent in many countries. The growth of export volume during the same period averaged 2.8 percent for Africa, compared with 6.5 percent for the non-oil exporting countries as a group. Per capita food production has declined by about 20 percent over the past two decades, causing commercial imports of grain to increase by about 9 percent per annum over the same period (Helleiner 1986, p.47). For thirty-three sub-Saharan countries for which data are available, twenty-one had debt equal to or greater than half the value of their GDP. Nine countries had debt greater than the entire value of their GDP. A total of sixteen countries from this same group has a debt-service ratio in excess of 20 percent.[1]

The combination of slow income growth, heavy debt burdens, and severe foreign exchange constraints, all in conjunction with increasing pressure from bilateral and multilateral donors, have stimulated many African countries to adopt profound economic policy reforms that feature, among other things, greater export orientation. (As part of the move toward involvement in the international economy, policy changes designed to create less regulated domestic economies have also been adopted.) For most sub-Saharan countries, the renewed emphasis on exports has caused agriculture to become a major focus of these reforms. Changes in exchange rate policy, pricing policies, export tax structures, and government licensing and marketing practices have been undertaken in an attempt to stimulate a supply response, typically meaning an increase in agricultural exports. At the same time, price and subsidy policy changes, combined with the progressive elimination of state intervention in domestic agricultural markets, are being adopted in order to stimulate food production.

Although not all countries have received identical prescriptions for policy reform, the similarities are considerable. Among the reforms that are of importance to the agricultural sector are:

1. Devaluation of local currencies in order to allow international prices to more directly affect production decisions in the agricultural sector (if domestic pricing policies are also reformed)
2. Pricing policy changes that are intended to raise farmgate prices and production of food and export crops
3. Reduction of those government marketing and trade interventions, e.g., subsidies, that distort local incentives
4. Central government expenditure reforms aimed at reducing the deficit and thereby making more financial resources available for investment (USDA/ERS 1986, p.17) and
5. Privatization of many functions previously performed by government in an attempt to increase efficiency

The United States has a genuine stake in the success of these reforms as a means of promoting political stability in the region and the economic growth needed to aid in maintaining that stability. Additionally, African countries, along with other developing countries, have the potential to be important trading partners with the United States, if and only if these countries can produce sustained and broad-based income growth. Many of the policy changes currently being undertaken have been major elements of the U.S. policy dialogue with African countries, frequently in conjuction with other donors/lenders such as the World Bank and the IMF. Therefore, the current African environment provides more opportunity to generate economic growth through the use of market-oriented approaches than has been possible for decades and is an important one for U.S. policy in Africa.

The success of Africa's experiments with policy reforms, that necessarily focus on the agricultural sector but are linked to macroeconomic reforms, depends on both economic and political factors. The economic benefits of and requirements for economic growth under a more open trade and more market-oriented development strategy have been extensively analyzed (see Krueger 1980; Krueger and Michalopoulos 1985; Lewis and Kallab 1986; and Bhagwati 1986).

Far less attention has been paid to the political requisites for successful economic change and the implications of successful policy reforms for the longer-term stability of the political order and success of development strategies.

Interaction between political and economic factors in an export-oriented strategy tend to undermine the economic order in the agricultural sector and thereby add to political instability. Any policy reform pro-gram that ignores this potential will be unsuccessful. There are two general considerations, beyond the strict economic requirements, that are of particular importance in ensuring the success of the current reforms. These are: (1) the existence of a viable domestic political coalition that is willing to, and capable of, supporting an open development strategy, and (2) a development strategy that is structured to ensure that the benefits of export-led growth are available to a suffi-ciently wide range of groups (Ruggie 1983). Current U.S. assistance decisions will influence, though not necessarily determine, the role these factors will play in the implementation of policy reform. Choices made now about the level of assistance and the design and nature of that assistance, will have major implications for the viability of market-oriented interests in African countries and, in turn, their ability to develop broad-based support for more open, market-oriented policies.

We take the view that while there are questions about the wisdom and viability of a policy that features a strong agricultural export orientation for African countries, it is a policy that is currently being pursued and is deserving of serious effort to make it work. In this discussion we will identify the reasons for greater emphasis on agricultural exports as a development strategy, some of the criticisms of that approach, and two problems with the export-oriented strategy that have not been addressed by policymakers.[2] Finally, we make some recommendations for modifications of current policy that, if undertaken in a timely fashion, can increase the potential for policymakers to take advantage of the unusual opportunity to influence the economic and political future of many African nations.

THESIS

Although the current policy reform movement in Africa presents an unusual opportunity to strengthen and redirect the economies of many African nations, it is necessary to view these changes in a broader context than simple adjustments to economic variables. Certainly the potential results from the reforms, e.g., avoidance of famine, debt repayment, the emergence of stable regimes, higher levels of economic growth, and market development are consistent with U.S. economic and political goals for the region. In order to achieve these goals, however, it is necessary to modify current policy to recognize three important factors.

The first concerns the importance of political coalitions in the policymaking process and the need for a realignment of these coalitions when significant policy changes are undertaken. The political and economic systems that emerged in post-colonial Africa had a set of policy goals and a coalition of interest groups that supported these goals. Although the range of groups incorporated in the governing coalition varied considerably among African nations, one of the common goals was the pursuit of some measure of development and/or economic growth. The development strategies devised in pursuit of this goal ranged from those that sought complete disassociation from the world economy (Guinea), to those that pursued aggressive export strategies (Kenya). Even countries with similar strategies regarding the degree of desired integration adopted different sets of domestic policies for attaining this goal. Despite the differences, a common characteristic was the need to construct a coalition that supported both the broad outlines of the strategy and the means of implementation.

The economic situation of recent years, characterized by slow growth, increasing debt service ratios, and foreign exchange constraints, precipitated a policy crisis in many African countries. The policies supported by the governing coalition were discredited by the growing economic problems in many countries. Donors responded to the crisis by creating new aid facilities that have provided donors, especially the World Bank and IMF, with a substantially greater role in policy formulation in many African countries. In order to take advantage of this type of assistance, however, it is necessary to modify existing policies and to accept the presence of donors in the policymaking process. The result is a critical and newly assertive external member of the governing coalitions in the form of donors acting together. To the extent that the policy reforms prescribed by the donors are in conflict with parts of the development strategy pursued in the pre-crisis era, the donors will find themselves in opposition to some of the other members of the coalition. Therefore, the success of the reforms depends crucially on the ability to establish and maintain a coalition that is able to support the new policies, in the face of what can be forceful opposition.

The recognition of the need to consider the viability of such a pro-reform coalition leads to the second point, how to support the reform-minded components of the coalition. Among the requirements for a successful transition from a development strategy that featured protection of domestic production, price controls, and subsidies to a more market- and export-oriented strategy are: (1) macroeconomic adjustments that are manageable, (2) policy changes that are perceived by the relevant coalition members as nontransitory, and (3) reforms that achieve tangible benefits in a short period of time. The first requirement means that the governing group(s) is (are) not forced to an antidonor policy in order to maintain a workable coalition. The second helps to create incentives for a more permanent realignment in favor of the development strategy advocated by the external sponsors. This realignment in favor of what is typically a more trade-oriented strategy, however, does not coalesce immediately. It takes time for the policy shift to be perceived as permanent or as one that requires adjustment by current coalition members.

This leads to the third requirement, evidence that the new policy prescriptions are workable and can be used to convince local groups of the merits of the revised strategy. In the case of an increased export orientation, which in Africa usually means increased agricultural trade, this requires a demonstration that export markets are available and accessible and that previous constraints on imported inputs, most notably, foreign exchange availability, are less binding than in the past. In addition, the potential political problems that accompany the move toward increased agricultural exports are made even more problematic by the fact that few African governments have developed effective mechanisms for coping with international economic instability. Successful open development strategies frequently rest on the ability to identify (often short-lived) market niches and to move quickly to realize the gains they offer, while limiting the exposure to adverse circumstances. The international economic "niches" available to African countries are frequently limited, focusing on the export of primary agricultural commodities or minerals. Economic policies that hold more promise for identifying and exploiting relatively narrow market niches will also place a high political premium on coping, and distributing risk, uncertainty and loss. This aspect of the problem allows for an important contribution by official development assistance (ODA), namely, assistance in the form of access to developed country markets and loans.

The third point we wish to make, and one that typically is not well appreciated by policymakers, concerns the longer-term risks of an export-oriented strategy, especially one featuring agriculture. Specifically, an agricultural export strategy leads to increased commercialization of agriculture as part of the transformation from subsistence agriculture to production for export. The commercialization of agriculture frequently results in a widespread alienation of peasant land holdings. The nature of export opportunities is such that the operation of an unfettered market environment frequently leads to a concentration of land holdings in the hands of a few, as smallholders are induced to sell or otherwise relinquish their claim to land. Although such alienation is not inevitable, it is especially difficult to resist. With the rate of return to peasant labor depressed as a result of the taxation of output, especially export crops, a lump-sum payment in return for relinquishing land is often an attractive option. Owners of large land holdings are able to justify the acquisition of additional land in order to take advantage of economies of scale. (Frequently, though not in all cases, economies of scale are available as a result of inappropriate factor intensity—for example, capital-intensive production amid excess supplies of labor. Reasons for this economically inappropriate use of factors range from a desire to avoid labor problems to a lack of awareness of alternative means of production.) It is also the case that owners of large tracts of land are typically better able to gain access to credit and other purchased inputs. This may allow owners of large holdings to achieve a higher rate of return than smallholders. This can be interpreted as providing apparent justification for a concentration of holdings. Finally, it is typically the case that the owners of large land holdings are better able to influence the formulation of policy in ways that benefit their interests. This adds to the appeal, for some, of increased land concentration.

The result of the alienation of small land holdings is frequently the creation of a group of very poorly paid employees or widespread unemployment. This has the result of excluding large numbers of individuals from the benefits of economic growth. Without economic power or a set of working democratic institutions, these peasants are left without political power. The dissatisfaction that results from this economic and political disenfranchisement leads to a deterioration of political stability. In order to offset the pernicious effects of this form of agricultural commercialization, it is necessary to design programs that take advantage of the efficiency of market forces, but that are able to protect the longer-term economic interests of the agricultural labor force. In addition to the issue of program design, it is imperative that the efforts to protect the agricultural labor force be timely. Once the process of disenfranchisement begins, it is difficult to reverse (witness the widespread failure to implement effective land reform policies in Central America in recent years). The interests that grow up around that large-farm policy are powerful and are able to resist efforts to reform land ownership and agricultural policy. Further, many of the institutions through which policy needs to operate, e.g., local government, suffer an erosion in their effectiveness as disenfranchisement proceeds. Therefore, it is crucial to the success of the reforms that they be implemented before the process of land alienation and concentration becomes entrenched.

AGRICULTURAL TRADE AND DEVELOPMENT STRATEGIES

The Move Toward An Export Orientation

Since the late 1970s, there has been renewed emphasis on the export potential of the agricultural sector in sub-Saharan Africa as a means of solving many of the problems facing the region. This represents another in what seems to be a continuing series of changing perspectives on agriculture's role in development. Agriculture was viewed initially by many development experts as outmoded and a sector to be swept away as part of an outdated era. Eicher and Staatz (1984, p.5) identify some of the reasons for the latter view:

> The propensity of development economists to give relatively little attention to agriculture's "positive potential in facilitating overall economic growth" was based in part on the empirical observation that agriculture's share of the economy inevitably declines during the course of development for at least two reasons. First, the income elasticity of demand for unprocessed food is less than unity and declines with higher incomes; hence, the demand for raw agricultural products grows more slowly than consumption in general. Second, increasing labor productivity in agriculture means that the same farm output can be produced with fewer workers, implying a transfer of labor to other sectors of the economy. Because agriculture's share of the economy was assumed to be declining, many economists downplayed the need to invest in the agricultural sector in the short run.

Not all thinking on the subject was as pessimistic about agriculture's role. Eicher and Staatz (1984, pp.6-7) describe the position of Johnston and Mellor (1961) and its impact on the profession of agricultural economics:

> Johnston and Mellor drew insights from the Lewis model to stress the importance of agriculture as a motive force in economic growth. They argued that far from playing a passive role in development, agriculture could make five important contributions to the structural

transformation of Third World economies: it could provide labor, capital, foreign exchange, and food to a growing industrial sector and could supply a market for domestically produced industrial goods.

The work of neoclassical agricultural economists during the 1960s stressed not only the interdependence of agriculture and industry and the potentially important role that agriculture could play in economic development but also the importance of understanding the process of agricultural growth per se if that potential is to be exploited.

The evolution of theorizing about the role of the agricultural sector was motivated in large part by the perceived failures of earlier development paradigms. Mellor (1986, p. 73) argues that the problems the green revolution encountered in Africa "spawned a 'basic human needs' approach that emphasized social welfare functions." He goes on to argue that the current export orientation is also a result of dissatisfaction with earlier import substitution or "capital-intensive" policies.

The failings of the capital-intensive strategies, dependent as they were on market interference, also prompted a trend quite separate from the equity-oriented basic-needs strategy: a renewed interest in a market-oriented strategy commonly emphasizing export promotion. With the gradual demise of the basic-needs orientation in the early 1980s, the strategy of export-led growth or export promotion became the new fashion. (Mellor 1986, p. 74)

Certainly Mellor's hypotheses of crisis-induced evolution in theory finds support in the tone adopted in the influential World Bank report on sub-Saharan Africa (World Bank 1981).[3] The report described an African economic crisis characterized by "slow overall economic growth, sluggish agricultural performance coupled with rapid rates of population increase, and balance-of-payments and fiscal crises" (World Bank 1981, p. 2). The report correctly recognized that the region's economic problems had both internal and external sources. Included among the internal forces are a number of structural factors: underdeveloped human resources, the economic disruption that accompanied decolonization, climatic and geographic factors hostile to development, and a rapidly growing population. External factors include commodity price instability, slow growth in world demand for most developing country exports, and the oil shocks of the 1970s. It goes on to describe the domestic policies that have aggravated the internal structural and external factors. Three areas are identified where policy has been weak:

First, trade and exchange-rate policies have overprotected industry, held back agriculture, and absorbed much administrative capacity. Second, too little attention has been paid to administrative constraints in mobilizing and managing resources for development; given the widespread weakness of planning, decision making, and management capacities, public sectors frequently become over extended. Third, there has been a consistent bias against agriculture in price, tax and exchange-rate policies. (World Bank 1981, p. 4)

By identifying these sources, especially the first and third, the report concentrated on those problems that can be addressed by donors through a process of policy reform.[4] Although the report advocates export-led growth, neither it nor other advocates of greater export orientation have adequately addressed the implementation or longer-term repercussions of such a policy reform. These include achieving a domestic political consensus on economic policy and creating policies that can be implemented to prevent the abuses of an export-oriented strategy that have earned it such a controversial reputation.

The Debate Over An Export-Oriented Strategy

There are two views that define the limits of the debate concerning the consequences of a more open economy, that of, for lack of a better collective term, dependency theorists and that of adherents of the more traditional neoclassical school.

Dependency theory and the Latin American example.[5] The term dependency theorists is used typically to identify those with the view that economic integration into the world market systems does not result in development, but rather underdevelopment. In the dependency paradigm, the concept of development is seen in a much broader context. Typically, most economists refer to development as centering on the income growth process, while voicing concern about income distribution, social transformation, and political participation. Dependency theorists use the term to describe a particular process of social, economic, and political transformation that took place in Europe at a specific time in history. They contend that this process cannot be duplicated at any other time or place, precisely because it has already occurred. Specifically, colonialism was part of that process, and as such it established social, economic, and political structures in Latin America that precluded the recurrence of the relatively synchronized European development process. In Latin America, colonialism left in its wake powerful agricultural interests that were typically not progressive. Colonialism also left behind centralized state structures in the hands of an agricultural oligarchy that prevented an industrialization process based on domestic markets. In other words, colonialism established structures that never required a relatively large internal population able to consume the output. A further characteristic of an underdeveloped economy is its inability to achieve self-sustaining growth. A big part of the reason for this failure is that the impulses for growth, i.e., increased demand, are external. This has caused dependency theorists to reject export-led strategies since they are seen as resulting in a loss of domestic control or even influence over the direction of development. It is this combined alignment of internal and external structures that dependency theorists refer to as underdevelopment.

In this view, export-led development schemes are seen as examples of ongoing underdevelopment. The argument is made that low-income countries will remain impoverished as a result of a process of unequal exchange with the industrialized capitalist world. Therefore, while some economists argue that the cause of poverty is the lack of a modern, productive agriculture sector, more radical economists argue that low incomes are the result of unequal trade relations between the agricultural sector and the domestic and international economies.

Advocates of the dependency view, including Cardoso and Faletto (1979), Dos Santos (1973) and Gunder Frank (1965), have dealt primarily with the Latin American examples. Two of the critical features of the Latin American experience that served to impress these authors and that are relevant in the African context, are the alienation of peasant landholdings and the *simultaneous* failure of the economic system to provide urban or industrial sector employment for those leaving the agricultural sector.[6] The first of these features was a consequence of colonial and post-colonial land policy. Cardoso and Faletto (1979, pp. 4-5) address the second feature.

> It is difficult to explain why the necessary measures were not taken to ensure continued development or why the measures taken were not effective. In some cases, the rate of economic growth was not sufficient to vitalize the more backward sectors of the economy, and the economy therefore could not absorb the pressure of population increase: it is well known that the demographic rate of growth is higher in depressed areas and among poor populations; with a low rate of investment, the offering of jobs can hardly meet the growing demand for them. The type of technology adopted by the most modern sectors used little labor and thus increased what seemed to be an overt incapacity to solve occupational demand through industrialization. The creation of new industrial sectors dismantled handicraft ones, destroying more jobs than creating new ones.

Ruggie (1983, p. 11) describes the dependency school solution to the problem of underdevelopment as one that

> does not seek the integration of the developing countries on any terms. On the contrary, to achieve development they deem it necessary to pursue dissociation and self-reliance.

This self-reliance is situated in the context of political and economic socialism. Self-reliance allows the economy to be structured and development achieved along the lines thought best by political leaders. While recognizing that disassociation from the international capitalist economy can be costly, some argue that such a policy will yield net benefits in the long run.

The export promotion view. The oft-quoted World Bank reports (World Bank 1981, 1984) played an important role in reacquainting many development planners with the merits of an export promotion strategy as a means of addressing many of Africa's economic growth and performance shortcomings.

The World Bank and the IMF (partly at their own initiative and partly under pressure from some developed country members) are strong advocates of the trade promotion approach to development. The World Bank is explicit in expressing the need for a shift in development emphasis.

> A reordering of post-independence priorities is essential if economic growth is to accelerate. During the past two decades most African governments rightly focused on political consolidation, . . . now it is essential to give production a higher priority. . . . Three major policy actions are central to any growth-oriented program: (1) more suitable trade and exchange rate policies; (2) increased efficiency of resource use in the public sector; and (3) improvement in agricultural policies. (World Bank 1981, pp.4-5)
>
> The agriculture-based and export-oriented development strategy suggested for the 1980s is an essential beginning to a process of long-term transformation, a prelude to industrialization. It is not a permanent course for any country, but one that in Africa generates resources more quickly than any alternative and benefits more people. Without these resources, the foundations of future development cannot be established. (World Bank 1981, p.6)

The position of the World Bank and IMF is, briefly, that developing countries can best improve their growth prospects by being active participants in international trade. This position has been defended even though countries that adopt this view are required to implement adjustments in monetary, budgetary, and exchange rate policies that frequently cause painful dislocations and do not always result in increased growth. Further, increased unemployment and reduction in expenditures on low-income groups, e.g., food subsidies, often add to political instability. Despite these problems, it is argued that the policy reforms that accompany structural adjustment loans and other credit facilities contain the best set of policies for longer-term development.[7]

Although many countries find the conditions that accompany these loans and the move toward increased export orientation uncomfortable, a number of African nations have accepted the need to move in that direction. Ruggie (1983, p. 16) acknowledges the importance and attractiveness of an export-oriented strategy.

> We pay closest attention to the "associative" posture, as we will call it for short, of an outward-oriented strategy designed to find a niche in the international economy based on comparative advantage. We do so because it clearly represents the hegemonic position. . . . It is hegemonic in part for the obvious reason that it reflects the principles of economic organization favored by the dominant economic powers. But its hegemony is also due to the fact that it is seen widely, and increasingly by the developing countries themselves, to come closest to embodying those forces that produce change in national economies and upgrade their status in the international division of labor. The newly found favor of this strategy among the developing countries no doubt is inspired by the growth in output and the extraordinary rates of growth in manufactured exports achieved by the newly industrializing countries, especially those in East Asia.

There is no question that the economic performance of a number of Pacific Basin countries, based largely on manufactured exports, provides a compelling example for African countries and one that appears worthy of emulation. We argue in the following section, however, that the implementation of policies designed to foster a greater export orientation raises doubts about how long such policies can be adhered to by many African countries. Further, the dynamic of greater emphasis on agricultural exports in Africa may well generate internal conflicts that threaten the viability of the development strategy.

THE POLITICAL ECONOMY OF TRADE-ORIENTED DEVELOPMENT STRATEGIES

In many ways, both dependency and neoclassical models of development are easy targets for criticism because each has serious shortcomings and because experience with each has produced some disappointing results. It is more difficult, however, to devise a means for taking advantage of the efficiency and growth potential of a market-oriented model, while avoiding the political problems of disenfranchisement of some groups. The balance of this discussion explores two areas encountered in a move toward greater export orientation that need to be addressed by policymakers. The first concerns the political requisites for successful implementation of greater export orientation. The second concerns the problems that can result from increased pressure for commercialization in agriculture.

Political Requirements

Developing countries vary significantly in their ability to adopt and maintain open, market-oriented development strategies. The most important factor in determining the ability of a country to adopt and implement any major policy revision is the support of domestic interests. In other words, economic policy formulation does not occur in a political vacuum. Sound economic strategies frequently fail because their supporters lack the political strength to implement the desired/necessary policies. Comparative analysis of open (associative) development policies have found that the political requirements for success are frequently difficult to achieve. Ruggie (1983) argues that the capacity to implement economic policies, that make optimal use of a nation's economic resources, generally reflects the *prior existence of certain political coalitions.*

> Devising domestic means to exploit the opportunities and control the adverse consequences of economic openness is not simply a question of devising optimal economic and social policies. To be sure, such policies are absolutely crucial to the compensating for small size and external dependence. However, the capacity to fully implement such policies itself reflects the prior existence of certain political conditions. In pure form, these conditions enable governing coalitions either to integrate the major sectional interests of society into the cooperative regulation of domestic distributional strife, or to insulate policymaking from their influence and to pursue state-defined national development objectives. History and experience offer variants of both and of their combination. But none exists in great abundance in the Third World at this time. (Ruggie 1983, p. 19)

Pursuing outward-oriented development strategies in the absence of these political requisites need not imperil short-term economic growth. Such growth tends to come, however, at the cost of exacerbating domestic cleveages. Under these conditions, the hope that market-oriented development will be associated with enhanced political stability becomes problematic. In sub-Saharan Africa, where sharp internal cleavages are common, and state structures are often poorly integrated into society, it seems likely that the high cost of implementing the economic reforms may exacerbate, rather than heal, internal cleavages. These domestic cleavages include differences between urban and rural groups, and between large- and small-scale farmers. Additionally, the divisive potential of an export-oriented strategy that emphasizes agriculture will certainly add to the stress felt by the country's political institutions and leaders. Unfortunately, there is no simple formula for predicting which cleavages will, in general, be aggravated, or the degree of political turmoil that might ensue. They seem to depend heavily on society-specific circumstances, e.g., the depth and scope of existing social cleavages as well as the configuration of state-society relations.

The agricultural policy now occurring in many countries has relatively weak domestic political support. Rural, agrarian interests are generally poorly represented in governing coalitions (Bates 1981). The political weakness of agrarian interests has been reflected both in agricultural export policies that are frequently designed to tax producers heavily and domestic food policies that are designed to subsidize politically important consumers, e.g., urban workers. The success of such reforms will depend largely on their ability to create coalitions of supporters endowed with the political skills to manage the inevitable distributional consequences of economic policy reforms.

In the short and medium term, the ability to manage conflict and generate an effective coalition in support of open, market-oriented development will depend on both the domestic perception of the reforms—whether they are perceived as permanent or transitory—and the initial success of the new policies in demonstrating that benefits can be delivered. If the involvement of the external member of the coalition is thought to be transitory, then the incentive to adapt to the wishes of that external member and its domestic allies is greatly reduced.[8] Similarly, the benefits of the reforms need to be made apparent quickly. This will help to serve as a demonstration that the reforms are workable and deserving of support. One obvious criterion for judging the viability of the new policies is the availability of foreign exchange. Since foreign exchange constraints often hindered importation of critical production and investment inputs, and consumer goods, relaxation of that constraint would be of substantial benefit to most developing countries.

Commercialization of Agriculture

Although the importance of constructing a domestic political coalition to support the reforms is critical in the longer-term, success of any development strategy will depend on the nature of agricultural commercialization. At present, the export promotion strategy receiving support from donors is attractive as an answer to the problem of stagnation. Such a strategy can address a number of short-term problems, e.g., high debt-service ratios, balance of payment disequilibrium, and slow growth rates. It can also give rise to fundamental conflicts within an economy. These conflicts manifest themselves in the medium and long run and are able to undermine the initial success experienced by policy reforms. Ruggie recognizes the limitations of simple export orientation:

> The theoretical scaffolding of the outward-oriented development strategies derives from neoclassical trade theory. Its lineage traces back to the model of Ricardo, as amended by Heckscher, Ohlin, and Samuelson, to make trade not simply of mutual advantages but an instrument for reducing international disparities. Though it is now accepted that there exist numerous anomalies to and asymmetries in the rule of mutually beneficial exchange. (Ruggie 1983, p. 14)

Further he argues:

> Openness toward the international economy creates opportunities, but also produces dislocating consequences. This is so irrespective of the institutional form within which international economic interdependence is embedded. A successful associative posture therefore requires devising means to exploit opportunities and to cushion the dislocations. (Ruggie 1983, p.18)

It is often argued that the means of income generation, i.e., increased agricultural exports, need to be established so that distributional issues can be addressed.[9] In the case of most African countries, such an export approach is unworkable. Since a large landed peasantry already exists in Africa, the issue is to what extent will that peasantry be included in the efforts to expand agricultural exports. The lesson of the Latin American case is that the peasantry is frequently excluded from such participation. If the peasantry is excluded, it can mean the loss of subsistence opportunities as well. The conflict that arises over access to land and agricultural export opportunities is made worse because most African countries have not created the institutions or mechanisms for resolving these confrontations to the mutual satisfaction of interested parties. This conflict is not merely a matter of the disruption of traditional economic relationships. Instead, it is centered on the loss of subsistence opportunities and the risk of political instability that results when a significant share of the population is excluded from or made worse off by the development efforts, and is denied legal or nonviolent political recourse.

The increased emphasis on agricultural exports can lead to a commercialization of agriculture that results in increasing aggregation of agricultural landholdings. In these instances an internal conflict will develop, as it has in many Latin American countries, and will center on access to factors of production, the most important of which are land and credit. Traditional or subsistence forms of agricultural production is the response of peasant producers to a specific environment and set of inputs. Although this method of production may not yield the maximum output or even the least-cost output, it typically does yield the most stable output stream under a set of variable climatic conditions. In other words, it will minimize the risk of food shortage in the face of drought and other climatic adversities. Despite the robust quality of smallholder agriculture, it is vulnerable to the pressures exerted by increased commercialization. Policymakers frequently judge the smallholder sector as being an unreliable source of supply for an international market that oftentimes demands consistent volumes of output. Further, there is the propensity of managers, who have been trained in a more technologically advanced environment, to choose methods of production that require input intensities ill-suited to local conditions. Add to these factors the natural proclivity of entrepreneurs to expand their holdings, and a considerable amount of economic and political pressure can be brought to bear on smallholders. An example of this pressure is the recommendation that is frequently attached to structural adjustment loan agreements for the formation of a market in agricultural land. It is argued that this will allow more efficient producers to expand their holdings. Although this may be correct, such policies do not make provisions to protect the rural poor who may alienate their access to land because of cash needs and imperfect rural credit markets.

The alienation of peasant land leads to the loss of subsistence opportunities and an excess supply of labor in the sector. If the rate of employment growth in other sectors is not rapid enough, which is difficult with the high rate of population growth in Africa, these disenfranchised individuals are then left without resources or an interest in the development strategy. The economic pressure engendered by these factors will inevitably be transformed into political pressure. (Bates [1981] has identified a number of factors that allow larger, well-organized interests, e.g., large landowners, to be more effective at influencing the policymaking process.) The absence of political institutions that allow representation in the decisionmaking process of a sufficient range of political interests means that those who have been injured by the current development process have no recourse within the existing political/legal framework.

Although obvious benefits are to be derived from the commercialization of agriculture, it is critical to avoid a large-scale displacement of smallholders from land unless suitable employment is available elsewhere, since such a disenfranchisement almost certainly means the loss of even subsistence opportunities and the creation of a potential political force that does not have a vested interest in the maintenance of the existing political system. Again the lessons of Latin American experience are telling. In the overwhelming majority of countries in that region there exist or have existed in the recent past, an active military resistance or "national liberation movements" opposed to the policies of the current government. In virtually all of these cases, access to arable land is an issue over which there is disagreement with the governing group.

For this reason Ruggie is correct that the central point for enabling an export-oriented strategy to be successful is the presence of political institutions that allow representation for a wide range of interests that can help to prevent the type of alienation described above.

> Devising domestic means to exploit the opportunities and control the adverse consequences of economic openness is not simply a question of devising optimal economic and social policies. To be sure, such policies are absolutely crucial to the accomplishment of both purposes and they can go some way toward small size and external dependence. However, the capacity fully to implement such policies itself reflects the prior existence of certain political conditions. In pure form, these conditions enable governing coalitions either to integrate the major sectional interests of society into cooperative regulation of domestic distributional strife, or to insulate policy-making from their influence and to pursue state-defined national development objectives. (Ruggie 1983, pp. 18-19)

It is our view that one of the significant threats confronting a development strategy that advocates an export-oriented approach in Africa, especially with a strong market component as advocated by the World Bank and others, is that it will commercialize agriculture in such a way as to exclude significant numbers of the agricultural labor force from the benefits of development.

CONCLUSIONS

The critical economic needs of sub-Saharan Africa have presented policymakers in both developed and developing countries with an unusual and potentially important opportunity to influence the patten and rate of economic growth in the region. The reforms undertaken as a result of donors' attempts to address the region's problems have met with some short-run success. The successful implementation of the reforms has been predicated on the ability of the World Bank and the IMF to offer financial assistance to the developing countries when acutely needed. As the immediacy of this need passes, the influence wielded by the donors will diminish. The central point we make here is that policy reform and the concomitant move toward greater market and trade orientation is a complex process, and thus far only the first step has been taken. The restructuring of economies being attempted must be seen by policymakers as going beyond changes in the volume and value of production and exports. It involves a realignment of political forces that alters the way that large sections of the population sustain themselves. It is not a simple matter. The situation is made more difficult by the fact that the political dimensions of the economic problems are frequently unappreciated by, or are viewed as outside the purview of, economic analysts.

In our view, the most practical alternative policy for most African economies, from both a political and economic viewpoint, is one that allows more integration with the world economy via increased agricultural exports, but one that calls for policies to prevent the abuses of a simple export promotion strategy. Although the advocates of dependency theory and closed-economy development raise a number of valid points about the nature of commercial relations with developed countries, in pragmatic terms, their recommendations are not likely to be a part of the current policy dialogue in most developing countries. As these theorists recognize only too well, existing political and economic interests impose boundaries on the range of policy options available to domestic policymakers.[10] These constraints mean that the transition to a closed-economy strategy or integration into the trade network among socialist countries, would require political and economic dislocation of a magnitude that most decisionmakers would not willingly undertake. This assessment is borne out by the willingness, albeit grudging in many cases, to implement the economic policies that accompany World Bank structural adjustment loans rather than pursue a disassociative option.

If the policy reforms are to be successful at promoting development, a number of modifications to current donor policy need to be made. Our recommendations are divided into two parts: those that address the need for supporting a coalition and those that address the longer-term issues of land tenure and commercialization of agriculture. As a matter of immediate policy concern, it is necessary to devise means of support for the coalition in each country that is willing and able to support the reforms. Although such a coalition can be self-sustaining in the longer term, it has an initial period during which it is heavily reliant on outside support. There are several ways that such support can be improved.

First, it is necessary to increase the level of assistance to those countries that are attempting to implement a reform program. Without such assistance, the investment programs of many of these countries would have been left in shambles. Even with continued assistance, the financing gap remains serious. A World Bank report "estimates that 29 low-income countries in the region will require $11 billion per year in concessional financing between 1986 and 1990 to support GDP growth between 3 and 4 percent."[11]

Second, the conditions attached to structural adjustment loans frequently require the implementation of politically unpopular policies, e.g., the elimination of subsidies on staple foods. Such conditions undermine support for the governing coalition and weaken its ability to implement the more fundamental features of the reforms. While not denying that such subsidies are expensive and inefficient, we argue that the benefit gained by their elimination is frequently less than the political costs imposed on the governing coalition. Therefore, it seems reasonable that more unpopular reforms be phased in over a number of years and that additional financial support be made available, if necessary, to accomplish that goal.

Third, greater care and responsibility needs to be exercised in the design and implementation of donor programs and projects. Too often it is the case that loans are made in order to meet a donor's quota for a country. Frequently, less emphasis is placed on the performance potential of a project than on the fact that the loan be made. It is this same mentality that contributed to the problems of many commercial bank loans in developing countries. It should be possible for donor officials to accept more responsibility for project successes and failures. Such a modification to current procedures would, after all, be in keeping with a greater market orientation.

Fourth, a longer planning horizon for donor funding commitments is necessary. In the present situation such a commitment would provide a demonstration of donor support for the reform efforts of the coalition. A planning horizon of five to ten years is necessary to allow a more permanent realignment in favor of those interests that support the policy reforms.

Certainly the recommendation that donor policy on foreign assistance be made more consistent and predictable is not new. The value of these characteristics to any foreign assistance policy has long been recognized. The opportunities that are currently available in sub-Saharan Africa, however, mean that the return to an improved and expanded assistance program for the region is especially high.

Stanley Please (1986, p. 113) made a similar point about the need for changes in donor policy toward Africa, specifically the need for greater awareness of the political dynamic of domestic policy reform, that helps to sum up this part of our argument:

> The Africa report has come up with what might be called reciprocal conditionality. There must, to begin with, be programs from African governments, but in addition there have got to be donor programs to provide adequate and sustained support to the African programs as they come to be formulated and prepared and implemented. If the donors are to provide this support, the issues are clear. There has to be less emphasis by donors on grandiose projects and on projects per se and more on rehabilitation and maintenance of existing capacity. There has to be more support for policy reform, which is extremely difficult to do politically and therefore requires a phasing of adjustment, during which much more support is required.

As important as the creation and support of a reform-oriented coalition is, it must be regarded as a necessary, but not sufficient, condition for viable medium- to long-term development. A coalition that implements an export-oriented trade strategy without mitigating the resultant domestic cleavages, can seriously damage the prospects for a successful strategy. This is perhaps the most important conclusion for Africa to emerge from the development experiences of many Latin American countries.

To avoid the disenfranchisement of large numbers of individuals and the accompanying political instability, it is necessary to ensure their continued access to the factors of production they need to be viable participants in export crop production.[12] The challenge to donors is to design and implement programs/projects that preserve peasant land rights and access to the other factors, but that are efficient and yield an internationally competitive product.

Two circumstances lead to the conclusion that donors, operating in conjunction with recipient governments, need to accept the responsibility for achieving this goal. First, market forces alone will not prevent the negative aspects of agricultural commercialization described above. Second, for an agricultural-oriented export strategy to work in developing countries there will need to be some liberalization of agricultural trade between developing and developed countries. Liberalization can be used as a device for encouraging development policies that help peasants. Evidence that the production and marketing of crops in developing countries are consistent with maintaining peasant agricultural rights could be linked with donor policies. The primary requirement for continued liberalization, and therefore access to developed country markets, would be evidence that such rights are upheld. While we harbor no illusions about the difficulty of implementing and enforcing such a policy, we argue that the combination of donor pressure and a tangible reward (access to export markets) will be enough to shape domestic agricultural policy so as to benefit the largest number of peasants and, therefore, do the most to foster broad-based development.

We have not argued here that an agricultural export strategy is the best option for the countries of sub-Saharan Africa. Instead, it is our view that such an orientation is inevitable in the near term. Since such policies are being and will continue to be pursued, it is reasonable that they be given the best possible chance for success. The modifications to current assistance policy that we recommend will not come about easily. There will be resistance from ODA recipients as well as from the donors. They are a reasonable step, however, in the direction of finding a solution to the problems of instituting and maintaining an export-oriented development policy that does not undermine its own goals in the long run.

NOTES

The views expressed here are those of the authors and should not be attributed to the institutions they are affiliated with.

1. While there is little question about the severity of the economic crisis in many African countries, there is less agreement on the causes of those crises. Most analysts would agree that four immediate causes are identifiable: (1) ill-conceived national policies, especially as applied to the agricultural sector, (2) the burden of debt repayment and the structural adjustments that accompany debt rescheduling, (3) low international commodities prices along with sluggish world demand for most of the region's exports, and (4) the various climatic hardships the region has suffered.

2. There are several features of donors' macroeconomic and sector policy reform programs that could be examined in this context. It is our intention, however, to concentrate on broad, long-term issues rather than on the short-term features of structural adjustment, e.g., privatization, and speed of adjustment. For additional information on these topics, see Christiansen and Stackhouse (1987) and Lele and Christiansen (forthcoming).

3. Mellor (1986, pp. 71-76) provides a succinct review of the agriculture

and industrialization debate. While Mellor does advocate a revitalized agricultural sector, he does not base the success of his recommended strategy on exports. Instead, he sees the expansion of rural employment, and therefore domestic markets for food and nonfood commodities, as the primary outlet for agricultural production. Eicher and Staatz (1984) also provide an excellent historical account of the role of agriculture in the development process.

4. The report does not attempt to analyze the forces that gave rise to these domestic policies. Instead, it treats them as a set of economic policies that can be corrected. The problem with this approach is that it fails to recognize that any set of domestic policies is a response by political interests to an issue. Consequently, it is necessary to consider more than just the economic dimension when considering the implementation of policy reforms.

5. We recognize that dependency theory evolved substantially in recent years and that it has been subject to criticism. The basic message of dependency theory, however, is still relevant. That is, development will be different and disadvantaged in those countries that were colonized. A worthwhile account of the merits of dependency theory can be found in Walton (1987).

6. Though some authors, most notably Amin (1972), have attempted to apply the analysis of dependency theory in Latin America to the African case, it has not been as well received as in Latin America.

7. The structural adjustment loan program is described in the *World Development Report* (World Bank 1986, p.153):

> With the structural adjustment loans (SALs), funds are disbursed in support of broad policy reforms rather than for a specific investment. Agreement is reached between the borrowing government and the Bank on specific measures of reform, and progress is monitored to form the basis for the release of funds.

8. This was the case in Malawi, which to date has had three structural adjustment loans (SALs). Among Malawian policymakers, the first SAL was perceived as temporary, after which development policy would return to its conditions attached to the first agreement. Late in the disbursement period of this agreement, it became apparent to both the World Bank and the Malawi government that an additional SAL would be necessary. As the negotiations for the second SAL began, the World Bank announced that it would not disburse the final tranche of the first SAL until compliance was obtained. Evidently, at that point perceptions changed and Malawi began to implement the policy changes desired by the World Bank.

9. The result is a pattern of inequity that over time resembles an inverted U. The pattern of distributional inequity increases during the early stages of the development process, but then decreases as income growth continues.

10. There are instances where political and economic interests prevent the implementation of policies that can effectively promote development. This appears to be the case in many Latin American countries where violent political conflict has been the result.

11. World Bank, *Financing Adjustment with Growth in Sub-Saharan Africa, 1986-90,* 1986, cited in *USDA/ERS 1986,* p. 16.

12. Obviously, the crucial ingredient for determining the distribution of benefits in an agriculture-based strategy is access to land. Land alone,

however, is not sufficient. It is also necessary to have access to appropriate seed and fertilizer packages, a marketing infrastructure, price incentives, secure transport routes, and credit.

REFERENCES

Amin, Samir. 1972. "Transitional Phases in Sub-Saharan Africa." *Monthly Review*, (May), pp. 52-57.

———. 1976. *Unequal Development: An Essay on the Social Formations of Peripheral Capitalism*. New York: Monthly Review Press.

Bacha, E.L. and R.E. Feinberg. 1986. "The World Bank and Structural Adjustment in Latin America." *World Development* (March), pp. 333-346.

Bates, R. 1981. *Markets and States in Tropical Africa*. Berkeley and Los Angeles: University of California Press.

Bhagwati, Jagdish N. 1986. "Rethinking Trade Strategy." In John P. Lewis and Valeriana Kallab, eds., *Development Strategies Reconsidered*. Washington, D.C.: Overseas Development Council, pp. 91-104.

Cardoso, F.H. and E. Faletto. 1979. *Dependency and Development in Latin America*. Translated by M.M. Urquidi. Berkeley and Los Angeles: University of California Press.

Christiansen, R. E. and L. A. Stackhouse, 1987. "The Privatization of Agricultural Trading in Malawi." Paper written for John F. Kennedy School of Government, Harvard University (December).

deJanvry, Alain. 1985. "Latin American Agriculture from Import Substitution Industrialization to Debt Crisis." Paper presented at the conference on "The Political Economy of Food," Brigham Young University, Provo, Utah, May 2-4.

Dos Santos, T. 1973. "The Crisis of Development Theory and the Problem of Dependence in Latin America." In H. Bernstein, *Underdevelopment and Development*. New York: Penguin.

Eicher, C. and J. Staatz, 1984. *Agricultural Development in the Third World*, Baltimore: Johns Hopkins Press.

Gunder Frank, A. 1965. *Capitalism and Underdevelopment in Latin America*. New York: Monthly Review Press.

Helleiner, G.K. 1986. *Africa and the International Monetary Fund*. Washington, D.C.: International Monetary Fund.

Jennings, A. 1986. "Measures to Assist the Least Developed Countries: The Case of Malawi." *World Development* (December), pp. 1463-1468.

Johnston, B.F. and J.W. Mellor, 1961. "The Role of Agriculture in Economic Development," *American Economic Review*, 51.

Krueger, A.O. 1980. "Trade Policy as an Input to Development." *American Economic Review* 70, (May), pp. 288-292.

Krueger, A.O. and C. Michalopoulos. 1985. "Developing-Country Trade Policies and the International Economic System." In E.H. Preeg, ed., *Hard Bargaining Ahead: U.S. Trade Policy and Developing Countries*. Washington, D.C.: Overseas Development Council, pp.39-57.

Kydd, J. and A. Hewitt. 1986. "The Effectiveness of Structural Adjustment Lending: Initial Evidence from Malawi." *World Development* (March), pp. 347-366.

Lande, S. and C. VanGrasstek. 1985. "Trade with the Developing Countries: The

Reagan Record and Prospects." In E.H. Preeg, ed., *Hard Bargaining Ahead: U.S. Trade Policy and Developing Countries*. Washington, D.C.: Overseas Development Council, pp. 73-94.

Lele, U. and Christiansen, R. E. Forthcoming. "Structural Adjustment Lending and Development Policy."

Lewis, John P. and Valeriana Kallab. 1986. *Development Strategies Reconsidered*. Washington, D.C.: Overseas Development Council.

Please, S. 1986. "Development Priorities for Sub-Saharan Africa." In *Recovery in the Developing World—The London Symposium on the World Bank's Role*. Washington, D.C.: The World Bank, pp. 107-117.

Ruggie, J.R. 1983. *The Antinomies of Interdependence: National Welfare and the International Division of Labor*. New York: Columbia University Press.

Saitoti, G. 1986. "A View from Africa: 1." In G.K. Helleiner, ed., *Africa and the International Monetary Fund*. Washington, D.C: International Monetary Fund.

Sandbrook, R. 1986. "The State and Economic Stagnation in Tropical Africa." *World Development* (March), pp. 319-332.

Sewell, J.W. and C.E. Contee. 1985. "U.S. Foreign Aid in the 1980s: Reordering Priorities." In J.W. Sewell, R.E. Feinberg, and V. Kallab, eds., *U.S. Foreign Policy and the Third World: Agenda 1985-86*. Washington, D.C.: Overseas Development Council, pp.95-118.

U.S. Department of Agriculture (USDA). 1986. Economic Research Service (ERS). *Sub-Saharan Africa Situation and Outlook Report*. Washington, D.C.: USDA (July).

Walton, John. 1987. "Small Gains for Big Theories: Recent Work on Development." *Latin American Research Review* 22 (No. 2), pp. 192-201.

World Bank. 1981. *Accelerated Development in Sub-Saharan Africa: An Agenda for Action*. Washington, D.C.: World Bank.

———. 1984. *Toward Sustained Development in Sub-Saharan Africa, A Joint Program of Action*. Washington, D.C.: World Bank.

———. 1986. *World Development Report, 1986*. New York: Oxford University Press.

CHAPTER 6

The Political Basis for Agricultural Policy Reform
Robert Bates

In recent years a consensus has formed in the international development community that many of Africa's agricultural problems possess "political origins." Those who view development as "efficiency and growth" point to studies by the World Bank that attribute retarded development and economic decline to the tendency of African governments to distort interest and exchange rates and to adopt public policies that undermine producer incentives in agriculture.[1] And those who give greater emphasis to distribution as an attribute of development stress the role of politics in promoting the formation of urban elites and in undermining the welfare of the poorest of the poor: the small-scale farmer in Africa.[2] I will summarize in this chapter the "political origins" thesis. And, accepting for purposes of argument its validity,[3] it poses the question: If Africa's farm problems possess political origins, then what is to be done to promote agricultural development in that continent?

THE NEW ORTHODOXY

The basic argument runs:

1. African farmers, like farmers elsewhere, are economically rational. They respond to economic incentives.
2. Government policies undermine incentives to farmers.
3. African policymakers are themselves rational. So when they inflict economic costs, they do so, because the value of the benefits exceeds the value of the costs.
4. Policymaking is dominated by politicians. It is therefore likely that the primary benefits of the policies chosen are political.

5. The policy origins of Africa's development problems therefore lie in politics.

Estimates of crop-specific elasticities of supply for African farmers provide the evidence in support of statement "1"; they tend to be positive in sign and of a magnitude not significantly different from those recorded for farmers elsewhere.[4] Given the quantity of the evidence, the sole remaining question of any significance concerns the magnitude of aggregate—as opposed to the crop-specific—supply response, particularly given the constraints imposed upon African farmers by their farming technologies. I have not observed evidence pertaining directly to this issue, but word of mouth among researchers suggest that statistical estimates support the inference of high levels of aggregate price responsiveness.[5]

The histories of the major agricultural industries in Africa provide further evidence concerning the economic rationality of African farmers. Narrative accounts of the rise of the cocoa industry in Ghana, the cotton industry in Nigeria, the groundnut industry in Senegal, and mixed farming in central and southern Africa—all suggest that in the face of adequate economic returns, African farmers work harder, save and invest, and transform their farming practices in efforts to secure increased incomes.[6] Where African farmers have not done so, the evidence suggests, the reasons have tended to be political. The numerous studies of the decline of peasant farming in southern Africa indicate that African farmers withdrew from the commercial production of foodstuffs because they were subject to systematic policies of economic repression—policies designed to undercut their capacity to compete with white farmers and to render the rural areas a source of cheap labor for white farmers and mining companies.[7]

The arguments adduced in support of proposition "2" focus upon the "low price" policies imposed upon farmers by governments. In the case of food crops, governments depress product prices by overvaluing their currencies while failing to impose barriers to "cheap food" imports. Many also attempt to impose prices administratively, although price controls are rarely effective.[8] In the case of export crops, African governments supplement policies of overvaluation with market regulations that tend to be effective, given the lack of alternative channels for disposing of such crops as coffee, tea, or cotton. Often the best that producers of such crops can do is to evade one government's monopsonistic market by selling their crops to a monopsony run by a neighboring government.[9]

While governments have sought to strengthen incentives for farmers by subsidizing the costs of farm inputs, such as fertilizers and mechanical equipment, these subsidies go to a small minority of farmers. In the face of declining revenues, moreover, such subsidies are less frequently paid.

Governments impose policies that increase prices of consumer items. Most notably, they protect domestic industries from competition from abroad and adopt policies that restrict the level of competition within the home market. The result is that inefficient firms survive, industries therefore operate at high cost, and consumers must pay high prices. In the underdeveloped economies of Africa, farmers make up the bulk of the consuming population.

Governments thus impose policies that lower the prices farmers receive. They adopt policies that increase the prices farmers must pay for consumer items. And while they subsidize farm inputs, the benefits of such subsidies are reaped by a privileged few. Overall, governments thus intervene in markets in ways that violate the economic interests of most farmers.

Why do governments make such policy choices? Given the costs of their policies, the presumption must be that the policies are chosen for reasons other than their economic merits. In particular, they appear to be chosen for political reasons. The story offered in defense of propositions "3" and "4" differs as between food and export crops.

Food Crops

With respect to food crops, the economic policies appear to represent the terms of a political pact between governments and their urban and industrial constituents—a pact in which the costs are borne by the mass of the unorganized: the small-scale, widely scattered, rural producers. Governments intervene in markets in an effort to guarantee the availability of food supplies in sufficient abundance and at affordable prices to groups that exercise significant control over their political fates: organized consumer interests. In effect, the economic costs incurred as a consequence of governments' efforts to control food markets represent a premium paid for political insurance. Governments devise agricultural policies so as to reduce political risks. Two lines of argument can be marshalled in support of these assertions.

Historical. Present governments in Africa are not the first to face political challenges mounted by urban dwellers when the costs of consumption necessities rise. Evidence from the nationalist period suggests that much of the impetus for the overthrow of colonial powers came from urban protests against the rising cost of living in the postwar era.[10] It is striking as well that in post-independence Nigeria, the basic elements of agricultural policy were devised by panels charged not with solving the problems of farmers but rather with resolving labor disputes—panels that sought long-term solutions to the problem of labor unrest in the urban areas and that concluded by recommending policies designed to lower the cost of consumer necessities: housing, clothing, transportation, and food.[11]

Analytic. Reasoning suggests the power of food prices as an issue in African politics. Most Africans are poor. People everywhere seek to safeguard the real value of their incomes. Poor people spend a large proportion of their incomes on food. They therefore support policy initiatives that seek to secure low food prices.

Not only is the demand for such interventions individually rational. It is also "coalitionally rational." Low food prices are demanded by those who draw their incomes from profits; for, all else being equal, the higher the level of wages, the lower the level of profits, and food is a wage good. Low food prices are also demanded by governments. Governments provide services, and wages therefore represent a significant proportion of the costs of government. In particular, governments provide unpaid services. Governments therefore cannot cover the costs of wage increases by increasing prices. The issue of food prices therefore promotes the formation of a coalition between workers, industrialists, and governments—a coalition whose interests in the short run sharply divide them from the interests of farmers.[12]

The reasoning implies a testable proposition that is strikingly counterintuitive: that socialist governments should be more likely than others to seek to control the price of food. The proposition is counterintuitive because the economic costs of "low price" policies fall upon the poorest of the poor in Africa—the small-scale farmer—and the ideology of socialism justifies governmental efforts to override market forces in terms of a government's greater ability to secure economic equality. But the line of reasoning developed in the "political origins" argument implies that socialist governments should act in ways that violate their own standards of economic justice. Because they aspire to provide a higher level of services, socialist governments pay larger wage bills. Because they tend to intervene more vigorously to regulate foreign investment and to promote industrial development, socialist governments tend to control more industries and therefore to be more directly affected by changes in industrial profits. They also have stronger political and organizational ties with labor movements than do governments based on nonsocialist parties. Their interests as governments and as the owners of industries and the preferences they form as a consequence of their political ties with labor movements therefore should render socialist governments more likely than others to intervene in food markets.

Export Crops

In elaborating on propositions "3" and "4," the "political origins" argument notes political dynamics which lead to "low price" policies. Nonetheless policies for export crops differ sharply from those for food crops. Basically, interventions in these markets appear to represent efforts at taxation. The economies of Africa are agrarian; in many, the preponderance of foreign exchange originates from export agriculture; and it is therefore unsurprising that governments in need of revenues and foreign exchange should tax export agriculture. Governments tax agriculture in part to secure development. They use the funds to start new industries, to provide better schools, or to mount programs of health care. And in part, governments tax agriculture so as to redistribute income. They use the funds collected from farmers to pay the salaries of civil servants and political elites and to subsidize urban industries.

A scarcity of data renders it impossible to test this interpretation directly.[13] An indirect test is provided, however, by examining coefficient of nominal protection, which measures the ratio of domestic to world prices. The smaller the coefficient, the further the domestic price lies below the world price. Such coefficients have been calculated for thirteen nations in Africa by the World Bank.[14] With so few observations, there is in fact little that can be done with the data. Nonetheless, I have been able to test the hypotheses that (1) the greater the demand for public revenues, the lower the level of nominal protection; and (2) the lower the supply of public revenues from nonagricultural sources, the higher the level of nominal protection. The rationale underlying both hypotheses is that price-setting behavior by African governments with respect to export crops is driven by the need for public revenues and that the disparity between domestic and international prices for exports provides a measure of agricultural taxation.

The percentage of the national labor force in public employment serves as an indicator of the level of demand for public revenues. The existence or nonexistence of commmercial petroleum deposits serves as an indicator of the adequacy of revenue supplies. The two variables account for nearly two-fifths of the variation in the pricing behavior of the thirteen African governments. Significance levels are low, however, which is unsurprising given the few numbers of observations.

POTENTIALS FOR CHANGE

The "political origins" position thus presents a coherent argument concerning Africa's development problems. Many in the development community find the implications of the argument disturbing, for insofar as it correctly captures major causes of Africa's development crisis, it then implies that what is needed is domestic political change. And there is, of course, very little that people in the development community can do to effect political reform.

In this section, I argue that such pessimism may be unwarranted, although for surprising reasons. Appropriate forms of foreign assistance may in fact yield political consequences that would lead governments to act in ways that promote the fortunes of farmers.

Learning

Some in the development community agree with the "political origins" position concerning the rationality of political actors in Africa. And they see in the assumption of rationality reasons for optimism. Being rational, they argue, politicians can learn. Pointing to the positions taken by governments in Africa at such important forums as the recent meetings of the United Nations General Assembly, they cite evidence in support of the contention that governments can learn from past mistakes. Having seen full evidence of the social costs of their economic policies, the optimists contend, governments will alter their policy preferences and choose a more socially rational set of agricultural policies.

I remain deeply skeptical of such arguments, because, as noted in the preceding analysis, African governments are not autonomous. They are not free to choose whatever policies they desire. The policies they might adopt would reject the need to accomodate the interests of powerful groups in their political environment. The consequence is that although governments may have learned and therefore revised their preferences with respect to public policies, political considerations may make it difficult for them to alter their actual policy choices.

The dilemma can be outlined more precisely using the example of food price policy. The substitution of political arrangements for market processes represents a basic element in the charter underpinning the coalition between government, labor, and industry in much of Africa. The magnitude of the dilemma facing a government that has become "enlightened" regarding the economic costs of market intervention can best be portrayed by outlining the nature of the task it would face were it to seek to replace government controls with unregulated markets.

Persuasion

To secure backing for this change in public policy, reformers must be able to communicate the costs of present policies and the benefits to be derived from more market-based alternatives. And, as *public* leaders, they must be able to do so at two levels: at the level of the collective, longer-term interests of society and at the level of immediate, shorter-term interests of particular groups. Both efforts require a mastery of economic reasoning and an ability to communicate economic arguments credibly.

The formulation of a justification for more market-oriented policies is not a simple task, particularly given the history of Africa. The task requires at least two fundamental changes in the thinking of informed elites. One is in the "technical" conception of how economies work; the other is in the conception of how the social interest is best served by governments.

Certainly in the case of Africa, which has experienced the slave trade, imperialism, and colonial government, it will be extremely difficult to communicate the welfare-enhancing properties of markets. Given the history of Africa, the introduction of markets in areas formerly controlled by governments is likely to be viewed as a triumph not for the collective welfare but for private interests: "neocolonial" forces, Western capital, or those who possess the wealth to secure a disproportion of the benefits to be gained from market transactions. Certainly any who stand to lose their position of privilege as a result of policy reform will be quick to point to the particular interests that may disproportionately benefit from such reforms.

In addition, well-developed, clearly articulated conceptions of how markets work dominate the mentalities of educated elites. These models hold that economic competition results in poorer quality of service, that unregulated markets result in explotation, and that gains by one agent must result in losses to another. The present patterns of intervention in African agriculture draw their legitimacy at least in part from such beliefs. Their replacement will require justification, much of which will have to be based on a reconceptualization of the behavior of markets.

Not only do present patterns of government intervention in agricultural markets derive their legitimacy from notions of the behavior of markets; they also derive from theories of how modernization takes place. Intellectuals and members of the elite tend to believe that economic growth must be based on industrialization;

that industrialization requires a reallocation of resources between town and country; that the capital for industrialization was seized from agriculture; that rural immiseration generated an urban labor force; that market-based processes of structural change promote private wealth and rural class formation; and that governmental transfers of resources between town and country are therefore preferred. The oppressive nature of present forms of government intervention in agriculture are in part legitimated by such conceptions of the development process.[15]

There thus exist in Africa well-developed economic doctrines that must be revised before "enlightened" governments can evoke consent for more market-based policies. But the challenge of persuasion is even greater than these arguments would suggest. For also required will be a reformulation of how the social interest is best served by governments. Elsewhere in the world, key groups—hegemonic interests—dominate societies, and see the social interest as best served by minimalist governments. They form parties of the Right and attempt to recruit mass support by advocating retrenchment and deregulation. Their program elevates the legitimacy of markets, of capital, of savings, accumulation, and investment.

In Africa, there exist few coherent movements of this kind. The calls for governmental retrenchment originate from abroad. Within Africa, contenders for power compete in terms of governmental activism. They recruit political support by promising more services or services of a higher quality or lower price. They focus on the benefits rather than the costs of government. Their vision of the public good does not include positive images of governmental restraint. It does not feature a providential role for governments.

To orchestrate changes in policies and to secure their legitimacy, political leaders may therefore have to restructure the reasoning that informs the way in which people analyze the behavior of economies, their notions of how development takes place, and their conception of the proper role of governments.

All that has been discussed thus far refers to acts of public communication. It refers to the rhetoric that governments must employ when communicating with broad audiences, be they the general public, the informed public, or the intellectual community. But policy changes also require acts of persuasion that are more finely tuned. Not only must policymakers alter general beliefs and collective values, but they must also persuade powerful economic interests of the merits of policy change. To secure the assent of particular interests, the governments must assess and communicate the costs inflicted upon each by present policies and the benefits to be reaped by each under alternative policies. Reform-minded officials must therefore possess a deep insight into the economic implications of reform proposals for key interest groups in their political environment. The reformers must be able to effectively communicate to those who control their political fate the magnitude of the benefits to be gained from the gamble of policy reform over the certain yield from present policy commitments.

This requirement underscores the necessity for large investments in a particular kind of economic knowledge. Those promoting reform base their arguments on models of the behavior of macroaggregates: models of employment, trade, aggregate price levels, or rates of growth of the gross domestic product. They fail to employ micromodels that could link a change in, say, the market price for a basic foodstuff to the real value of the incomes of a particular segment of the labor force or the revenues of a particular firm or parastatal enterprise. Those advocating reform therefore fail to furnish African political elites with the means by which to make credible argument to key political actors. Political leaders must be provided with well-researched evidence of the incidence of the costs and benefits of policy change. In the absence of such evidence, the economic risks associated with change are converted into political risks for its proponents. While cognizant of the collective benefits of policy reform, political leaders are unlikely to champion them if deprived of the means by which to shape credible appeals to the economic interests of key segments of their political environment.

Large investments in economic research are therefore required to equip policymakers with the information they need to pursuade key interest groups of the merits of policy reform. It is necessary to measure the microlevel impact of policy changes on specific industries and portions of industries and on the incomes of those who supply different factors of production to them. Not only must these costs and benefits be measured, their assessment must be communicated in a knowledgeable, persuasive, and credible manner. These efforts are essential if governments are to act as leaders of policy reform.

Enforcement

Reform-minded elites thus face a formidable challenge in seeking to persuade their constituents of the merits of policy reform. They must be able to persuade key groups of the beneficial impact of reform to their particular interests and convince the wider community of the legitimacy of market processes as a way of allocating resources and inducing development. And they must legitimate a providential role for government. Given the impact of historical experiences upon the mentalities of African elites, the transformation of their basic conceptions of self-interest and the way in which their collective interests are secured poses a challenge of such magnitude as to call into question the capability of even the most gifted leadership to accomplish it.

Further calling into question the likelihood of internal reform is that successful policy change will require not only persuasion but also enforcement. The advocates of policy reform may be right. It may indeed be the case that each economic interest would be better off were public policies altered, and each key group may come to learn that in the long run its economic welfare would be improved by the adoption of new policies. But none of these interests can risk "moving first," that is, unilaterally altering its policy position. To secure the benefits of reform, changes must be orchestrated.

The dilemma can be outlined more precisely. Food policy can be seen as representing the terms of an alliance between labor, industry, and government, in which short-run political gains are achieved at the expense of rural producers. Rural producers, however, adjust in the longer run. They grow less, which leads to scarcities, higher food prices, or shortages of foreign exchange. All members of the alliance may therefore come to realize that the short-run advantages of "low price policies" are not in the longer run sustainable. *But no member, including government, can afford unilaterally to alter its advocacy of the present set of policies.* No labor leader, for example, would demand a repeal of price controls without compensating adjustments by industry or government—nor would industry, without some guarantee of wage restraint by labor or of protection of its profits by government. For any party to shift its position and to accede to change, it must be certain that others will make compensating adjustments. The adjustments must therefore be organized.

In securing policy reform, then, the government must be able to make credible promises; it must be able to secure deals and then to convince each party to the deal of its ability to deliver concessions on the part of the others. The significance of this requirement can perhaps best be communicated by envisaging a scene in which, say, Kenneth Kaunda, president of the Republic of Zambia, is appealing to the leaders of the business community to accept the abolition of NAMBoard and the movement to market-determined prices for maize. It is certain that business would seriously doubt Kaunda's ability to secure from labor credible commitments to withhold wage demands or to prevent work stoppages should the change in policy lead to higher food prices. The government of Zambia simply cannot deliver such assurances. And without them, the leaders of business are in no position to endorse policy reform in agriculture.

Governments in Africa may have learned from past mistakes. But the changes in their policy preferences may not result in changes in their policy choices. The situation within which they seek to retain power requires that to secure change they must alter basic beliefs and values, enlighten other major groups as to where their interests lie, and orchestrate reciprocal adjustments among them. Economic reconstruction poses daunting challenges to political leaders, and we can deservedly be skeptical of the prospects of success.

There is, of course, evidence that some policies have changed in recent periods, particularly pricing policies. But they have changed in large part because of the fiscal crisis that faces the states of Africa. Governments lack the funds to subsidize production or to import food so as to defend prices that lie below market-clearing levels. Should prosperity return to Africa, then powerful groups no doubt will find politicians still willing and once again able to employ the government to alter markets in ways that accomodate their interests.

MEASURES BY OUTSIDERS

One can despair, then, for the prospects for internal reform. There are, however, constructive measures that can be taken. They aim not at comprehensive political reform but rather at more limited objectives. And they are of such a nature that outsiders can contribute to them.

Tax Reform

One measure would be to alter the system of taxation. In the case of export crops, the preference for a "low price" policy represents an induced preference, one adopted because of the need for public revenues. Driven by the imperative of revenue production, governments possess a vested interest in opposing policy reforms that entail higher producer prices. Higher prices to farmers result in lower tax rates and, all else being equal, in lower government revenues.

It would therefore appear that altering the system of taxation could lead to a change in the policy preferences of governments. If, for example, governments taxed the goods farmers bought—i.e., levied revenues by means of excise taxes, sales taxes, or tariffs—instead of the goods which farmers sold, then governments would have less reason to oppose higher prices for farm products. They would instead have an incentive to support higher prices for farmers, because richer farmers would be able to purchase more goods and so pay more taxes. Alteration of the way in which public revenues are generated may therefore produce a change in the willingness of governments to alter agricultural pricing policies.

Casual evidence in support of this contention can be adduced by comparing the role of the Treasury in Uganda and Kenya. In the case of both countries, the World Bank has recently negotiated structural adjustment programs; and, as in the case of many such programs in Africa, the Bank sought to achieve price policy reforms in the agricultural sector. In its negotiations, the Bank sought the support of Treasury. Other ministries are likely to be expenditure-oriented or behoven to constituencies with vested interests in existing governmental policies, whereas treasury departments tend to be dominated by economic technocrats who think in terms of aggregate measures of economic performance. Unless the Bank has Treasury on board, it has little prospect of carrying the day in its efforts to secure policy reform. It is notable that Treasury in Kenya has consistently been more likely to support Bank demands for pricing policies that strengthen farmer incentives than has Treasury in Uganda. Indeed, in the case of coffee pricing, at least, Treasury in Uganda has resisted the raising of producer prices.

Differences in the revenue structure of the two countries help to explain why the Treasury favored positive pricing policies in the one and opposed them in the other: pricing policies had completely different implications for the level of government revenues. Government revenues in Kenya come from sales, customs, excise, and income taxes, whereas in Uganda they come from taxes on export crops. Raising farm prices in Kenya would therefore generate richer farmers, whose incomes could be taxed or who would spend more on taxable consumer goods, and so add to the coffers of the state. Raising farm prices in Uganda, by contrast, would cut into the government's share of the earnings from agricultural exports. With costly commitments to economic reconstruction and the salaries of soldiers to pay, the Treasury in Uganda opposes measures that threatened its revenues.

The significant general point of these comments is that for too long it has been assumed that the need for tax revenues in Africa, where the tax base often lies in export agriculture, necessarily implies the adoptions of "low price" policies. The link between the revenue imperative and pricing policy is spanned by the system of taxation, and different forms of taxation induce different preferences over pricing policies. The significant implication is that if foreign donors wish to alter the incentives for governments and to induce, as a matter of governmental self-interest, a public sector preference for more favorable pricing policies, then they want to achieve that goal by reforming the system of taxation.

Food Security

Those asking governments to switch to "free markets" in grains are asking them to take enormous political risks. Present methods of market management possess the virtue of giving governments physical control over grain stocks, which they can channel at times of shortage to groups that possess the power politically to overthrow them. To ask governments to replace regulatory controls with market mechanisms is to ask them to let loose from their grasp the means to shape their political fate at moments of subsistence crisis. And given that Africa remains an agricultural continent and one of rain-fed agriculture at that, every drought threatens to generate such a crisis. What foreign donors need to do, then, is to put in place an alternative form of political insurance.

Toward this end, members of the international donor community that have access to surplus grain could negotiate programs that would guarantee food deliveries when certain criteria were met (see chapter by Raymond Hopkins). These criteria include:

- the number of days without rain during the planting season
- the quantity of food in storage and the rate of depletion of stocks
- the percentage loss of crops during a drought
- the level and rate of increase in prices in key grain markets
- some combination of these indicators.

When agreed-upon triggering levels were breached, the donor governments would supply deliveries of grain sufficient to maintain adequate food supplies. In the face of such guarantees, African governments would face a lower level of political risk. They may therefore be willing to alter their agricultural policies.

It is to be noted that this proposal for "food relief" fundamentally differs from present programs that bear that name. Existing programs protect African governments from the risks of their "low price" policies. As currently conducted, programs of food aid compensate governments for shortfalls that result at least in part from the way in which their controls over grain markets weaken producer incentives. The programs therefore lessen the incentives for governments to alter their agricultural policies. The alternative offered herein would instead provide insurance for governments that have adopted market pricing policies. It would insure against the risks that hitherto have deterred governments from relying upon markets and would therefore promote, rather than weaken, the cause of policy change.

Technical Change

African governments want lower food prices. African farmers want profits. Under present conditions, the result is a deadlock, as farmers withdraw from markets rendered unprofitable as a consequence of government pricing policies.

It is, of course, possible for the interests of both parties to be served. Prices could decrease and profits increase were the costs of farming to decline. Investments in technical change therefore represent a way of "decoupling" the central political conflict between farmers and the state in Africa.

Agricultural research appears to have declined in Africa. Research programs that once thrived have been run down and few new varieties are "in the pipeline," it would appear. Investments in biological and technical research, designed to enhance the productivity of farming, would not only improve the economic welfare of producers and consumers but would also improve the political climate within which public policies are made. In the present context in Africa, such research would represent not just applied science but also a constructive form of political intervention.

Within the ranks of many donor agencies, development specialists debate the relative merits of "project-based" assistance. And in many, the devotees of project-based approaches have been muscled aside by those seeking policy reform. In the United States Agency for International Development (USAID), for example, public choice theorists and advocates of the "miracle of the market" now dominate and seek to use the diplomatic power of the United States to forge international alliances of donors, capable of forcing African governments to withdraw from agricultural markets. In seizing control of the policymaking councils of USAID, these activists have chased from its upper ranks an earlier generation of policy advocates: those championing project-based lending. Foremost among the vanquished stand those drawn from the ranks of the agricultural research and extension services, who had in an earlier era advocated development assistance structured along the model of agricultural research stations in the United States. The thrust of the present argument is that policy reformers would do well to look once again at their bureaucratic rivals. A key to policy reform may lie in the hands of those who can secure technical progress in agriculture.

Historical evidence and recent events suggest that the link between productivity increases can in fact lead to the relaxation of market controls; the proposal, in short, is implementable. In the case of Kenya, for example, market controls were briefly abandoned in the late 1970s, when a combination of high prices and the diffusion of hybrids led to quantities of production so great that government warehouses became glutted. Unable financially or administratively to deal with the glut, and assured of adequate supplies for consumers, the government relaxed controls over the market. In the present period in Kenya, public officials once again are calling for the relaxation of market controls, and once again because of the massive grain surpluses. It would also appear that a major reason for the reduction of governmental controls over agricultural markets in India was the burden placed upon grain marketing bureaucracies by the flood of production generated by the green revolution.[16]

With increased productivity, then, governments can obtain low prices even while farmers earn increased profits. In addition, the costs of public regulation rise, as increased production overwhelms the regulatory bureaucracy. Investments in agricultural research may therefore generate changes that will induce governments to withdraw from agricultural movements.

Economic Literacy

Another appropriate investment would be in economic literacy. Many top policymakers in Africa fail to grasp even the rudiments of economic reasoning: the process by which prices are formed, the role of prices in allocating resources, and the operation of markets. Equally to the point, their constituents are poorly versed in economics. The result is that ill-advised policies get proposed and those who bear their costs often fail to oppose them. They therefore get adopted.

In eighteenth- and nineteenth-century Europe, political economy represented a field not only of scholarship but also of public debate. Learned economists wrote, published, and engaged in public controversies, and they commanded an influential audience. These debates often centered upon the role of governments in agricultural markets, and featured the leading economists of the time: the Physiocrates in France, for example, and the classical economists in England.[17]

It is very difficult to assess the influence of popular ideas on public policy. But it would appear that the withdrawal of governments from agricultural markets in Europe resulted at least in part from a growing popular awareness of the magnitude and distribution of the costs and benefits of government intervention. The ability of the Physiocrats and the classical economists to maintain a public dialogue with policymakers and their constituents helped to lay the groundwork for economic restaint by governments.

In Africa, there is little economic pamphleteering. The journals and newspapers carry little economic analysis, learned economists are not retained as contributors to the popular press, and economic societies operate sporadically, if at all, and rarely provide forums for assessing the making of government policy. The result is that there is less economic appraisal of government policy, fewer opportunities for members of the public to determine where their interests lie, and fewer political incentives for governments to act with economic restraint.

Foreign governments interested in promoting economic reforms could invest in the training and education of African decisionmakers. They could also promote curriculum reform and preparation of materials for use in schools and universities. In the long run, these investments may produce better public policy.

CONCLUSION

This discussion has formulated the "political origins" argument concerning Africa's development crisis. A position frequently taken is that if the current problems of Africa have internal political origins, then there is very little that external donors can do. In rejecting such a position, I have suggested several interventions that would affect the behavior of African policymakers.

I have noted that there is serious difficulty in making the benefits of market relations apparent to different social groups. Since African leaders face various webs of policy constraints, their implementation of tax reforms, reduction of parastatals, or opening of markets will come only through difficult adjustments. These adjustments will more likely occur if states are supported by sustained donor commitment. This would allow for not only policy reforms but also new initiatives in agriculture that could provide a more secure foundation for economic growth.

The situation facing African states and donors is such that only a coordination between donor support and policy reform can be effective. This chapter's review of the political origins explanation for failed agricultural policies indicates the embedded interests and interrelated factors that prevent the adoption and implementation of new policies. Existing opposition to policy reforms is often tied to the present political relations within most African countries. This opposition can be overcome through the creation of new alliances that benefit from the reforms undertaken through shifts in pricing policies, market orientation, and tax structures. To make such change feasible, governments need assistance from donors that make the promises of economic growth via reform credible. The coordination of these reforms with political changes and growth-oriented policies is a task that will continue to challenge states and donors in the coming years.

NOTES

1. See, for example, International Bank for Reconstruction and Development (IBRD), *Accelerated Development in Sub-Saharan Africa*, Washington, D.C.: World Bank, 1981.

2. That patterns of governmental intervention harm the interests of the small-scale farmer in Africa is argued by Robert H. Bates in *Markets and States in Tropical Africa*, Berkeley and Los Angeles: University of California Press, 1981. See also the special issue of the *Review of African Political Economy*, 34, 1985, entitled "Market Forces."

3. The reader should consult criticisms of this position, such as that contained in *IDS Bulletin*, 14: 1, January 1983, "Accelerated Development in Sub-Saharan Africa: What Agenda for Action?"

4. See data collected in Hossein Askari and John Thomas Cummings, *Agricultural Supply Respsonse: A Survey of the Econometric Evidence*, New York: Praeger, 1976.

5. A related issue, but one that is not directly relevant, is whether under present economic conditions agricultural supplies would increase were price incentives strengthened. In the absence of farm inputs or consumer goods to buy, the argument runs: Why would farmers seek to produce more in response to higher prices? Clearly, positive pricing policies are sufficient only when other elements of the farmer's economic environment are in place. But the question at issue is the farmer's desire to respond to economic incentives, not the sufficiency of price intervention.

6. See, for example, Polly Hill, *The Migrant Cocoa Farmers of Southern Ghana*, Cambridge: Cambridge University Press, 1963; J.S. Hogendrorn, "The Origins of the Groundnut Trade in Northern Nigeria," in C. Eicher and C. Liedholm, eds., *Growth and Development of Nigerian Economy*, East Lansing: Michigan State University Press, 1970; Donal B. Cruise O'Brien, *The Mourides of Senegal*, Oxford: Oxford University Press, 1971; Robin Palmer, *Land and Racial Domination in Rhodesia*, Berkeley and Los Angeles: University of California Press, 1977. See also Kenneth R. M. Anthony, Bruce F. Johnston, William O. Jones, and Victor C. Uchendu, *Agricultural Change in Tropical Africa*, Ithaca, N.Y.: Cornell University Press, 1977.

7. Palmer, *Land and Racial Domination* (note 6). See also Giovanni Arrighi, "The Political Economy of Rhodesia," in *Essays on the Political Economy of Africa*, New York: Monthly Review Press, 1973.

8. See the data contained in United States Department of Agriculture, *Food Policies and Prospects in Sub-Saharan Africa*, Washington, D.C.: USDA, 1980.

9. IBRD, *Accelerated Development* (note 1).

10. See the material contained in Dennis Austin, *Politics in Ghana 1940-*

1960, Oxford: Oxford University Press, 1970; and Elliot J. Berg, "Real Income Trends in West Africa, 1939-60," in Melville J. Herskovitz and Michael Harwitz, eds., *Economic Transition in Africa*, Evanston, Ill.: Northwestern University Press, 1964.

11. Republic of Nigeria, *Report of the Anti-Inflation Task Force*, Lagos: Government Printer, 1975; *Second and Final Report of the Wages and Salaries Review Commission, 1970-71 (Adebo Report)*, Lagos: Government Printer, 1971; and *Public Service Review Commission: Main Report (Udoji Report)*, Lagos: Government Printer, 1974.

12. Crawford Young, *Ideology and Development in Africa*, New Haven: Yale University Press, 1982.

13. But see David Bovet and Laurien Inneverhr, "Agricultural Pricing in Togo," World Bank Paper No. 467, 1981.

14. IBRD, *Accelerated Development* (note 1).

15. For examples of such reasoning see the position summarized and critiqued in Rene Dumont, *False Start in Africa*, New York: Praeger, 1969, and in Kwame Nkrumah, *Ghana*, New York: International Publishers, 1976.

16. See Robert L. Paarlberg, *Food Trade and Foreign Policy: India, the Soviet Union, and the United States,* Ithaca: Cornell University Press, 1985.

17. See, for example, Steven L. Kaplan, *Bread, Politics and Political Economy in the Reign of Louis XV*, 2 vols., The Hague: Martin Nijhoff, 1976, and Boyd Hilton, *Corn, Cash, Commerce: The Economic Policies of Tory Governments, 1815-1830,* Oxford: Oxford University Press, 1977.

CHAPTER 7

Food Aid and Policy-Based Lending to Africa: Dilemmas for States and Donors
Raymond Hopkins

Food aid can be a valuable resource in improving African states' economic performance. However, the current rules and attitudes regarding food aid pose serious dilemmas for using this resource. Neither African states nor overseas donors have adequately realized the potential of food aid. The more classic roles of such aid—famine relief and projects providing food—consequently remain the major uses in Africa. Yet these uses, as well as food sold for support of programs, are guided by structural rules that are in tension with macroeconomic needs. The economic problems of Africa and trends in development prescriptions for financial aid make it timely for the role of food aid to be reconstrued. Let me explain why.

Rich people do not starve: this is the central truth of the African famine of 1984-1985. The starvation that threatened people in dozens of states merely dramatized the growing poverty of Africa. In many African countries people are less well off than they were twenty years ago; even in states where there have been positive gains in per capita income, the rate of growth has shrunk.

It is important to recognize that the economic crisis in Africa, now widely discussed by the UN, World Bank, and Organization of African Unity (OAU) (UN 1986; World Bank 1986; OAU 1985), has been building for some time and will not easily or quickly be overcome. Economic degeneration has become almost intractable. In contrast to the sharp drama of famine, it is a kind of silent crisis.

Disturbingly, in 1984/85 debt servicing alone outpaced public and private capital inflows. Net official development assistance (ODA) fell by 9 percent. Transportation, communication, and service infrastructure in Africa have deteriorated, while recurrent costs for running large public enterprises, such as power plants and processing factories, and maintenance costs for effective infrastructure cannot be met.

What has been the response of African states to this crisis? What has been the response of the external donor community? In addressing these questions, I want to focus principally upon a major anomaly in the response of these two groups—namely, the insignificant role they have assigned to food aid.

African states have been hesitant to propose a role for food aid in addressing long-term economic needs. The 13th Special Session of the UN called for $40 billion of external aid to Africa in 1986-1990, and debt relief of $48 billion in meeting upcoming repayment obligations without mentioning food aid. Africa's Priority Program for Economic Recovery, 1986-1990 (OAU 1985, p. 15) states:

> A lasting solution to [problems of] . . . the unbalanced structure of the African economy . . . will not depend on short-term emergency measures such as food aid but on the structural transformation of Africa economies with the emphasis on the mobilization of financial resources.

Most donor organizations have also not viewed food aid as very important for long-term economic transformation and growth. The World Bank, for example, did not cite food aid as a resource for structural adjustment problems or a way to bridge the "resource gap" in 1986-1990 in their special Africa study (World Bank 1986a, pp. 11-29, 36). The 1986 *World Development Report*, in pointing out inefficiencies of food aid even erroneously remarks that "since food aid cannot legally be converted into cash, much of it has to be distributed in kind" (World Bank 1986c, p. 148). In fact, for over thirty years the largest share of all food aid has been sold. In spite of such reservations and misunderstandings some attention among donors has been given to the economic role of food aid. For example, the Development Advisory Committee (DAC) of the Organization for Economic Cooperation and Development (OECD) has recommended a development role for food aid:

> Food aid must be integrated into other forms of financial and technical assistance and closely related to national programs and policies . . . .
> It is essential that emergency food aid does not weaken efforts to deal with structural deficit problems. (DAC 1985, p. 287)

At a 1986 seminar on food aid for African Development sponsored by the African Development Bank and the World Food Program a similar theme was struck.

Despite the at best lukewarm interest in food aid, it seems likely to remain a significant resource available to Africa over the next decade. This is especially so in light of the low per capita food availability in Africa, and the rising tide of food imports, and the greater political support for food aid compared to other aid forms in donor countries. This last factor arises thanks to the current grain surplus situation in North America and Europe combined with the humanitarian appeal of food as a resource of special value to the most needy.

In light of this it is somewhat anomalous that donors and African states have done little to link food aid to efforts to eliminate deeper, more abiding causes of the economic crisis—most centrally bad policies and weak institutions. Recently the bulk of donors' food aid to sub-Saharan Africa has gone as relatively untied emergency relief or as inputs to specialized projects. Program food aid that could help with debt and adjustment burdens amounted to less than 30 percent of total African food aid in 1984/85, although this portion can easily grow. With a demand for food on commercial terms, the way is open for food aid to do more in assisting long-term structural adjustment.

My argument here is threefold. First, there are common conditions that have shaped changes in the pattern both of financial aid and of food aid. Second, food aid can contribute importantly to successful structural adjustment efforts in Africa. Third, the current regime governing food aid poses some problems and dilemmas for such use.

BACKGROUND

The causes of Africa's economic failure have been widely debated (see OAU 1985). Virtually all analysts agree that aspects of the crisis result partly from large-scale, inertial forces—largely forces out of the hands of any one state. For example, the international economy provided external shocks from oil prices in the 1970s and, in the 1980s, high interest rates, stagnating aid levels and declining earnings for most primary product exports. Even countries initially well off from oil earnings, such as Nigeria, have been hurt. Other inertial forces include high population growth rates, deterioration of land, forests, and capital assets, and recurrent drought. While many of these factors can be affected by changed policies, most require either long-term external investment before substantial results can be seen or broad international collaboration to manage markets, an action for which no political consensus exists. Thus, of the factors outside African states' control, donor policies on short-term aid and debt can quickly affect African economies; and action here still requires concerted steps by a few donor countries.

Analysts also lay part of the blame for Africa's economic crisis on African governments. Again, many of the problems are rather entrenched: weak skills, corruption, tribal rivalries and instability from military rule, expensive and inefficient bureaucracies, and state controls over the economy (Sandbrook 1985). Such qualities are not changed overnight, even, and perhaps especially, by a military takeover. In addition to political weaknesses, many countries have followed a set of policies that systematically disadvantaged rural peasantry. The result has been to discourage agricultural production and encourage a retreat by the peasantry towards subsistence and black market economies (Hyden 1980; Bates 1981).

The emergency food needs of some twenty-five countries in 1984/85 were thus rather more symptomatic than fundamental. They revealed in dire terms the results of drought on societies fundamentally plagued by economic failure. People and countries were simply too poor, or too committed to funding other endeavors, to secure the food needed to ward off starvation of the weakest among them. Put another way, the famine conditions were caused by poverty not food shortages (see Sen 1981). External and internal factors had led to the exhaustion of economic and political capital in many countries. Short of declaring bankruptcy and seeking a foreign takeover, African states had little control over their affairs except for formal government policies. Their dependence on the external world for money and legitimacy was large (Jackson and Rosberg 1982).

The major response to this condition has been a movement toward major structural reforms. This movement has been mutually engineered. Both African states and donors have agreed that the results of the 1970s and early 1980s were disastrous and that new courses of action must be pursued. In light of the economic crisis, most African states have responded by drastically curtailing budgets and appealing for more aid and better trade and financial arrangements. They have pledged reforms and in return offered target levels for additional aid at the 1985 OAU meeting and 1986 UN Special Session on Africa (OAU 1985). Metaphorically, they are trying to keep their respective ships of state afloat by lightening their loads and sending out SOS signals.

Donors, in turn, have responded by seeking greater coordination of their efforts, reducing support for projects with high recurrent costs, and shifting their aid toward rescue support. In exchange for recipients' agreement to follow new, more liberal economic policies, donors have given funds for general budget support. The International Monetary Fund (IMF) has been more tolerant, in some cases providing its short-term balance of payments adjustment assistance. It has also sought to work with the World Bank, recognizing that some international payment problems are rather longer term. The World Bank's concessional "adjustment loans," now nearly 20 percent of new International Development Association (IDA) lending, are seen as particularly apt for Africa. This phenomenon of policy-based lending is not only novel in the traditional banker's sense, since rate of return is no longer a key test, but it is explicitly political. Policy-based aid goes directly to help governments meet domestic payrolls, pay foreign debts, and import key commodities. This approach is also subject to considerable criticism, especially its forcing Africans to meet their debt and policy distortion problems through measures that are unfairly severe to the poor and weak.

The rise of policy-based lending is to a large extent a result of structural imperatives: in the 1980s the need for quick changes became an imperative affecting the economic policies of African governments and the lending policies by donors. To mobilize financing for adjustment lending, the World Bank has taken a lead role. Its major resource, IDA lending, accounts for about $3 billion or 10 percent of ODA from the OECD countries. This is roughly the same level as total food aid (OECD 1985). Both aid flows now go disproportionately toward Africa. Indeed states in Africa get four to ten times the per capita aid of South Asia. Although the World Bank has provided program loans in association with adjustment policies and even IMF lending, for a number of years, e.g., the 1975 $30 million loan to Kenya, it was only after 1980 that IDA lending has been consciously and increasingly aimed at promoting structural adjustment (see Killick 1984). As of 1986, little food aid has been used in this way. Despite this dichotomy in orientation, both food and financial aid have encountered similar problems in Africa.

THE COMMON PROBLEMS CONFRONTING FINANCIAL AND FOOD AID

There are several parallels between food and financial flows to Africa. As noted, the World Bank and other donors have shifted their concessional financial aid towards Africa; at the same time there has been a shift of food aid towards Africa. Food aid rose from 2.7 percent of ODA to sub-Saharan Africa in 1970 to over 20 percent in 1985. In 1984-1986 over 40 percent of all the world's food aid went to the sub-Saharan region. Right alongside this growth of food aid, financial aid for structural adjustment also grew.

What explains these concurrent shifts? There are four reasons. First, African governments became increasingly unable to sustain national policies that proved to be deleterious to incentives and successful projects. Second, and in addition, economic deterioration, debt burdens, and food supply shortages in many countries led to a felt need for broader, more drastic emergency measures. Third, a multitude of donors and projects engulfed African states. The effort to be helpful and efficient increasingly required coordination and linkage among such projects, especially if basic reforms were to be realized. Fourth, difficulties of maintenance and high recurrent costs of projects gave impetus to a search to reduce the project approach. Let me elaborate on how each of these problems was a reason for some aspect of the shifts occurring in African aid flows.

Bad Policies

Throughout Africa the responsibilities assumed by the state sector expanded during the 1960s and 1970s. This led to the creation or reinforcement of powerful groups with a stake in this expanded state role. As the regulator of many economic exchanges, the state increasingly became the instrument for providing divisible, targeted benefits. For example, agricultural subsidies aided the powerful Muslim Marobouts in Senegal, while food subsidies, as in Zambia, gave employers, including parastatal bodies, protection from wage demands that might arise from the pressure of higher food prices. Unfortunately, these policies were often unable to work as conceived, few people obeyed them voluntarily, and such policies discouraged productivity. In many cases governments became hostage to powerful, rapacious groups that tended to promote and perpetuate exploitative policies. Analysts came to see such policies as undermining the potential success of classical project assistance. Thus, a consensus emerged that such bad policies should be reformed.

It is easy to see how state policies, meant to help the economy through providing collective public goods, created a strong vested interest in their maintenance. Once policies proved too ambitious or significantly out of adjustment with market forces, benefits could be "hijacked" by intermediaries too powerful to be curbed, or siphoned off by insiders with preferred access. Benefits that were too small to share with all had a regressive effect. For instance, privileged farm groups not only got access to subsidized credit and equipment but they also treated loans as if they did not have to be paid back. Defaults, for example, were higher among richer farmers than poorer ones. Finally, there were urban employers and workers. Workers were protected by minimum wages and food subsidies. This created an urban overprivileged group. Access to jobs became a marketable item. While employers gained some stability and protection from wage demands, thanks to the subsidies, a large unemployed labor pool surrounding the urban worker also kept workers docile. Moreover, strikes and labor unrest were increasingly curtailed by the establishment of state-controlled unions and the intimidation or cooptation of labor agitators.

As rural production first began to falter and problems in marketing arose in the late 1960s and 1970s, external agencies stepped in to help. In 1969 in Senegal, the French and the World Bank encouraged a large increase in the state's role in agriculture through boards that would subsidize imports and monopolize purchases (Waterbury 1985). In Ethiopia in 1974, an FAO study recommended establishing the Agricultural Marketing Cooperation (AMC) with a view to displacing local traders and helping integrate a national cereals market. Under the revolutionary government of Mengistu, the AMC became the sole legal buyer of grains, and, as such, has concentrated on supplying grain to key groups, principally the cities and the military.

There are many instances where donor agencies have provided the advice and funds that encouraged the expansion of the state into agriculture, but with inadequate planning for the continuing supply of skilled personnel and resources that would be needed to make the intervention work as outlined. Whether state expansion took place without the push of external aid as in Guinea, or with outside encouragement as in Tanzania, Ethiopia, and Senegal, virtually all African states have expanded their reach in ways that have proved regressive, inefficient, and economically depressing.

Emergencies

The second reason for changes in aid flows is that in the 1980s the African debt crisis and food crisis presented a new set of challenges. Donors of financial and food assistance found themselves facing parallel "emergency" problems, that of providing quick cash aid to prevent financial strangulation of debt-ridden countries and that of providing quick food aid to prevent famine deaths in food-shortage countries. In both these cases the pattern was to offer grant assistance—quickly dispersed, targeted on specific cash- or food-starved domains, and aimed at short-term relief until internal capacity came into balance. The IMF, which normally provides the short-term adjustment loan, has, of course, played a role, but the need for concessionality in the African case gave the World Bank's IDA facility a special role. Moreover, the problems to be addressed were longer-term issues. The debt situation is especially bad, as per capita debt is two to three times higher than in Latin America, even though debt servicing cost is lower because most debt is based on low-cost public loans.

With the world's highest per capita debt and the lowest per capita food availability, sub-Saharan African states were especially vulnerable to financial and food shortages. The response of donors as the crisis grew in the 1980s was to provide balance of payment relief, debt reorganization, and policy-based loans to bail out bankrupt states, as well as to provide more funds to repair damaged economies and seek a better public/private balance. With variations in form and timing, by 1986 Ghana, Mauritius, Togo, Guinea, Mali, Mauritania, Niger, Sudan, Senegal, Tanzania, and Zaire had moved to accept these new loans and associated policy changes. During this same period some of these same governments, and others in Africa, received large amounts of emergency food aid, provided on the most generous of terms and dedicated to minimizing famine and the economic dislocations associated with it. In the case of emergency food aid, however, the attachment of policy reforms as a condition of their provision was not considered. Doing so, in fact, would have been a violation of the policy legislation of many donors. In spite of this different approach to conditionality, the injection of both money and food into ravaged African economies should be seen as a complementary and parallel exercise; both were bail-out exercises to alleviate transient crises built upon chronic problems.

This analysis suggests that conditionality should be attached to emergency food aid. The argument for it is sound, I believe. Nevertheless, it must be recognized that the major countries receiving emergency (and refugee) assistance are not identical with the top indebted countries. Rather they are mostly countries faced with major civil strife—Sudan, Chad, Ethiopia and Mozambique. The top debt burden states have arrived at their situation rather less as a result of internal and/or external military challenges to state authority.

Donor Coordination

In response to the importance of a suitable policy framework and the rise in emergency situations, enhanced coordination has been sought. The problem of many small, uncoordinated projects was identified as the need for greater coordination among donors and with recipients. This seemed the logical way to improve efficiency and prevent actions that work at cross purposes. Some small governments were asked to deal with dozens of donors and hundreds of projects. Coordination strategies have been emphasized in World Bank reports on Africa (1981, 1983, 1984, 1986), in the UN special session on Africa, and in such regional consultative groups as the Club du Sahel, Comité Interétats de Lutte Contra la Sécheresse (CILSS), and the Southern African Development Coordination Conference (SADCC). In recent years food aid donors have made efforts to better coordinate their policies through informal meetings, through in-country representative meetings, and through occasionally having food aid's role in development lending considered in Consultative Group and United Nations Development Program (UNDP) Roundtable meetings, especially when food aid officials were invited, usually World Food Program (WFP) personnel.

Unsuccessful Projects

Officials designing grants and loans to Africa, especially project-based ones, have found that the assets created by projects have a short duration. Projects have sometimes been abandoned shortly after the funding period for lack of domestic support or lack of maintenance. To work successfully, a project must leave some asset, whether a physical one such as a road, or an institutional legacy such as techniques for information gathering, that can generate revenue directly or indirectly for its recurrent costs. Otherwise the asset will wither. As a result of past project mistakes African states and donors try especially to avoid white elephant projects. Now undertakings thought to have high recurrent costs are unlikely to be put into a project pipeline. What, of course, may undermine a project's success are policies that lower its use rate or prevent ways for users to be taxed on the benefits they receive.

The same problem of project failure and low sustainability occurs for food aid projects. However, a concern to screen out projects that will not be self-maintaining has not been as readily applied to projects using food aid, especially those mounted by agencies with a strong humanitarian, food security, and human welfare orientation. Feeding and food subsidy programs have especially high, ongoing costs; the subsidies of wheat alone have amounted to $30-40 million in Sudan (1982). Subsidies in particular, have been the subject of sharp criticism in recent years, and food aid has been seen as supporting these through marketing boards and fixed nationwide prices (World Bank 1981; Hopkins 1985). Thus, agencies designing projects using food aid, although these are equally subject to the negative effects of unmet recurrent costs, have been slower to incorporate a concern for sustainability.

A rural credit scheme, upgraded port facilities, a nutrition project, or a food security stock all can equally go awry when the incentives and legal constraints on their transactions are widely different from those assumed to be governing behavior in the initial design. Currency-financed projects such as loans go to less productive farms as favors and never are repaid, while rehabilitation projects that require expensive capital imports quickly deteriorate, again because the maintenance of valuable equipment is not tied to income nor does anyone bear the cost of depreciation of such a good. Food-financed nutrition programs fail to show much gain either in human capital or in improvement in nutritional status, while food aid given for security stocks has disappeared as part of regular stock uses. Distortions of real costs and benefits is the result of a weak state, where informal "economies of affection" and personal ties of loyalty govern public-private transactions, where rule enforcement is weak, and where care and maintenance of "technical" equipment is novel for most people (Hyden 1980; Sandbrook 1985). In such a context project proposals cannot be evaluated with confidence and their success is doubtful. Thus all types of donors have shifted toward seeking policy reform and strengthening a leaner, more reliable state.

FOOD AID'S POTENTIAL ROLE IN POLICY-BASED FUNDING

There are only two useful things to do with food: eat it or sell it. With food aid one needs to determine which is the main goal. If the goal is consumption of food, then a design is needed specifying who the target consumers are, the rationale and terms for receiving it, the cost-effectiveness or other criteria for selecting the target group, and the arrangements for delivering the imported food, or the equivalent in swapped local food, to them. When the objective of food aid is to sell it, the major concerns are the effect of the sales on the overall food market and the use of the sale proceeds. Food aid can be used either in its consumption or its sales mode in collaboration with structural adjustment. In the first case, by using it directly or indirectly in compensatory feeding programs, it can ease adjustment burdens on the most vulnerable. In the second case, by selling it to augment government revenues, it can be used as a resource for almost any priority task. In the latter case, it is especially important that the food aid substitute for commercial imports, thereby saving foreign exchange and having an assured local demand at attractive prices. Of course, there are mixed-type uses, notably food-for-work projects where food is used as a wage good, saving a government cash expenditures and offering employment to those especially in need of food. Since, in Africa, I know of no food-for-work schemes without food aid, it seems reasonable to consider this a feeding rather than a sales goal, although the results can be identical to cash-funded projects as in reforestation and irrigation efforts. Let us elaborate on these two examples of how food aid can assist in adjustment, first through consumption and second through extra cash.

Compensatory Measures

One critical thing food aid can do in supporting structural change is to address the problem of "losers." It can do this in two ways: (1) by protecting certain groups already badly off; (2) by making it politically easier to induce and sustain change.

When food prices are adjusted, among the first to lose are the poor who find themselves priced out of the food markets at the same time that their employment and incomes have yet to rise. Food aid can be used to support targeted programs to mitigate partially the negative effects of economic "medicine" on the truly vulnerable. Policies with this food compensation in mind have been followed in Sri Lanka, Argentina, and Egypt in association with their economic liberalization.

The World Bank has been rather sanguine on the issue of the effects of structural change. A recent report on sub-Saharan Africa declares:

> The distributional effects of devaluation . . . are likely to benefit lower-income groups in many African countries. . . . Rarely will the poor be the principal losers from devaluation. (World Bank 1986a, p. 13)

The Bank concludes this on the basis that rural producers, who constitute the largest portion of the poor, will gain, especially from improved urban-rural terms of trade. However, urban poor and rural landless who are food purchasers, and subsistence farmers who trade very little will not benefit. Even if food production stimulated by higher prices eventually grows sufficiently that market prices decline, some groups of the very poor are likely to be worse off at some time. This is especially true if government employment shrinks while private sector employment does not quickly grow to absorb this labor.

What can food aid do for such vulnerable groups? Without some exchange entitlements to food, such people could starve; at a minimum they will become further malnourished and, as a result, lose their social roots. Basically, as mentioned before, people starve not because there is insufficient food, but because they cannot afford it. One possible response, using food aid, is to set up national nutritional programs. Effective nutrition programs can be targeted to these vulnerable groups during the early stages of adjustments. Special programs using foods eaten by the poor, such as sorghum, millet, or maize, can be made available, perhaps in rationed amounts at low prices, even while prices of preferred cereals such as wheat and rice rise dramatically. This could be a way to protect nutritional goals in the structural adjustment process. Because food aid often is available as wheat or rice, commodity-swap arrangements might allow a donor's wheat, for instance, to be traded for an appropriate larger amount of lower cost, domestically produced coarse grain. This would then be milled and used for special nutrition projects and/or sold at low prices to poor, often urban-based, consumers. By increasing demand for local cereals in this way, rural producers are also likely to get positive price incentives. Alternatively, targeted food distribution might simply accompany general sector and food price reform, as in Morocco where $60 million of food aid is planned to be used to compensate 3 million people most hurt by food price rises. Finally, food-for-work projects might be mounted in the most vulnerable rural areas, or even in urban slums, to expand employment and offer food as part of the wage.

The "losers" also pose a political problem for successful adjustments. Often urban groups have benefited from structural distortions. It is no accident that cereals marketing boards frequently have a mandate to supply key groups, including cities and the military, with food grains. Cheap, assured food supplies to urban groups take pressure off wages and keep volatile elements from protest demonstrations. African heads of state are not oblivious to the fact that the last coup in Niger and the military-led revolution in Ethiopia, both in 1974, were triggered by immediate discontent arising from national food shortages and mismanaged relief efforts. Neither are they likely to forget that in 1979 a threatened rise in rice prices resulted in a riot in Liberia that set the mood for the military revolt a year later. Nor do they overlook that President Niemary of Sudan was overthrown in April 1985 when people took to the streets of Khartoum protesting food price increases. These examples of political failure following policy price reform are but more dramatic instances of the issue of "sustainability" of structural adjustments. They are not a complete picture, however, as studies have shown that food price rises did not result in riots in a majority of cases, and even where this did occur, most governments weathered the storm (Gersovitz and Bienen 1985). Nonetheless, the ability to moderate the losses reform measures bring to politically powerful groups by moving gradually on consumer food prices could be a major asset in helping a government sustain its adjustment steps.

As in the Morocco case of agricultural sectoral adjustment, food aid, because it is a tied commodity, is most appropriate for assisting in particular adjustment sectors. The cereal markets restructuring, begun in Mali in 1982, has explicitly used food aid as a resource by which OPAM, the government's national monopoly buyer and seller of rice and millet, the key foods in Mali, was able to begin a step-by-step withdrawal from controlling prices and trade. In the Mali case also, the government got the donors' permission to put responsibility on the group of donors for "reforms" that might be unpopular. Food aid provided a source of financial income as proceeds from the sale of the food went into a special fund to help pay expenses caused by subsidies of deficit-ridden OPAM. In turn, the OPAM reduced its staff by about 25 percent and streamlined its transportation and storage facilities. Food aid also gave the Malian government a level of food security that made it politically acceptable to reduce the size of required purchases from the country's major rice-growing schemes and to eliminate required sales in other cereals. Unfortunately, the 1984 drought that led to a large extra inflow of emergency food aid, followed by a bumper harvest in 1985, has postponed the planned step-by-step set of policy changes and the expected rise in producer prices. The sectoral project, however, has food aid support from the United States, Canada, and the European Community and the WFP, and uses food aid with a feeding objective that supports economic adjustment sensibly. Of course, this requires donor cooperation.

In Kenya a contrasting situation has unfolded. The World Bank proposed some changes in the operation of the National Cereals and Produce Board (NCPB) in 1982-1983 that would, like the Malian case, have reduced the NCPB's formal role as a monopoly grain buyer and price enforcer. Many donors agreed with the idea, as did some Kenyan officials. However, the proposal did not go forward because of donor agriculture and political-military interests, primarily those in the United States, that continued to supply program food aid. This effectively undercut policy reform on this issue. If food aid is to be used to help in economic reform, donor political and commercial interests will need to be encouraged to see their long-term advantage in assisting healthier economies in Africa, rather than in pursuing the short-term considerations and blocking effective donor coordination.

Resource-augmenting Measures

Selling food is the alternative to its being used directly or indirectly for nutritional and redistributional purposes, as just discussed. Food aid sold for its full value on local markets is a rather efficient means for a government to raise revenue. Where a government has been running deficits and where it has a significant dependence on taxes from agriculture, often collected as export duties, it is difficult to achieve reform. A government is asked to reduce the tax burden on agriculture in order to encourage greater production, and at the same time is required to reduce deficit spending. In this situation, where alternative revenue sources are critical, the possibility of revenue from sales of imported food is especially attractive. Such food is bought by groups that are otherwise hard to tax, and collection costs are low compared to domestic income and excise tax collection. For purposes of my argument here, the food aid provided is assumed to be a pure substitution for commercial imports, and the commodities relate to effective demand, even after exchange rate adjustments have raised the price of food imports. In reality, of course, a "pure" case may be hard to maintain in the face of changing prices and possible political pressure from export interests of donor states to maintain commercial imports rather than aid exports. In any event, providing food for revenue generation works much better than providing other surplus goods from donor countries such as cars or furniture.

Unlike cereal swaps or nutritional projects, the food aid resource in this scenario goes diffusedly to help the state and the general structural adjustment process. Proceeds from sales that accrue to the Egyptian government from its sale of PL480 wheat (or from the maize it imports under the U.S. Commodity Import Program), are accounted in a general fashion to agricultural development expenditures, and at least offset the cost of food subsidies. If it were additional it would, of course, have price implications. Such food for cash, it is sometimes argued, can deepen or maintain a dependency on imported grains. Given the rise in commercial imports in countries like Nigeria, however, where oil income raised purchasing power in the 1970s, this seems to be an argument regarding distortion towards imports only for countries that continue in economic decline. Economic growth, not food aid, creates long-term effective shifts of consumer taste towards imported food.

The revenue from sales, referred to as counterpart funds, can be managed in a number of ways. It can be simply a general budget support item justified in light of the policy reforms being undertaken and conditioned on their continuation. Alternatively, it can be earmarked with varying degrees of seriousness and detail to particular development undertakings of the governments. The World Food Program, for example, has new projects of this nature in Grenada and Rwanda. If the U.S. wheat food aid to Egypt were not part of a major food subsidy system, it would also be a good case of general budget support with earmarking. In any event, what real sales proceeds do accrue to the Egyptian government from its sale of PL480 wheat, or for that matter, from the maize it imports under the U.S. Commodity Import Program are attributed in a general fashion to agricultural development expenditures, and at least offset somewhat the cost of food subsidies. In Egypt, food subsidies play a central compensatory role in maintaining political support for the economic liberalization introduced under Sadat in 1976 (Alderman 1984; Hopkins 1985).

In the negotiations between donors and recipients over the level of resources and debt forgiveness donors will provide, and the type and timing of policy reforms recipients will undertake, food aid can be added to the package. Its value as a function of the whole, especially in smaller African states can be significant, ranging from 10 to 25 percent of a package. Of course, if it is to become part of a package, greater coordination among donors would be required and practices on conditionality for food aid would need modification.

As a sweetener in the negotiations themselves, food aid can be attractive not only as an economic help by relieving foreign exchange indebtness, but also, as I noted earlier, a political asset. Food aid makes the package more politically attractive by allowing important groups to be protected temporarily during the pain of adjustment and/or by giving the government with its weak tax administrative capacity, an efficient source of local revenue.

DILEMMAS IN USING FOOD AID AS POLICY-BASED LENDING

Food aid poses some dilemmas for structural adjustment situations. This is not, as some might think, due to its being tied to commodities. Basically, food aid as a resource is no different than other aid. Indeed, financial aid has concrete value only after it is turned into the import of some kind of commodity or technical assistance. Moreover, many financial aid arguments specify the commodities to be imported and even the countries from which imports may come. This is true either specifically for project aid or for more general program aid, including much of the World Bank's African Development Fund. The dilemmas posed by food aid arise from the historical principles and rules that have guided its use. In law or by convention these establish certain practices by which food aid is to be used that contradict the formulas and goals associated with policy-based structural adjustment lending.

I find five dilemmas in policy-based uses of food aid. First, food aid usually encourages increased subsidies, which is the very opposite goal of most policy-reform efforts in structural adjustments. Second, policy-based lending usually monitors policy performance and provides funds in tranches as policy reform proceeds. In contrast, program food aid donors usually monitor specific undertakings funded either by counterpart funds or directly through food. Conditionality is linked to project implementation not macropolicy. A third dilemma is over the public/private sector division. Most reform efforts seek to reduce the role of the state in the economy and the size of states' large payrolls. Food aid usually does the opposite. Fourth, food aid, to be most valuable, needs to be countercyclical, able to vary from year to year in response to changes in local production and food availabilities. In contrast, there is a more stable schedule for loan disbursements and repayment obligations. Finally, there is a symbolic dilemma for Africa. Using food aid even to support reform efforts seems counter to the professed goal of current reform pledges to increase agricultural and food production and decrease food imports. Food aid is seen as a symptom not a solution.

These five rather interrelated problems pose true dilemmas. They are not merely problems that can be solved in the existing circumstances, but rather require difficult choices. Essentially, either some desirable effects of food aid must be traded off against some other desirable ones or, alternatively, certain of the rules and procedures of food aid must be changed. Examples of changed rules include those on project conditionality and the requirement that countries maintain usual commercial food imports, even when their economies are sinking. These changes, while desirable, still would not overcome the tension inherent in all of the dilemmas. I will try to illustrate my argument briefly on each dilemma.

Food Subsidies

Food subsidies can distort urban-rural terms of trade through implicit taxes on producers to pay for them. This was often true in the 1970s. They may also be a direct fiscal cost to the budget, leading to inflation and/or to government funds being diverted to buy consumption goods from investment accounts. Marketing inefficiencies may also be fostered by state agencies' actions to control directly the purchase, transport, storage, and sale of grain in ways that cost more than the same activities handled by the private sector. The gains that explain this economic "irrationality" are added security of supply to targeted consumers (often politically important groups), exclusion of pariah minorities from grain trade, and fulfillment of political expectations that a state should handle grain stock as evidence of its power. In addition, parastatal operations can prove a convenient mode for moving public assets into the private holdings of public officials (World Bank 1983).

The dilemma is how can food aid, which in the 1970s often aided governments in expanding their market control over trade, now somehow do the reverse? The Mali restructuring exercise, and Tanzania's use of the income from wheat sales income to subsidize maize flour, may be instances of how trade-offs may be drawn. Both reduced the cost of subsidies to the state, without eliminating them. African states and donors need to steer a politically viable course through belt-tightening macro economic measures and general liberalization (Jaycox 1986, p.22). Food subsidies may be one of the last and most sensitive elements a state may wish to eliminate. Food riots, however unlikely, are occasions no African government would wish to experience. Thus, there is a rationale for maintaining some subsidies. In addition to political factors, some subsidies are desirable to compensate those least able to afford high food prices created by an adjustment (World Bank 1986b). Finding the right trade-off between liberalization and subsidies should be an important consideration in structural adjustment negotiations. The major argument over the "right trade-off" will be between nutrition targets to maintain a "human face" on adjustment, and political-economic considerations that will search for a cost minimizing, but risk adverse form and some of the subsidies.

Conditionality Requirements

Food aid requires that food be given free or in exchange for work, school attendance, and so forth; or if the food is sold, generated counterpart funds must be used for specified purposes. The latter are often linked to improving a country's food self-reliance. Structural adjustment lending encourages the avoidance of earmarked funds. Because this lending seeks its quid pro quo in reformed fiscal and monetary policy, devalued exchange rates, and public sector austerity, it seeks to avoid protecting any one activity. The new U.S. Food for Progress program may provide a model for resolving this dilemma. By changing the older food aid rules, the United States can now provide Title I food as a grant and not the normal concessional sale to countries adopting policy reforms. Rice is to be provided to Guinea and Madagascar under agreements for FY 1987. Rice sales in these countries aim to minimize project conditionality and illustrate how the dilemma may be resolved. Similarly, WFP projects in Grenada and Rwanda, agreed upon in October 1986, offer general budgetary support with no real targeting, although the Rwanda project has funds attributed to salary payments of personnel in agricultural research. The problem is not that the rule against a diffuse use of counterpart funds is being waived. In Egypt, for instance, this has been a de facto reality for the last decade. Rather the issue is whether it is appropriate for the country in question to receive food aid and whether the potential manner of using the food aid can support structural adjustment. Obviously the reverse should be true—that adjustment, if successful, can provide for a better environment for regular project-oriented food aid. Aside from ending all project ties as conditions, food aid can support sectoral reform. The effort to provide a price wedge and period of adjustment to more market-determined prices has been reasonably effective in one case outside Africa—Bangladesh, which moved to open-market sales under a U.S. PL480 Title III (Food for Development) multiyear agreement. Similar sectoral conditionality seems to be congruent with policy reform in Africa. Mali and Senegal have coordinated food aid for step-by-step moves toward freer market conditions. Even in Madagascar, mentioned earlier as a "pure" case, domestic rice prices have been raised.

Emergency aid is much like program aid, but it is given on easy, quick terms. It, also, should be linked to policy reform. Such conditionality should be a normal procedure, just as adjustment requirements are imposed with "emergency" bank loans. Of course, exceptions should be made in the case of dire emergencies such as refugees or people already in a near famine state. In such cases, direct feeding with UN and voluntary agencies delivering services is usually the case. But there are chronic emergencies, as in Mozambique and Ethiopia in the 1980s, where policy conditionality would be appropriate. Even in "variable" emergency cases, such as Kenya in 1984, policy reform would be an appropriate condition to associate with the aid.

Overhead Costs

As a commodity, food is most naturally used for targeted nutrition interventions. Such use seeks to avoid disincentive effects and to arrive in countercyclical fashion when it is well managed. Management, however, entails substantial costs. Even oversight and bookkeeping of food and counterpart fund accounts takes resources. This increases the need for government employees to provide such management and runs directly counter to the conditions in Africa where there are few trained accountants, warehouse supervisors, and grain specialists. This effect runs counter to recommendations to accomplish a reduction in a state's expenditures. Furthermore, the recommended policy changes suggest ending or at least limiting parastatal operations, reducing public services, and eliminating price and internal trade controls, which have enforcement costs: The idea is to shrink the state to a point where its interventions can be sustained by domestic government revenues. Food aid, in contrast, tends to encourage or sustain public sector activities. Rules governing food aid require that such aid be differentiated from other kinds of commercial imports and its uses be carefully planned and overseen. Thus, food aid requires substantial local management so that it can be targeted and so that it can avoid depressing prices of local food producers. In addition food-for-work projects require substantial costs in nonfood inputs and management. While policy reforms aim to reduce public sector costs, food aid is often associated with public and social services.

The solution to this dilemma, as in the case of conditionality rules and practices discussed above, is to simplify the food management requirements per se through program sales. This, however, can eliminate the value of the food as a nutrition, humanitarian resource, and as such raises questions about why food aid should be supported by donors at all.

Variable Food Needs

Food import needs in Africa vary substantially from year to year. This contrasts with the total cash needs for local government costs or foreign exchange for all imports.

Manufactured goods imports, whether for existing or planned activities, can be forecast with some precision and a modicum of reliability. However, since most Africans lack adaptive ability (thanks to chronic undernourishment) food aid needs, leaving aside the smaller feeding projects that require imported food, can vary greatly. For example, in 1984 Kenya and Niger had grain production shortfalls of 20 to 50 percent. They were in great need of food imports. Twenty months later they were able appropriately to export grain to neighboring states. It is unwise, therefore, to lock in food aid promises to specified amounts over a several-year period, especially if it is to be a resource to support long-term reforms. Food aid needs to arrive in neither too little nor too great amounts in any given year. Of course, this is less true for "structural deficit" commodities, usually wheat, rice, and cooking oil. In many countries these cannot be produced economically, but they have an established and predictable local demand.

The European Economic Commission has a rule that allows up to 10 percent of its budget for food aid to be given as cash if the targeted recipient's food import needs change. Adjustment assistance using food aid needs such flexibility. Another prospect is to be able to purchase local food in years of surplus food in the project. Adoption of these principles and practices among all donors would be a useful step. Further budgetary amendments are needed to create an ability to shift in time the schedule of actual food deliveries without forfeiting the allocation. This also would help maintain needed support for planned government measures without bringing food imports at a bad time, i.e., just after a bumper harvest. Future markets could possibly be used, putting food aid commitments in a kind of escrow account. This could be earmarked for a set of fluctuating food import needs and relatively fixed food aid donor budgets.

Negative Attitudes

The comparative lower priority accorded food aid by donor and recipient officials makes use of food aid and pressure for rule changes difficult. As noted earlier, African states have long given rhetorical priority to food and agriculture. This became more widespread and vocal in 1980 in the Lagos Plan of Action. As fears over food shortages and losses of export revenues have grown, budget allocations and pricing policy have also changed toward providing greater returns to agriculture. There have been real changes in the 1980s in a number of states. Looking back, many African leaders associate food aid with the problems they seek to escape. Donors, too, are skeptical about food aid historically, wondering whether program and emergency aid may not create policy disincentives (Hopkins 1986). By relieving pressure to acquire grain for urban groups, food aid can lower the impetus for reform of policies biased against rural areas. A case for such effects having occurred may be made in some countries, e.g., Zambia, Mali, and Tanzania in the 1970s.

The seeming contradiction between food aid and the goal of long-term self-reliance is a major barrier to interest in using food aid in policy-based lending situations. Fear of the food undercutting a will to transform economic policies seems well justified when one looks at cases where food aid, indeed emergency food aid, arrived at the same time adjustment measures were rejected. In Tanzania in the 1970s and early 1980s, emergency food aid was used to keep the cereals board (NMC) supplied with food to meet urban demand. In the 1980s, of course, producers' prices and the efforts of the NMC have been much more rural-oriented. In Tanzania, as in Ghana, the urban population suffered relatively more economic recession. Probably the only solution to the attitudinal and analytical skepticism toward food aid is closer and more candid examination and discussion of food aid's actual effects on policy. Perhaps if the problems of ignoring food aid are seen, as well as those associated with its special commodity and humanitarian rules, the negative attitudes can be directed to constructive efforts to resolve some of the dilemmas food aid poses for policy-based lending to help economic adjustment. In any case, a principle that food aid should be withheld from countries rejecting policy reform deserves examination.

CONCLUSION

If food aid is to play a significant role in longer-term African development, as it can and should, several changes are required. First, emergency food aid should be treated in a parallel fashion with structural adjustment lending by the IMF or the World Bank. Policy conditions should be attached to it. This conditionality could be waived for famine relief aid channeled directly to nongovernmental groups. In such cases, conditions for how these groups will work in specific feeding efforts would be agreed upon in advance; even so, these conditions would take into account problems of disincentives and the issue of local government policy toward famine victims. Second, the negative media positions held in some development circles toward food aid, viewing it solely as a surplus disposal mechanism with high transfer costs, must be altered. Skepticism is healthy; uniformed prejudice is not. Third, some food aid rules need changing—for example, commercial marketing requirements for the poorer African countries should be waived, at least partially. In adjustment lending, commodities to be imported should be chosen for their highest transfer value rather than their end-use suitability as nutrition resources for the poor. Fourth, research to design efficient and self-limiting food subsidy schemes is needed so that structural adjustment does not choke on self-expanding subsidy schemes that, once induced by food aid, end up counterproductively supporting the better off. Fifth, counterpart fund generation should be based on the commercial market value of sales—so-called open-market sales—of the food commodities. These funds should be part of a coordinated donor government revenue resource dedicated to high-priority expenditures. Sixth, recurrent costs and rates of return on projects associated with food aid should be estimated initially and monitored during the course of a project. If projects look expensive or later begin to fail, food aid can be shifted to a program mode. Seventh, program/structural food aid should be available for variable (transient) import needs as well as structural deficits. This, too, requires rule changes. Eighth, efforts that strengthen the state's capacity to establish a reliable framework for market activity (e.g., contract enforcement, information, public service assets such as rural transport and communication facilities) should be built up, if necessary at the expense of less productive public goods.

There are some analysts who advocate large rural public works projects in Africa, using food-for-work techniques as successfully fostered in Asia. Ethiopia has a large reforestation food-for-work project and this approach is certainly possible. Africa, however, has far less of a tradition of payment-in-kind for labor; it has less surplus labor in rural areas, especially not in concentrated groups; and the institutional and human resource capacity for successfully developing such food-for-work projects is limited. Hence, for the time being, food aid in Africa needs to move toward strengthening states and supporting economic reform.

NOTE

In this essay I refer basically to sub-Saharan Africa, but often shorten this reference simply to "Africa." On food use see FAO 1986 and earlier World Food Programme and FAO reports.

REFERENCES

Alderman. 1984. *The Effects of the Egyptian Food Ration and Subsidy on Income Distribution and Consumption.* Washington, D.C.: International Food Policy Research Institute.

Bates, Robert. *Markets and States in Tropical Africa.* Berkeley: University of California Press.

Development Advisory Committee (DAC). 1985. *Report.* Paris: OECD.

Economist. 1986. "The World Bank." September 27, pp. 7-42.

Food and Agriculture Organization (FAO). 1986. *Food Supply Situation and Crop Prospects in Sub-Saharan Africa.* Rome: FAO (September).

Gersovitz, Mark and Henry Bienen. 1985. "Turmoil and Structural Adjustment." *International Organization* (Winter 1985).

Hopkins, Raymond F. 1986. "Food Aid: Solution, Palliative, or Danger for Africa's Food Crisis." In Stephen Commins, Michael Lofchie, and Rhys Payne, eds., *Africa's Agrarian Crisis: The Roots of Famine.* Boulder, Colo.: Lynne Rienner.

Hyden, Goran. 1980. *Ujamaa.* Berkeley: University of California Press.

Independent Commission on International Humanitarian Issues. 1985.

Famine: A Man-Made Disaster? London: Pam Books.

Jackson, Robert and Carl Rosberg. 1982. "Why Africa's Weak States Persist?" *World Politics* (Organization of African Unity) vol. 35.

Jaycox, Edward V.K. 1986. "Africa: Development Challenges and the World Bank's Response." *Finance and Development* (March), pp. 21-26.

Killick, Tony, ed. 1984. *The IMF and Stabilization: Developing Country Experiences.* London: Heineman.

Organization of African Unity (OAU). 1985. *Africa's Priority Program for Economic Recovery.* Addis Ababa: FAO.

Sandbrook, Richard. 1985. *The Politics of Africa's Economic Stagnation.* London: Cambridge University Press.

Sen, Amartya. 1981. *Poverty and Famines.* New York: Oxford University Press.

Waterbury, John. 1985. *Senegal.* Manuscript, Princeton University (June).

World Bank. 1981. *Accelerated Development in Sub-Saharan Africa: An Agenda for Action.* Washington, D.C.: World Bank.

———. 1983. *The Effects of Corruption on Administrative Performance.* World Bank Staff Working Papers, No. 580.

———. 1986a. *Financing Adjustment with Growth in Sub-Saharan Africa, 1986-90.* Washington, D.C.: World Bank.

———. 1986b. *Poverty and Hunger: Issues and Options for Security in Developing Countries.* Washington, D.C.: World Bank.

———. 1986c. *World Development Report, 1986.* New York: Oxford University Press.

PART III

Problems of Political Economy

CHAPTER 8

Political Economy and Policy Reform in Sub-Saharan Africa
Carol Lancaster

Increasingly in recent years, major foreign aid donors, led by the World Bank, have tied their aid to African governments to policy and institutional reforms by those governments. At the same time, African officials have increasingly acknowledged the need to change government policies and institutions if recovery and growth are to occur. Reforms typically include demand management policies, changes in the structure and function of governments, improvements in production incentives, and better management of aid and debt. All of these reforms share a fundamental aim—improving the efficiency with which national resources are used to promote economic growth.

Major changes in macroeconomic policies and government institutions inevitably have an impact on incomes and access to resources of individuals and groups in the reforming country. Reforms can also carry implications for prevailing economic ideologies and priorities underlying government policies. And they can make heavy demands on a government's administrative abilities in formulating and implementing reforms.

Not surprisingly, the process of policy reform has not always been a smooth one. Even where the link between economic reform and improved efficiency is clear and uncontroversial (by no means the case with all reforms), those government officials favoring reforms have often had to deal with resistance from other parts of their governments, from private interests, and even from their political leaders. Where there is a consensus on the need for reforms, there have occasionally been problems of inefficient or ineffective implementation. And sustaining an ever-broadening series of reforms has raised concerns about "adjustment fatigue" and a growing resistance to reform in government and among affected groups. While a number of reform programs have been successfully implemented and sustained, there have also been cases where government leaders, although persuaded of the need for particular reforms, have failed to implement them fully or have been unable or unwilling to sustain them. It is important for policy reformers in Africa and in donor agencies alike to address problems of managing and sustaining reforms. To do so, however, inevitably carries one beyond the field of economics and into considerations of public administration, politics, and social structures in which government policies and institutions are embedded.

During the past several decades, the field of political economy has been resurrected as mainstream political scientists, and a growing number of economists, have begun to ask questions about the interrelationships between government and society, politics, and economics.[1] In this chapter I will describe the major approaches in political economy over the past twenty-five years and analyze the insights that body of work offers about the nature of African government policies and institutions, and implications—seldom explicit—for the implementation and sustainability of reforms and for the role that foreign donors can play in supporting such reforms.

POLITICAL ECONOMY TODAY

Once upon a time, economists were called "political economists." Adam Smith, James and John Stuart Mill, Thomas Malthus, Jeremy Bentham, and others all viewed themselves as political economists. They asked questions "concerned with directing governmental policies toward the promotion of the wealth of the government and the community as a whole."[2] Eventually, political economists in the last century narrowed the focus of their work to elaborating the concepts and analytical tools that would advance their understanding of the working of markets. Those studying government—precursors of today's political scientists—frequently concentrated their attention on constitutions, laws, and the structure of governments, or on political philosophy. For many decades, practically the only individuals who continued to examine the link between economics and politics were the Marxists.

Today, the field of political economy includes several different types of work by economists and political scientists. One approach developed over the past several decades rests on applying analytical tools of economics to explain political phenomena. The work of the recent Nobel laureate James Buchanan falls into this category. Another, rather different group, composed largely (but not exclusively) of political scientists, has begun to examine interrelationships among economic, politicial, and social phenomena as economies develop and modernize. A diverse group of political scientists has explored the nature of the state in an effort to explain policy choices.

The differences among these approaches often turn on assumptions about the nature of the state and how government decisions are made. Modernization theorists concerned with interrelationships between economic, political, and social phenomena barely deal with the state, thus implicitly assuming that government policies and institutions reflect broad economic and social influences. Among those who focus explicitly on the nature of the state are some who view it as "autonomous," that is, having its own objectives and making decisions based on its own goals as well as on outside pressures. Others view the state and its policies as controlled by dominant classes, external forces, social and economic structures, or modes of production. All of these approaches differ from the basic assumption, often implicit in neoclassical economic analysis, that the state is a welfare maximizer, with goals of promoting national economic welfare and implementing policies intended to achieve those goals.

Before turning to an examination of several of the major areas where work on "political economy" has been undertaken in recent years, it is worth pointing out that such work has infrequently focused explicitly on policy change or on the management of policy reform. Rather, it has usually examined broader questions such as the economic analysis of political choice, the relationships between political modernization and economic development, the relationship between African economies and the world economy, or the nature of the African state. We shall therefore have to tease out of these works any insights they offer for policy reform.

ECONOMIC TOOLS FOR POLITICAL ANALYSIS

Since the 1950s, a growing number of scholars, mainly economists, have sought to use the concepts and analytical tools of economics to explain and predict political phenomena. Although the questions they have asked and the tools they have used differ, they tend to focus on political choices by individual groups or governments, and to assume that such choices are made by those bodies rationally, on the basis of self-interest or utility maximization. Analysts often define "utility" in largely economic terms.[3] They have employed tools such as cost-benefit calculations, input-output matrices, indifference and transformation curves, and concepts involving "exchange," "competition," and "free rider" to explain political phenomena.[4]

The major insights this work has provided economists and political scientists is that political beings, like economic beings, act to advance their own interests (i.e., rather than "national interest") and work to influence government to adopt policies that will benefit those interests. It emphasizes the critical role of interest groups in influencing public policy and tries to predict the actions of such groups and their probable effectiveness in influencing public policies. It differs from work by political scientists on the influence of interest groups on public policy by attempting to impart a rigor to such analysis that economic concepts and tools provide.

Much of this work has focused on the function of Western industrial democracies, with their typically pluralistic economies, open political competition, and periodic voting. As a result, this analysis tends to provide limited insights into politics in developing countries, particularly in Africa, where economies are less pluralistic, political competition is anything but open, and formal and free elections are rarely permitted. There has, however, been some effort by political scientists to adapt the tools of economic analysis to understanding public policies in developing countries. Perhaps the best-known effort to apply economic concepts to political analysis regardless of the degree of development or government structure, was undertaken in the early 1970s (but apparently not often applied to specific cases).[5] It attempted to redefine political phenomena in economic terms, employing such concepts as political resources, infrastructure, accumulation, or inflation, to provide a framework for rational political choice. The reason this work has been so little applied may be that its concepts are too limited and lack the nuances to capture the diversity of political phenomena, particularly in developing countries.

This "economistic" school of political economy has provided suggestive insights into the realities of public policymaking to those economists or political scientists who have tended to regard government as an institution functioning to "provide the greatest good to the greatest number" and choosing policies based on a concept of national interest. This may seem a naive insight to today's less innocent generation of political scientists, Africanists, or development specialists, but it has not been so long ago that these assumptions reigned and indeed may still influence thinking by analysts in both professions.

However, this approach suffers from a fundamental limitation. By attempting to inject greater rigor (and often quantification) into political analysis, it tends to exclude important variables that do not lend themselves easily to cost-benefit analysis or quantification—for example, the influence of beliefs and convictions that may not always be coterminous with the self-interest of the individual or group. A basic problem is the definition of "utility" for political purposes. As soon as it is expanded to include all relevant political phenomena, it begins to lose its rigor. But if it does not include relevant political phenomena, it loses its power to explain and predict. The world of politics may be messier than the tools of economics permit.

MODERNIZATION THEORY

In the late 1950s and early 1960s, when an increasing number of developing countries were becoming independent, a stated goal of the political leadership in these new countries was rapid economic development and improvement in the welfare of their populations. Looking back on the economic and political science literature of the period, it was a time of considerable optimism among economists and policymakers who believed that with sufficient capital and technical expertise, economic development would occur. Political scientists became interested in the governing of these new countries. By and large, they accepted the preeminence and even the inexorability of the development process. They went on to ask several questions: What was the likely impact of economic development on national political structures and functions? What were the political, social, and psychological preconditions of development? What was the relationship between economic development and political change?

The answers political scientists attempted to give to these questions varied widely, so widely that it would be inaccurate to speak of a body of theory covering modernization or "political development." They shared with economists a fundamental problem—there were relatively few cases of successful economic development in non-Western societies on which to base their research and conclusions. As a result, much of the empirical material they drew upon was based on the experience of Western Europe with economic development and political change.

Not surprisingly, there was much disagreement on what constituted political development. In 1966, Lucien Pye listed ten diverse concepts that were then being used to define political development, including the creation of political preconditions (or removal of political obstacles) to economic development; behavior by governments that was "rational" or "responsible," like that typical of industrialized countries; or the establishment of democracy.[6] The models of political development were seldom value-free. Some of the most influential political scientists working on these issues viewed political development as the creation of political structures and functions in developing countries similar to those of Western democracies. In effect, the goal of political development was democracy.

In addition to the variety of concepts of what political development or modernization was or should be (and many did not even agree that political development and modernization were the same), there was a diversity of opinion on the interrelationship between economic and political development. Some argued that economic development would result in the creation of pluralistic societies or middle classes that would in turn demand democratic government. Others argued that political development had to precede or at least accompany economic development. Psychological attitudes toward government itself would have to change (i.e., become secular, rational, based on the needs of the nation state rather than ethnicity or family units) if economic development was to proceed. One theory put forth by a number of Africanists was that economic development would lead to a diminution of ethnic loyalties and a transfer of those loyalties to the nation.

Academics working on political development were never able to create a generally accepted set of definitions, models, or body of theory to explain the relationship between economic development and political change. Meanwhile, the approach was criticized as being ethnocentric, deterministic, and wrong.

More from the unfolding of events in developing countries than from advances in analysis, political scientists in the late 1960s increasingly acknowledged that the process of economic development was neither inexorable nor easily understood. The direction of political change in developing countries was unpredictable and did not necessarily produce democracy or political stability. Fragile democracies in Latin America and Africa were overwhelmed by military coups, or undermined by repressive leaders; outbreaks of political violence within developing countries grew; and corruption and governmental inefficiencies became more evident if not widespread. In Africa specifically, it became clear—particularly in the wake of the Nigerian civil war—that economic development could exacerbate rather than diminish tensions arising from ethnic loyalties.[7]

Not surprisingly, scholars began to lose interest in political development. As military coups and conflict began to replace inherited democracies in newly independent states, some scholars turned to analyzing questions of political stability rather than political development. Perhaps the best known of these writers is Samuel Huntington, who argued that economic change can provoke political instability unless political institutions are flexible enough to respond to new expectations and demands made upon them.[8]

The work of modernization theorists, even that still read and used by political scientists, appears to have relatively little to say to today's policy reformers. With its emphasis on underlying economic and political trends, and its relative neglect of the state in the policy process, modernization theory tells little about which policies to reform and how. Modernization theorists have chosen to work on a broader canvas (analyzing major economic and political processes) than have policy reformers. But, most significantly, modernization theorists gave up looking for interrelationships in the confusion and disillusionment of the late 1960s as coups and conflicts became common in much of the developing world. Considering the complexity of change and the time it takes change to manifest itself, they may have given up too soon.

IDEOLOGY

Policy reformers, particularly in Western aid institutions, frequently point to the prevailing economic and political ideologies in African countries as important factors in promoting or impeding reforms. The role of ideology in determining economic policies and structures in Africa has received some attention from political scientists working on Africa. Their interest in the connection between political ideologies and economic structures and policies was sparked by the general tendency among African politicians in the years after independence to declare themselves "African socialists" and to characterize their policies as African socialism. It quickly became clear that African socialism included an extraordinary variety of economic policies and structures, from those of relatively capitalist-oriented Ivory Coast to those of heavily state-controlled Guinea or, after 1967, Tanzania.[9] What this variety of socialists had in common was an emphasis, at the level of rhetoric at least, on equitable development and a leading role for government in that development. More basic, perhaps, was a generally shared distaste for free markets and private enterprise, and a fear that such markets would not support and could well impede equitable national development. Many did not trust the "invisible hand"; others believed that the early stage of development in their countries made a leading role for government in their economies inevitable.

The common preference for a major role for government in African economies may also have been part of a broader tendency of newly independent political leaders to protect their positions by expanding their control over political activities as well as economic resources. Thus, a belief in socialism, or at least in a major role for government in the economy, was justified both in terms of practical politics and in terms of larger principles. African politicians could do well politically by doing good economically.

The key question for policy reformers, particularly where proposed reforms involve reducing the role of government in the economy and expanding opportunities for private sector activities, is to what extent does ideology or a preference for government-led development pose a barrier to reform. And if such a barrier exists (as many working on reform programs in Africa believe), how can it be removed?

Despite the appearance of a major change in the thinking of African officials about the appropriate role of government in their economies, we do not know how deep a change has taken place or even whether officials are simply manipulating foreign aid donors. Unfortunately, there is little work by political economists on existing attitudes of political leaders, government bureaucrats, or the public in African countries, or on what factors produce changes in such attitudes—all areas of critical interest to policy reformers. The work on policy reform currently underway appears to focus little on the role of ideology or commonly held beliefs in influencing the implementation and sustainability of reforms.

One recent study on ideology comes to the conclusion that ideology and economic structures have had little relevance to development performance in Africa. In his book, *Ideology and Development in Africa*,[10] Crawford Young assesses the performance of capitalist-oriented, populist-socialist, and Afro-Marxist regimes in terms of six criteria: growth, equality of distribution of income, autonomy and self-reliance, human rights, political participation, and "expansion of societal capacity", i.e., the ability of the state to adapt to changing needs. His conclusion was that ideology did not appear to be a determining factor in development performance. A variety of performances—vigorous as well as poor—existed within the three ideological groups. What appeared more important to development performance was "capacity," a quality that Young left undefined. While Young's conclusion may appear controversial, it has yet to be definitively challenged in scholarly publications.

DEPENDENCY THEORY

In contrast to many Western development experts, dependency scholars view ideology as irrelevant to development in Africa, since African countries are all part of a global capitalist system and it is this relationship that is the determining one for their economic development.

Dependency theory was elaborated first in Latin America and somewhat later applied to Africa, most notably by Samir Amin.[11] This approach explains underdevelopment in poor countries as a result of the asymmetrical economic relationship between those countries (which are on the "periphery" of the world capitalist system) and developed capitalist countries (which are "central" to the world capitalist system). Peripheral countries are linked to the center through trade, capital transfers, and other economic ties. These relationships are, in turn, based on "unequal exchange" in which surplus in the periphery is not retained there for reinvestment but is transmitted to the center in the form of low export prices, repatriation of profits, capital flight, and so on.

Amin argues that the key element in underdevelopment throughout Africa is the subordination of the interests of peripheral African countries to those of countries in the capitalist center. Until the peripheral countries rupture their links to the world capitalist economy, their condition of underdevelopment is unlikely to change. Dependency analysts have further argued that the African state and those who lead it are essentially part of a "comprador" class, supporting the goals and deriving the benefits from their links with foreign capitalists while having little interest in the development of their own countries. Development requires the removal of this class as well as the foreign capitalists on which it depends. Unlike modernization theory, dependency theory views the state as neither benevolent nor irrelevant to development. The state and the class interests it reflects are seen as an obstacle to development because of their relationships to central, capitalist countries. Foreign aid, with its procurement ties and other conditions, was simply another link between Africa and world capitalism.

Dependentistas have had a significant impact on the thinking of many Africans and foreigners on the causes of African underdevelopment and on the rhetoric of change, if not on the reality of government policies. For obvious reasons, no African government has seriously considered a complete rupture of its relationships with the Western capitalist system. (There are many examples of governments reducing the role of foreign capital in their economies through nationalization of private foreign investment. But such nationalization falls far short of what the Dependentistas had in mind as a rupture in links with world capitalism.)

In addition to voluminous academic writings on various aspects of African dependency, the Lagos Plan of Action, signed by the heads of state of the Organization of African Unity (OAU) in 1980, appears to owe much to dependency theory, especially in its emphasis on collective self-reliant development through the eventual creation of a continentwide common market. (The Lagos Plan has remained an expression of African governments' goals but it, too, has had little apparent impact on policies. Experiments in regional integration abound on the continent but have thus far made little progress toward creating larger markets.)

Dependency theory offers policy reformers and their supporters relatively few insights of practical use. Dependentistas would argue that incremental reforms in government policies are irrelevant to Africa's basic problems, which can only be solved by revolutionary change in relationships with the world capitalist system and in the leadership of African countries. In contrast, one of the major thrusts of the policy reform movement is to increase rather than diminish incorporation of African countries into the world capitalist system through expansion of their exports and larger amounts of private investment in their economies, including foreign investment.

In any case, the heyday of the dependency school of analysis of Africa's economic problems appears to have already passed. In addition to a variety of criticisms of the theory made by academics (i.e., that it is tautological, illogical, sloppy in its use of facts, obscure, and unreflective of African realities), its prescriptions for policy have been universally ignored and even at the level of rhetoric and official statements, African politicians appear to have begun deemphasizing self-reliant development. They, too, have begun to point to the need for policy reform and an expansion in the role of the private sector in their approaches to economic recovery and growth.

THE ROLE OF THE STATE IN AFRICAN DEVELOPMENT

As the economic crisis facing Africa deepened during the 1970s and it became clear that African government policies had contributed to that crisis, political economists began to turn their attention to the nature of government and politics, and their impact on economic development on the continent. The role of the state in African economies has grown since independence.[12] African politicians sought to control political activity in their societies through the creation of one-party states, the banning of competitive or opposition political groups when these could not be controlled or coopted, the suppression of a free press, and often the elimination of an independent judiciary. Government officials in many parts of the continent have pursued policies that allocated national resources not on the basis of efficient promotion of economic growth but largely for their own political or personal gain.

Political scientists examining the nature of the African state have produced individual case studies as well as some general treatises on its character and state-society relations on the continent.[13] While scholars have used different models of the state, they share some common views. First, there tends to be a general agreement that the African state has become overextended. It has undertaken commitments and responsibilities that it cannot fulfill and, increasingly, cannot afford to fund. Parastatals, often inefficient and unable to function without continuing subsidies from government, are frequently singled out as exemplifying the overextension and incapacity of the typical state in Africa. Second, a number of observers agree that the African state is "soft,"[14] i.e., unable to implement effectively its policies, or in some circumstances even to provide for law and order. For these and other reasons, African states have generally become impediments rather than promoters of growth on the continent.

Students of the African state differ from earlier modernization theorists in that they do not regard the state as autonomous, acting to promote development and, where it is flexible enough to do so, responding to new demands from its citizens. They differ also from the dependency theorists and orthodox Marxists who regard the state as "instrumental," i.e., dominated by foreign economic interests or domestic, economically based classes who promote their own interests. They tend to view the state as affected by domestic and foreign interests and pressures but also as acting in the interests of its own leadership (often centralized in a charismatic individual) and bureaucracy to maintain power and its own access to resources.

Within this general framework, scholars have emphasized the key role of personal rule and the objectives of that rule. For example, in a widely read recent work, *Personal Rule in Black Africa*, Carl Rosberg and Robert Jackson state:

> In African countries governance is more a matter of seamanship and less one of navigation—that is, staying afloat rather than going somewhere. This is a source of considerable dismay to planners, economists, and policymakers (among others) who want African governments to initiate a rational and concerted assault on

poverty, ignorance, disease, and other problems of underdevelopment.[15]

National economic resources (government revenues and expenditures, foreign aid, and access to national resources through licenses or permits) are distributed as rewards or bribes to cement political support by followers. The general public, and particularly the unorganized rural masses, are exploited to extract resources. They have been "depoliticized," deprived of a political voice by suppression of periodic elections or of opportunities for legitimate political activity (outside a single party). And because governments control political life and politically sensitive information, they are relatively unaccountable to their publics. Politics is essentially conducted in the form of patron-client relationships. In the most extreme cases, the state and national resources controlled by the state are "hijacked" by political elites and pillaged to benefit themselves.

Several scholars have sought to explain the evolution of the patrimonial state in Africa in historical terms. One sees it as a version of early modern European states and thus likely to change relatively slowly whatever reforms in structure are made.[16] Another scholar views it as an outgrowth of inherited state structures and behavior patterns established in the colonial period and extended after independence by opportunistic politicians (who faced resistance from relatively few organized interest groups).[17] These suggest that time and the development of pluralistic economies may be necessary before African politics becomes more institutionalized and less dependent on the often capricious whims of charismatic rulers who are inefficient and exploitative of their people. The implications for policy reforms appear pessimistic. Policy reforms to benefit the mass of the population (for example, small farmers) are unlikely to be initiated by rulers whose support is rarely drawn from potential beneficiaries.

Another analysis of the African state puts somewhat less emphasis on the peculiarities of political leaders and more on the policies they adopt to maintain their positions. As in the preceding approach, economic resources are distributed to groups and key individuals in the dominant coalition to ensure continuing support.[18] Some view African states as acting primarily to balance diverse economic and regional claims by ethnic groups and to minimize political tensions through the redistribution of national resources.[19] Typically, coalitions include bureaucrats, the military, urban middle and working classes, and influential individuals from rural areas. Those paying for but not usually sharing in the benefits enjoyed by this coalition are small farmers who are seldom organized or in a position to influence government policies.

Analysts favoring these approaches seldom include recommendations on policy reforms in their published works. But a major implication of their analyses is that policy reforms, if they are to be sustained, must generate active political support in the reforming country. Conversely, they can adversely affect the political support of government. By redistributing national resources, such reforms could upset ethnic or political balances and could lead to political instability. Reforms could be undermined or made difficult to sustain through the resistance of vested and powerful interests, especially where the intended beneficiaries of reforms are relatively powerless (for example, small farmers) or few in number (for example, indigenous industrial entrepreneurs).

A small group of analysts has emphasized the role of cultural factors in explaining the inefficiency of African countries. Hyden describes the African "economy of affection" in which Africans retain their traditional obligations to one another (i.e., to share resources, to promote the interests of family, village, clan, or other group) even when in public office.[20] Indeed, Africans may expect that when in public office, individuals should appropriate public goods to fulfill such obligations, hence the inability of African states to implement policies efficiently (or at all), and the high incidence of appropriation of public resources for private purposes. Intended to explain behavior at all levels of government rather than just at the top, Hyden's analysis has much of interest in it. The implication of this particular aspect for policy reformers is, however, not reassuring. Training, improved equipment, bureaucratic reorganization, and other essentially superficial changes are not likely to have a significant or immediate impact on the behavior of African officials or the efficiency of African governments as long as attitudes toward public service and traditional obligations do not also change.

IMPLICATIONS AND APPLICATIONS

It is now time to see what relevant implications work in political economy has for policy reformers in the Western development community, in African officialdom, and elsewhere. However, it may be useful first to examine the approach of policy reformers for implicit assumptions relevant to the work of political economists. What do the groups have to say to one another?

Policy reformers are actually a varied lot. As a group, they draw their inspiration from neoclassical economics, but many also recognize "structural" obstacles to growth.[21] These obstacles include limitations of physical and human infrastructure, organizational impediments, and the absence of viable technical packages to expand production, which must be eased along with "getting prices right" if recovery and growth is to resume in Africa. Policy reformers share an assumption that by and large economic beings are rational and act to maximize their own interests. Over time, economic incentives will induce a response in the same direction worldwide, though the extent and timing may vary greatly. Policy reformers occasionally divide on whether free markets are necessary to ensure efficient resource use. The World Bank has emphasized in its official statements that governments can operate to allocate resources efficiently, and reforms in government policies can enhance such efficiency. The examples of state-led development in Korea or Brazil are often cited. In contrast, the United States has emphasized the absolute importance of free markets and private enterprise if growth is to occur. Some observers have suggested that conditions peculiar to Africa today (e.g., Hyden's "economy of affection") may make greater reliance on the private sector for efficient resource allocation unavoidable. In recent years, it appears that there is a growing consensus between the Bank, the United States, and other donors on the need for a reduction in the role of government in African economies, especially in controlling or directly managing productive activities, and for freer markets if national resources are to be used efficiently.

In their official statements, policy reformers in the World Bank, in the United States, and elsewhere underline the importance of the "policy dialogue" with African officials in developing reform programs.[22] This dialogue aims at persuading African officials to discuss with aid donors the need for and efficacy of reforms (and, ideally, to educate donors on African government views of policy reforms as well). Behind this assumption lies another—that a lack of understanding of the impact of government economic policies is often an important reason for inefficient policies and can be overcome through improved information, education, or persuasion. Western development officials often emphasize that if African government officials are not convinced of the need for reforms or are not committed to such reforms, the reforms will likely not be implemented or sustained. It is also recognized that in some cases, where governments have little real interest in using their resources efficiently to promote growth, aid without policy reform is likely to be wasted.

The relationship of aid to policy reform is explained in a number of different ways, not all of which are mutually consistent. Aid can "lubricate the process of reform."[23] This seems to mean that aid can ease the pain of reforms by, for example, ensuring that plentiful stocks of imports are available at the time of a devaluation to modify the impact of a devaluation on import prices. Another rationale for aid tied to reforms is that such reforms will not work to promote recovery and growth without an increase in the imported goods that such aid finances. For example, increasing producer prices will not promote expanded production without increased imports of needed inputs. Finally, aid conditioned on reforms provides aid-givers a "voice at the table" in government discussions of policies, development strategies, and change.[24]

It is more difficult to infer assumptions about the sustainability of policy reforms from official donor statements since few of them deal with the problems of sustainability at all. If anything is assumed, it appears to be that reforms will be sustained on the basis of their effectiveness in promoting recovery and growth. If reforms are effective, their beneficiaries—the general public, farmers, entrepreneurs (who, it is assumed, would appear or expand in number to take advantage of freer markets)—would presumably support the reforms and government officials would be convinced of their desirability.

Of course, individuals from aid agencies and African governments engaged in developing packages of policy reforms usually see the world in far more complex and nuanced terms than those described above. Unfortunately, however, the "theory" and assumptions on which the policy reform movement is based have not been elaborated by foreign aid donors except in the most simple of terms. Policy reformers in the Western aid agencies appear to believe that the views of African officials and appropriate economic policies play a critical role in policymaking and can be changed through discussion and persuasion; that the same kinds of reforms will have roughly similar impacts in different societies; and that policy reforms can, with enough time, work to promote recovery and growth.

Political economists today are less optimistic and less universalistic in their approach than policy reformers. They see human behavior as prompted or constrained by a variety of economic and non-economic factors and goals, including relationships of power and interest. They view government structures and policies as reflective of historical, social, and political phenomena, including conflicts among ethnic, regional, or economic groups and classes for power. By implication, effective and sustainable economic reforms will have to take into account the non-economic factors underlying economic policies.

Several political economists have studied ways in which the implementation of policy reforms can be eased through public persuasion by government officials, and through planning the timing and extent of reforms to minimize the extent of likely opposition.[25]

This empirically based work by political economists is among the most directly relevant to policy reformers in providing insights into how reform programs can be implemented with a minimum of political resistance or reaction. In this regard, an argument continues between political economists who argue that democratic regimes can more easily implement reforms once they have obtained a degree of national consensus versus those who argue that less democratic regimes can more easily and quickly implement reforms since they do not have to develop such a consensus.

In looking at the impact and sustainability of policy reforms, some political economists will emphasize the importance of balancing advantages and disadvantages among ethnic and regional groups to avoid exacerbating national tensions. For example, in the case of countries with Lebanese or Asian minorities, it may be necessary to ensure that opportunities opened up by "privatization" are not monopolized by these minorities. Others may raise questions about the possibility of elite appropriation of the benefits of reforms, e.g., where government bureaucrats use their power and influence to acquire land or businesses that have become attractive as a result of reforms.

Political economists have also raised questions on the sustainability of policy reforms when the beneficiaries are weak or unorganized politically and those adversely affected are politically influential. How can the powerful be prevented from undermining such reforms and reestablishing policies and institutions benefiting them? Some scholars have argued that nothing short of full democratization of the political process will ensure that economic recovery and growth occur.[26] Others have argued that efforts to empower the weak, e.g., through promoting political organizations representing them, may be necessary if reforms are to be preserved. There is little speculation on how such empowerment can take place or whether Africa's political leaders, always jealous of their power, would welcome the creation of politically active groups not under control.

A particular problem arises as regards reforms involving greater private sector activities. Urban middle classes and civil servants can be disadvantaged by such reforms through a reduction in the size and responsibilities of government. Yet the beneficiaries—the private entrepreneurs who it is assumed will appear to exploit new opportunities—are often not present or are present only in small numbers. Those that exist are frequently experienced in commerce or in small-scale production but rarely in large-scale productive activities. Yet, the opportunities that appear to be in the minds of policy reformers include the large-scale production and distribution of goods and services. There is considerable debate on why African entrepreneurs operating large-scale, productive enterprises have been relatively few in number. Reasons given include cultural obstacles (e.g., the responsibilities of the extended family deterring the accumulation of capital),[27] historical obstacles (e.g., Africans prohibited in colonial times from operating businesses), and social obstacles (e.g., the disinclination of Africans to sell their labor to others).[28]

Whatever the explanations, the paucity of African entrepreneurs can present a problem for sustaining policy reforms intended to advantage the private sector. It may take time for entrepreneurs to appear who can exploit new opportunities and ultimately provide support to sustain such reforms. Meanwhile, there will be disadvantaged groups that will presumably press for a reversal of the reforms and an expansion in the size and responsibilities of governments.

These and other questions raised by the work of political economists really point to several basic issues in policy reforms. What political, social, cultural, and historical factors are significant in shaping current government policies and structures? And how can sustainable change take place, not just in policies and institutions but also in attitudes of policymakers, in political organizations participating in the political process, in coalitions supporting government, and ultimately in relationships between the state and its citizens? Thus far, political economists do not have answers to these questions; they have only begun to raise the questions.

There is a final issue confronting foreign aid-giving institutions involved in policy reform. If the questions raised by political economists are important to understanding and supporting the effective management and sustainability of policy reform, to what extent should foreign aid donors take them into account in their own approaches to policy reform? To what extent should they inform themselves on salient political, social, and cultural factors in reforming countries? To what extent should their own advice on reform take such factors into account? To what extent should they seek to change these factors through the types of aid they provide and the conditions they attach to their aid?

There are no easy answers to these questions. The World Bank, for example, does not at present have the staff or the staff expertise to address these questions on a systematic basis in each country in which it operates. Additionally, lending programs encumbered with a panoply of economic and other conditions could well become unwieldy and difficult to implement, even with good will on all sides. Finally, the directors of the World Bank—representatives of developing countries—and recipient governments themselves would likely object strongly to World Bank programs that had explicit political and social conditions in them. Yet, some of the questions raised by political economists suggest that without addressing political and social as well as economic issues in its reform programs, the Bank may find that the reforms it has promoted are ineffective and unsustainable. Programs of policy reforms are highly interventionist. Some aim at nothing less than restructuring African economies. To what extent can policy reformers promote and maintain fundamental economic change without at the same time promoting political, social, and cultural changes as well?

NOTES

This essay is based on a paper undertaken for the Economic Development Institute of the World Bank for a workshop on Political Economy and Policy Reform in Africa, December 1986.

1. Two early and excellent articles that reflected a renewed interest in political economy both by political scientists and economists were "The Resurrection of Political Economy," by James Coleman in Norman Uphoff and Warren Ilchman, *The Political Economy of Development*, Berkeley and Los Angeles: University of California Press, 1972, and "Political Economy and Possibilism," by Albert Hirschman in *A Bias for Hope*, New Haven: Yale University Press, 1971.

2. Webster's Third New International Dictionary, cited in Coleman, *ibid.*

3. This concept is the foundation for the work of the recent Nobel laureate James Buchanan. See, for example, *The Calculus of Consent*, which he wrote with Gordon Tullock, Ann Arbor: University of Michigan Press, 1969. Mancur Olson has utilized the same concept, combined with cost-benefit analysis and the concept of "free rider" in his examination of decisions of collectivities, e.g., interest groups, in his *The Logic of Collective Action*, Cambridge: Harvard University Press, 1971. An interesting application of some of these concepts to explain governmental regulatory policies is found in the work of another Nobel laureate, George Stigler, who argues that special economic interests seek regulation for their own benefit. See, for example, his *The Citizen and the State: Essays on Regulation*, Chicago: University of Chicago Press, 1975. One wonders how Stigler would analyze the array of regulations and regulatory bodies in Africa designed not to benefit the regulated but to exploit them.

4. See, for example, Anthony Downs, *An Economic Theory of Democracy*, New York: Harper, 1957, or Charles Lindbloom, *Politics and Markets*, New York: Harper, 1977.

5. See, for example, Norman Uphoff and Warren Ilchman, cited in note 1.

6. Lucien Pye, *Aspects of Political Development*, Boston: Little, Brown, 1966.

7. See, for example, Howard Wolpe and Robert Melson, "Modernization

and the Politics of Communalism: A Theoretical Perspective," in *The American Political Science Review*, vol. 66, 1972.

8. Samuel Huntington, *Political Order in Changing Societies*, New Haven: Yale University Press, 1968.

9. For an exploration into African socialism, see Thomas Callaghy and Carl Rosberg, *Socialism in Sub-Saharan Africa*, Institute of International Studies, University of California, 1979. It was not until the mid-1970s that African socialist regimes began to look more like traditional Marxist-Leninists. See David and Marina Ottaway, *Afro-Communism*, New York: African Publishing Co., 1981.

10. Crawford Young, *Ideology and Development in Africa*, New Haven: Yale University Press, 1982.

11. See, for example, Samir Amin, *Neo-Colonialism in West Africa*, New York: Monthly Review Press, 1973, or his *Unequal Development*, Los Angeles: Harvest Press, 1976. For critiques of Amin's work, see, for example, Jonathan Schiffer, "The Changing Post-War Pattern of Development: The Accumulated Wisdom of Samir Amin," in *World Development*, vol. 9, no. 6, 1981, or Sheila Smith," The Ideas of Samir Amin: Theory or Tautology?", *Journal of Development Studies*.

12. See the chapter by David Abernethy, "Bureaucratic Growth and Economic Stagnation in Sub-Saharan Africa," in this book.

13. See, for example, Thomas Callaghy, *The State-Society Struggle: Zaire in Comparative Perspective,* New York: Columbia University Press, 1984; Crawford Young and Thomas Turner, *The Rise and Decline of the Zairian State*, Madison: University of Wisconsin Press, 1985. It is striking how many analysts of the African state, particularly those with the most pessimistic outlooks, are experts on Zaire.

14. The phrase is Gunnar Myrdal's. See his *Asian Drama: An Inquiry into the Poverty of Nations*, New York: Pantheon Books, 1968.

15. See Carl Rosberg and Robert Jackson, *Personal Rule in Black Africa*, Berkeley and Los Angeles: University of California Press, 1982, p. 18.

16. See, for example, Thomas Callaghy, "The Patrimonial Administrative State in Africa," in Zaki Ergas, ed., *The African State in Transition*, New York: St. Martin's Press, 1987.

17. See Crawford Young, "Africa's Colonial Legacy," in Jennifer Whitaker and Robert Berg, eds., *Strategies for African Development*, Berkeley and Los Angeles: University of California Press, 1986.

18. See, for example, Robert Bates, "Governments and Agricultural Markets in Africa," in D. Gale Johnson and G. Edward Schuh, eds., *The Role of Markets in the World Food Economy*, Boulder, Colo.: Westview Press, 1983.

19. See, for example, the collection by Donald Rothchild and Victor Olorunsola, eds., *The State Versus Ethnic Claims: African Policy Dilemmas*, Boulder, Colo.: Westview Press, 1983.

20. See Goren Hyden, *No Shortcuts to Progress*, Berkeley and Los Angeles: University of California Press, 1983.

21. Ian Little, in *Economic Development: Theory, Policy and International Relations*, New York: Basic Books, 1982, describes himself and Hollis Chenery as viewing the neoclassical and structuralist approaches as fundamentally contradictory (see Chapter 2 for a discussion). One nevertheless sees a mixture of both approaches in much that is written about policy reform. See, for example, John Mellor and Chris Delgado, "A Structural View of Policy Issues in African Agricultural Development," in *American Journal of*

Agricultural Economics, December 1984.

22. For an official statement (unusually frank in places) by a donor of that donor's approach to policy reform and the nature of the "policy dialogue," see USAID Policy Paper, *Approaches to the Policy Dialogue,* Washington, D.C.: Agency for International Development, December 1982.

23. The phrase is drawn from *Accelerated Development in Sub-Saharan Africa,* Washington, D.C.: World Bank, 1981.

24. This rationale bears an interesting resemblance to that often given by U.S. diplomats for U.S. aid programs in small African countries. Without such a program, "the telephone stops ringing."

25. Joan Nelson has probably done more than anyone in this area thus far. See, for example, her "Politics of Stabilization," in Richard Feinberg and Valeriana Kallab, eds., *Adjustment Crisis in the Third World,* Washington, D.C.: Overseas Development Council, 1984.

26. Claude Ake has come close to making this case in print in "Why is Africa Not Developing?," in *West Africa,* 1985. Ake has made this case explicitly in a discussion on the World Bank in Africa at the Woodrow Wilson Center, Smithsonian Institution, August 1985.

27. The success of the Bamileke people of Cameroon as entrepreneurs is explained in terms of values limiting obligations to the extended family and so permitting the accumulation of capital, in USAID Evaluation Special Study No. 15, *The Private Sector: Ethnicity, Individual Initiative and Economic Growth in an African Plural Society: The Bamileke of Cameroon,* Washington, D.C.: Agency for International Development, June 1983.

28. See John Iliffe, *The Emergence of African Capitalism,* Minneapolis: University of Minnesota Press, 1983.

CHAPTER 9

Bureaucratic Growth and Economic Stagnation in Sub-Saharan Africa

David Abernethy

The emergence of a global system of formally sovereign states during the past four decades has been paralleled by the emergence of a global consensus that the economic development of these polities is both possible and desirable. In wealthy and poor, old and new states alike, ever-growing portions of the population have come to expect that their economic well-being will steadily improve—and have come to judge political leaders and institutions by the extent to which that improvement in fact takes place. National leaders hope to benefit politically from economic development, whether this be due to their own policies or to factors beyond their control. The converse is also true: leaders fear being blamed—and perhaps ousted—if for whatever reason the pace, character, or distributional pattern of economic development fails to meet popular expectations. Because their own hold on power has come to be so intimately connected with the performance of the economy, many national political leaders are understandably inclined to reduce the risks of losing power by expanding the public sector's control over the domestic economy, and by exerting whatever limited influence their governments may possess over events in the international economic arena.

To this factor, which helps to account for the enlarged scope of government activity in all contemporary countries, may be added a reason more specific to the world's poor ones. The private sector in many Latin American, African, and Asian countries consists of groups of people who may be unable or unwilling to act in ways that stimulate rapid, internally integrated, equitable, self-sustaining economic growth. A country's rural populace, for instance, may be too poor to mobilize a high volume of domestic savings, too bound to past traditions, and too close to the margin of survival to adopt and diffuse untried new yield-increasing agricultural techniques. At the other end of the economic scale, foreign entrepreneurs and foreign-owned companies often control large segments of a poor country's modern private sector, with strong incentives to establish capital-intensive enclaves oriented more to the export of commodities and profits than to the productive employment of the country's urban or rural poor. Members of the indigenous bourgeoisie involved in commerce and the professions, who are economically and socially situated between the indigenous small peasantry and large foreign-owned corporations, may be small in numbers and lack the experience and incentives to finance and manage their own productive enterprises. These individuals may prefer instead to play a subsidiary role to foreign enterprise, or to invest in import/export and speculative real estate ventures, or to transfer their savings to more secure havens outside the country. In these ways the national bourgeoisie may actually reinforce the external dependencies and internal inequalities that constitute structural barriers to long-term national development.

Under such conditions, it is tempting for a poor country's rulers to construct the following syllogism as a guide to policy: (1) For a host of powerful and mutually reinforcing reasons, our citizens must escape from their current deplorable condition of poverty and low productivity. (2) The groups comprising the private sector cannot or will not perform this task as rapidly and equitably as the country requires. (3) Therefore, a greatly expanded public sector is a necessary condition of development. We should rely heavily on direct government initiatives as well as policies closely regulating the private sector in order to attain our national economic objectives. In effect, government is deemed the only means available to achieve the desired end of development. Consequently, government must be able to achieve that end.

One need not quarrel with the normative perspective of the first part of this syllogism, or even with the empirical premises of the second, to question the policy conclusions of the third. Suppose that a poor country's private sector does indeed feature all the weaknesses and distortions attributed to it. Is it not also possible that a probing and critical examination of the country's public sector will reveal different but equally serious weaknesses and distortions there as well? That a particular sector of the economy may not appear likely to stimulate development does not in itself demonstrate that another sector is able to do so. As Gabriel Roth put it in his study of *The Private Provision of Public Services in Developing Countries,* "the possibility of 'government failure' as well as 'market failure' must be considered. The private market may be faulty, but the government 'remedy' may be worse."[1] Moreover, the activities of public sector institutions, like those of private sector actors, could well constitute a sufficient condition for *failure* to develop. It is even conceivable that under certain conditions *neither* the private *nor* the public sectors will be able effectively to stimulate economic development. The policy implications of such a situation are not entirely clear—or, if clear, hardly pleasant to contemplate. Nonetheless, an analysis of development options that attempts to be equally critical of all of them may ultimately prove more helpful than a prescription for one option that proceeds essentially by attacking the feasibility or desirability of the alternatives to it.[2]

Extensive public sector activity to stimulate economic development could be counterproductive for three principal reasons. First, the high costs of such activity, the general tendency (noted by Adolf Wagner a century ago) for government expenditure to rise as a proportion of national income, and the need to finance public expenditures by extracting financial resources and recruiting talented individuals from a country's private sector—all these factors presumably reduce the capacity and will of the private sector to save, productively invest, and generally share the burdens of risk-taking. The high costs of government represent high opportunity costs for those not in government.

Second, public officials must consider many non-economic factors when they formulate and attempt to implement public policy, and these other factors are likely to conflict with what might be considered economically optimal decisions. Politicians in power must at all times consider the effect of their decisions on their ability to retain and consolidate that power.[3] Civil servants must at all times take the harsh imperatives of bureaucratic politics into account. There is no inherent reason why politicians and bureaucrats, for whom such concerns are in effect essential components of the job description, will make policy decisions that are automatically the most direct, effective means to the end of national economic development.

Third, patterns of thinking and acting within government agencies may keep the developmental benefits provided by these agencies quite small in relation to the fiscal costs and time delays incurred. A civil servant trained to revere the cumbersome procedures of a large bureaucracy, and temperamentally averse to personal or organizational risk-taking, may be quite the wrong sort of person to take charge of a parastatal agency mandated to generate and aggressively market some new product or service. It is difficult to expel incompetent but well-connected civil servants, and it is easy for civil servants to succumb to the temptations of corrupt behavior. The tendency of public enterprises to monopolize their particular national market breeds the same inefficiencies and neglect of consumer interests that socialist writers properly note when critiquing private sector monopolies. For these and other reasons, governments may be particularly cost-ineffective instruments for implementing even the best-designed development strategies.

In wealthy market-oriented countries, current criticisms of the economic role of government usually focus on the first of these three factors. The concern over costs is understandable, for government's capacity to extract from the populace, and pressures from the populace for more and higher-quality government-financed services, both tend to increase as per capita income rises. In the years before 1945, the increase in the public expenditure/gross domestic product (GDP) ratio in many Western capitalist countries was uneven, with major international crises such as the world wars and the depression tending to push the ratio rapidly upward to record levels.[4] In the post-1945 period the rise has been more steady, and less a function of international events. But the magnitude of the increase has nonetheless been quite striking. A study by Frank Gould shows that total general government expenditure averaged 29.5 percent of GDP for thirteen OECD countries in 1960-1962, rising to 43.3 percent in 1977-1979.[5] This trend has in turn stimulated efforts by politicians such as Ronald Reagan and Margaret Thatcher to reverse it. But it is noteworthy that the central government expenditure/GNP ratio rose by over 5 percentage points in the United States and by over 8 percentage points in the United Kingdom between 1972 and 1985.[6] What appears to be an ineluctably upward-bound trend has stimulated widespread discussion of the potential inability of the modern welfare state to finance both its socially redistributive and its economic growth objectives.[7]

These soundings of alarm may well be overstated, however. This is because a high proportion of public expenditure in a wealthy market-oriented state is simply allocated back to the private sector in the form of transfer payments, subsidies, and contracts enabling private agencies to perform public functions. Gould estimates that about half of 1977-1979 general government expenditure for the OECD countries in his study consisted of transfer payments.[8] Referring to the United States, Murray Weidenbaum has noted a growing reliance on "a combination of contracts and grants-in-aid to involve private industry, state and local governments, and non-profit institutions in the federal government's activities."[9] To an extent the federal government operates as a recycling agency, redistributing resources extracted from some segments of the U.S. private sector to other segments. In this respect it does not necessarily deprive the private sector as a whole of resources. One may debate, of course, whether the pattern of public redistribution to various groups and organized interests (e.g., the poor, children, the elderly, defense contractors) is likely to stimulate the desired pace and character of economic development. But the argument that spiraling government expenditure is per se detrimental to private sector-led growth in wealthy market economies is not particularly persuasive.[10]

By way of contrast, the argument mounted against government as an economic actor in poor countries tends to focus less on the sheer magnitude of its expenditures than on its faulty policies and the cost-ineffective behavior of its employees. This again is understandable. The government expenditure/GDP ratio is lower (generally in the 15-20 percent range) for poor countries than for wealthy ones, which makes the sheer cost burden of government appear relatively manageable. At the same time, the abysmal economic conditions in many poor countries, their lack of national integration, and their vulnerability to external events inevitably heighten the insecurities of political leaders, while the lack of fit between indigenous cultural norms and the frequently imported norms of officialdom tends to produce in extreme form the pathologies to which large bureaucratic structures everywhere are susceptible. Politicians and civil servants operating under such conditions can be routinely expected to make policies that development economists might consider suboptimal, if not downright irrational. Bureaucratic pathologies may also be expected to generate inefficient, wasteful, and corrupt behavior at the individual and institutional levels.[11]

It would be a mistake, however, to focus on what governments in poor countries *do* and *do not do*—to the extent that public policies constitute economic sins of commission and omission—while ignoring altogether the question of what such governments *cost*. For one thing, poor countries vary greatly in their ratios of public expenditure to GDP, with some of these countries exhibiting considerably higher ratios than economically well-developed ones.[12] Wagner's well-known "law of expanding state activity" may be generally true for a given country over-time, but it is clearly invalid if it implies that late-developing countries will not attain the expenditure ratio of wealthy countries until they reach the per capita income levels of the latter.[13] Indeed, if we compare government expenditure not to GDP but to the income of the wage-labor force in the monetized portion of a country's economy, ratios in poor countries (which feature a large subsistence sector) are often higher than those for wealthy countries. If a high government expenditure/GDP ratio does in fact constrain economic growth, the problem is posed for high-ratio countries at all levels of development, not simply for countries in upper-income brackets.

Second, poor countries have generally experienced in recent years a dramatic rise in the public expenditure/GDP ratio. For many Asian and African states the impact of political independence following 1945 was the functional equivalent of the impact of the world wars on Western market economies during the 1914-1945 period. Domestic pressures to expand the new state's role in industry, mining, agriculture, the social services, defense, and general administration have been and remain extremely strong. As these pressures are unlikely to diminish in the future, the general trend is apt to be one of convergence between slowly growing rich-country ratios and more rapidly growing poor-country ratios. Consequently, an increasing number of poor countries must directly confront the issue of whether their public sector simply costs more than their domestic economies can afford.

Third, a relatively high proportion of public expenditure in poor countries is devoted to maintenance and expansion of the public and parastatal sectors, rather than recycled to the private sector through transfer payments, subsidies, and contracts as in wealthy welfare states. For government agencies as for all organizations, first things must come first: the "basic need" is to cover their expenses in recruiting, remunerating, promoting, pensioning, and managing their own personnel. Resources available after that basic need has been met may then be devoted more explicitly to the organization's formal agenda to alter the society around it in some fashion. Given the paucity of resources in poor countries, internal organizational demands consume a relatively high proportion of government's recurrent budgets. Funds available to implement the government agenda for the rest of society—for example, stimulating economic growth—are correspondingly reduced. In this respect there is a tendency for goal displacement to occur. The government may consider itself the institutional means to the end of economic development. Yet its own needs for institutional self-maintenance and growth are such that meeting these needs becomes a primary, albeit unstated, objective. Civil service salaries and perquisites need not, of course, be economically counterproductive if bureaucrats are performing important tasks that would not otherwise be fulfilled (or fulfilled as efficiently) by others, and if they spend a high proportion of their income on locally produced goods and services. To the extent that these conditions do not apply—and frequently in developing countries they do not—civil service personnel expenditures can constitute an obstacle to growth rather than a stimulus to it.

These observations suggest that a serious examination of the public sector's effects on poor countries' prospects for development should take into account not simply the policies and behavior of public officials but also the cost of government activity relative to GDP. They further suggest that the personnel component of government expenditure is a particularly important variable to consider if one wants to specify the conditions under which public sector spending may contribute to or detract from a country's economic performance. The remainder of this discussion will analyze trends in the recurrent expenditures of African governments, with special attention to the level and distribution of salaries and benefits for public sector employees. In considering the historical factors causing the particular pattern of public sector remuneration that has developed in sub-Saharan Africa, I argue that this pattern is the product of four powerful, converging forces. The first two were at work in the colonial era, the last two in the post-colonial (roughly post-1960) period:

1. Externally-imposed European colonialism, based on inegalitarian, racist, and elitist assumptions
2. Indigenous African anticolonial nationalism, based on egalitarian, antiracist, and populist assumptions
3. Domestic political imperatives—and opportunities—to expand public sector employment following the attainment of independence
4. Institutions from the international environment, whose role as policy-setters and as "reference groups" affects both the size and the remuneration levels of African public sectors

This analysis suggests a paradox: The first two forces noted, which so often were openly at odds with each other in the political and philosophical arenas, actually complemented and reinforced each other in the bureaucratic arena. Another paradox is posed by the fourth factor. While international institutions have taken the lead in the 1980s in pressing for a more modest and lower-cost African public sector, the existence of these same powerful institutions, with their own elevated salary scales and expensive ways of conducting operations, has contributed to the very problem their policymakers are now attempting to resolve. International agencies that preach austerity but do not practice it are likely to produce, at best, resentful compliance on the part of African governments hard pressed by these agencies to pare budgets already pitifully small by current world standards.

I conclude that trends in the cost of government—and in the

remuneration of public employees—probably have had on balance a negative impact on Africa's development record. But this is not to say that the African private sector, as presently constituted, offers particularly bright prospects for an alternative path to growth. Although a good case can be made for privatization of several activities currently in the hands of government ministries and parastatal bodies, one should not ignore the tragic possibility that *neither* the private *nor* the public sector is well positioned to stimulate the kind of development Africans in all walks of life feel is desperately needed.

ECONOMIC STAGNATION/BUREAUCRATIC GROWTH

Sub-Saharan Africa merits special attention because in a number of key respects its economies have ceased to advance. Indeed, of the thirty-six sub-Saharan countries on which the World Bank has relevant data, nine experienced negative per capita growth rates during the 1960-1981 period, while twelve had negative rates from 1965 through 1985.[14] Relative to other regions in what is often termed the "developing world," African growth rates are unusually low. As Table 9.1 indicates, Africa grew more slowly than all other developing regions from 1950 to 1981, with the exception of the half-decade from 1960 to 1965. Africa is the only region in which growth rates have consistently fallen since 1960-1965, and its rate for 1970-1981 is by far the lowest of all regions during the three decades for which data are available.

If anything, the record in the 1980s is even more disturbing. The World Bank estimates that per capita income for the twenty-nine African countries eligible for its IDA loans has fallen over 2 percent annually from 1981 through 1985.[15] The Bank notes that

> the decline in Africa's per capita output during the 1980's together with the decline in the 1970's, will wipe out all its rise in per capita output since 1960. As a result, low-income Africa is poorer today than in 1960. Improvements over those years in health, education, and infrastructure are increasingly at risk. For the first time since World War II, a whole region has suffered retrogression over a generation.[16]

Two-thirds of Africa's labor force works on the land. Yet the region's per capita production of food probably declined by 20 percent between 1960 and 1980. Food imports into this eminently rural continent have risen enormously in the last decade and a half. While Africa accounted for 11 percent of food aid to developing countries in 1974/75, it absorbed 40 percent of such aid a decade later.[17]

The contrast with the growth trajectory of East Asia and the Pacific

Table 9.1 Annual Average Percentage Growth, Per Capita Gross Domestic Product, by Region, 1950-1981

Years	Sub-Saharan Africa	Middle East & N. Africa	East Asia & Pacific	South Asia	Latin America, Caribb.
1950-1960	1.2	1.8	2.7	2.0	1.9
1960-1965	2.7	1.3	3.0	1.9	2.0
1965-1970	2.3	3.1	5.5	2.5	3.4
1970-1981	0.4	4.1	5.6	1.6	2.7

Table 9.2 Annual Average Percentage Growth, Public Consumption, by Region, 1960-1981

Years	Sub-Saharan Africa	Middle East & N. Africa	East Asia & Pacific	South Asia	Latin America, Caribb.
1960-1965	7.5	0.4	2.6	7.8	3.3
1965-1970	8.1	5.9	8.2	6.9	5.7
1970-1981	6.6	11.0	8.7	5.4	6.0

Table 9.3 General Government Consumption as Percentage of Gross Domestic Product, at Current Market Prices, by Region, 1960-1981[a]

Years	Sub-Saharan Africa	Middle East & N. Africa	East Asia & Pacific	South Asia	Latin America, Caribb.
1960	9.7	13.7	11.2	7.7	9.8
1965	11.6	15.3	6.8	9.7	9.6
1970	12.8	17.4	11.5	10.0	10.3
1981	14.3	17.7	12.3	10.0	12.1
Increase, 1960-1981	4.6	4.0	1.1	2.3	2.3

Source: World Bank, WORLD TABLES, 3rd ed., Vol. 1 (1983), pp. 485, 493, 501.

[a]"General government consumption" includes all current expenditure for purchase of goods and services by central, regional, and local government agencies, as well as capital outlays on defense. Outlays on public nonfinancial institutions are excluded.

is particularly striking. This contrast raises questions about the utility of continuing in the 1980s to conceptualize all the geographic regions listed in Table 9.1 as belonging to the same category, be it "developing," "underdeveloped," or "Third World" countries. If African economies are stagnating, if not in fact retrogressing, can one honestly still call the continent a "developing" area?

It would be foolish to hazard a single-factor explanation for the region's current economic calamities. While those most familiar with the situation might quarrel over the relative weight to assign various contributing factors, there would be general agreement that several factors converge and interact in complex ways to produce what might be termed a creeping continental catastrophe. These factors include:

- Rates of population increase that have risen by 1980-1985 to 3.3 percent annually, a level of endogenous growth not equaled by any continent in modern world history
- Widespread drought in a region unusually dependent for its water upon rainfall
- Deterioration of fragile ecosystems on which farmers and herders are utterly dependent
- Central government neglect and/or exploitation of the rural populace
- Civil wars and interstate conflicts, which divert scarce resources to military ends and transform millions of peasants into refugees
- A dramatic decline in both the volume and the unit value of many of Africa's agricultural and mineral exports, as recession and the "synthetics revolution" in economically developed countries constrain world demand for many of the commodities on which Africa concentrated during the colonial era.

The structure of public sector remuneration on which I focus in this discussion is but one among these contributing causes. It is worth particular attention, however, not only because the subject has been relatively neglected in academic and journalistic accounts, but also because the remuneration structure helps to explain why the public sector has so often exacerbated Africa's economic problems and so seldom taken effective action to resolve them.

We may begin by noting that general government consumption in sub-Saharan Africa grew very rapidly from 1960 until the early 1980s, both in absolute terms and relative to GDP. As Table 9.2 indicates, Africa's growth rate in this respect was the highest of any developing region during the 1960s, its first independence decade. During the 1970s the rate fell behind East Asia/Pacific and the Middle East/North Africa, two regions whose relatively strong showing in per capita GDP growth permitted them much more easily to afford increments in their rates of government expenditure. Table 9.3 shows that the percentage of GDP accounted for by general government consumption rose more rapidly for Africa than for the other regions between 1960 and 1981. Thus, while Africa lagged behind all regions save South Asia at the start of the period, two decades later it led all regions save the Middle East/North Africa.

A critically important causal factor in these trends is the rapid rise in the numbers of people employed by African governments. Two examples may indicate the magnitude of change in recent years. Kenya's civil service, which employed 14,000 in 1945 and 45,000 a decade later, rose to 63,000 in 1965, 84,000 in 1971, and 170,000 by mid-1980.[18] The Senegalese government employed 10,000 shortly before independence in 1960, 35,000 in 1965, and 61,000 by 1973.[19] Parastatal organizations with important economic responsibilities have grown in number—and in numbers employed—with striking speed. That their net expenditures are not counted as part of "general government consumption" indicates that Tables 9.2 and 9.3 are likely, if anything, seriously to understate the actual costs of government. At independence in 1957 Ghana possessed few state-owned companies. By the time of Kwame Nkrumah's overthrow nine years later there were 53 state enterprises, 12 joint public-private enterprises, and 23 public boards.[20] Zambia had 134 parastatal bodies by 1970, Nigeria about 250 by 1973, Tanzania about 400 by 1981.[21] In a recent World Bank study employing data from the late 1970s through 1985 for thirty African countries, John Nellis counted almost 3,000 financial and nonfinancial public enterprises—an average of 100 per country.[22]

A rough estimate is that employment in regular-line agencies of central and local governments in the region grew from 1.9 to 6.5 million between 1960 and 1980, i.e., about 240 percent over two decades. If one adds nonfinancial parastatal organizations, public sector employment rose from about 3.8 to approximately 10 million (i.e., about 160 percent) over this same period. By 1980 the public sector, including parastatals, probably accounted for 3 percent of the region's population and half the number in nonagricultural employment.[23]

Less obvious than the increase in numbers—but nonetheless a crucial part of the explanation—is the unusually high level of civil service salaries relative to per capita national income. Table 9.4 presents the ratio of the average central government wage to per capita GDP, using data for 1980 or near it, for forty-five countries studied by Peter Heller and Alan Tait. Salaries at the top of the civil service scale are even more strikingly elevated above per capita GDP. As of 1963/64 the ratio of the former to the latter was 73:1 in Malawi, 82:1 in Kenya, 96:1 in Tanganyika, 118:1 in Nigeria, and 130:1 in Uganda.[24] This pattern is in sharp contrast to that of the United States, where the ratio is well under 10:1—most likely under 8:1.[25] If we translate African ratios at independence into contemporary American terms—admittedly a procedure of dubious validity—a top American civil servant earning one hundred times U.S. per capita income would receive (in 1985 dollars) a salary of about $1.7 million a year! Adding the value of civil service perquisites to salaries significantly increases the gap between bureaucrats and the peasantry at the base. These perquisites include heavily subsidized allowances for housing, transportation, pensions, medical care, and vacation leave. The Uganda Treasury noted in 1963,

Table 9.4 Average Central Government Wage as a Multiple of Gross Domestic Product Per Capita

OECD industrial countries (n:16)	1.74
Africa (n:16)	6.05
Asia (n:5)	2.90
Latin America (n:8)	2.94

Source: Peter Heller and Alan A. Tait, *Government Employment and Pay: Some International Comparisons* (Washington: International Monetary Fund, Occasional Paper #24, revised March 1984), p. 18.

for instance, that fringe benefits for those in the public service equaled 35 percent of base salary for those paid up to Sh266 a year and exceeded 45 percent of salary for those paid over Sh945 a year.[26]

Another distinctive African feature is the large spread between salaries at the top of the civil service hierarchy and those at the base. As of 1963/64 eight English-speaking African countries had ratios ranging from 22:1 to 40:1, the mean being 29.7:1.[27] These figures may underestimate the real spread because they do not include perquisites whose monetary value as a proportion of salary tended, at least as of the early 1960s, to rise as salary increased. The general pattern in the post-independence years has been to reduce this particular gap by holding top salary scales relatively constant while raising those at the base. Nonetheless, the extent of current inequality within the public sector is still striking if African figures are compared with those from other parts of the world. Using data from the late 1970s and early 1980s, Heller and Tait found that the highest-paid 10 percent of government employees received 22 percent of government salaries in Kenya, 24 percent in Swaziland, and 26 percent in Senegal. These were (with the exception of Guatemala, at 29 percent) the highest percentages in a five-continent sample of fourteen countries. Figures for the five economically developed countries in the sample ranged from 14 percent to 20 percent.[28]

A final feature to note is the unusually large proportion of total government expenditure devoted to the wages and salaries of public employees. As Table 9.5 indicates, the African percentage as of 1980 was about twice that for the world as a whole, twice that of Asia, and roughly 50 percent higher than Latin America and the Caribbean. Moreover, the African figure essentially stabilized at 30 percent from 1974 through 1980 (the last date for which African regional data are available), while the industrial market countries and Asia slowly but steadily reduced their percentages. Only the oil-exporting countries, which could more readily afford both an expensive civil service and funds for development, had ratios in the 1970s equivalent to Africa's. Compared to other "developing" regions, African governments are thus unusual in the degree to which they devote public resources to the basic maintenance costs of the public sector.

COLONIAL BUREAUCRACIES

What accounts for these features of the African bureaucratic landscape? A necessary point of departure is the experience of European colonial rule, which was terminated only twenty-five to thirty years ago in most of the region's countries. One must examine on the one hand the character and policies of the governments established by European colonial rulers, and on the other hand the initiatives taken by Africans as they coped with the condition of being ruled by racially and culturally distinctive foreigners. The role of the European outsiders was crucial: during the last two decades of the nineteenth century they effectively rewrote the political map of the continent, arbitrarily fixed the boundaries of new territories, named these territories, and established the rudiments of an administrative apparatus to make good their initially overstated claims of sovereignty over the indigenous population. To rule a colony is to administer it; the essence of the colonial situation is authoritarian rule by bureaucrats. And the structures, procedures, and norms of the administrations established to rule the colonies were in many respects exported from the European metropole to the colony, examples of institutional and value transfer from the outside world to the political center, so to speak, of the new colonial territory. The transfer process was clearly an aspect of international politics. At the same time, the European exercise of

Table 9.5 Current Expenditure on Wages and Salaries as a Percentage of Total Expenditure and Lending Minus Repayments

	1972	1974	1976	1978	1979	1980
World	18.3	16.6	15.3	14.8	14.7	n.a.
Industrial (market) countries	16.6	15.5	14.0	13.3	13.0	12.3
Oil-exporting countries[a]	31.2	18.7	19.0	23.1	30.4	n.a.
Africa	35.2	30.9	28.5	28.8	29.2	29.7
Asia	n.a.	18.9	17.4	15.8	15.3	14.7
Middle East	n.a.	n.a.	14.5	16.4	15.0	n.a.
Western Hemisphere[b]	22.1	20.6	21.3	21.1	20.8	n.a.

Source: International Monetary Fund (IMF), *Government Finance Statistics Yearbook*, Vol. 4, 1980, pp. 43-44 for 1972 data only; Vol. 6, 1982, pp. 47-48 for 1974-1980 data.

[a] Africa's most populous country, Nigeria, is included under the "oil-exporting" and not the African heading.
[b] "Western Hemisphere" refers to the developing countries of Latin America and the Caribbean.

power through these transferred institutions affected—indeed, it defined—the character of a given colony's *domestic* political life. It is in the study of colonial administration that two analytically separable subfields of political science—international relations and comparative politics—converge and in fact overlap.

The Europeans' principal contribution to what would eventually become the conspicuously consumptive African state was to set salary scales and terms of service for the top of the hierarchy at a level sufficiently high to attract well-educated, competent Europeans into the colonial administrative service. It was self-evident to the new colonial rulers that the top generalist and specialist posts should be in the hands of Europeans from the metropole, who would have a direct personal stake in maintaining the metropole's rule and in reinforcing the carefully projected image of whites as powerful dynamic agents of "civilization."

But how could Europeans be recruited from the home country to work in culturally quite different societies offering limited amenities, serious hazards to health, and the ever-present potential for political unrest? To be sure, colonial administration promised a number of significant nonmonetary rewards: the exercise of considerable power, an opportunity to act out of a sense of service and duty, relative autonomy in making decisions, and an exciting and challenging alternative to a more mundane existence at home.[29] But such inducements were not sufficient by themselves to attract the desired quantity and quality of talent. A necessary condition for recruiting the individuals who would actually construct the edifice of empire was a salary at least as high, for equivalent formal education and experience, as one obtainable at home.

The level of remuneration in Europe inevitably became the reference point for the level of remuneration offered Europeans serving in Africa. In the British case, for instance, the Secretary of State for the Colonies, concerned that nine of the first twelve candidates offered appointments to East Africa had refused them, in 1910 appointed a committee to examine the problem. The committee recommended a substantial increase in pay scales, a recommendation that was promptly accepted. Subsequent pay increases designed to attract and retain colonial administrators were put into effect in 1920 and again in 1930, when a unified British Colonial Service was established.[30]

Moreover, because tropical Africa was defined as a "hardship post," conditions of service had to be offered that if anything were *more* generous than an equivalent post in Europe. European administrative officers in British West Africa and Somaliland during the 1930s, for instance, were provided such perquisites as free quarters, a generous pension plan, seven days of paid vacation at home for each month of service in the colony, free passage to and from the metropole for officers and their wives going on leave, and a bonus for length of service.[31] Lord Hailey noted of Portuguese authorities in the 1950s that

> by comparison with British standards the pay is low, but the majority of Administrative officers are supplied with furnished houses of a good standard, free of rent, and officers down to the rank of Chefe do Posto have free cars.[32]

A pattern begun at the outset of colonial rule continued through it. Salaries and "perks" for European colonial administrators in the years after 1945 shifted upward as economic conditions in Europe improved and as inflation reduced the real value of salaries in the metropole. In 1948, for instance, salaries for the (virtually all-European) *corps des administrateurs* in French Africa were raised to bring them in line with officials of the same rank working in France, following a period during World War II when upward adjustments had not been made.[33] In the terminal phase of colonial rule, metropolitan governments were anxious that salaries, pensions, and other forms of compensation for European colonial administrators be set sufficiently high to induce these individuals either to stay on if requested by the new African government or to return to the metropole in a reasonably comfortable financial state.[34] Indeed, much of what was described as "foreign aid" in the early years of independence consisted of grants or loans from the ex-metropole to the ex-colony to buy off departing European civil servants at rates deemed equitable within a European frame of reference.

In one sense, market forces were at work in setting compensation levels for Europeans in the colonies. But the market was the *metropole*, not the colony. Within the colony the determination of salary scales was on the basis of *nonmarket* forces. European administrators had the power by virtue of their control of the state apparatus to fix their own compensation, and they were happy to exercise this power in their own interests.

Even in settler territories, however, Europeans were never sufficiently numerous or influential to administer their colonies by themselves. Indigenous people were needed to occupy a wide range of subordinate administrative positions.[35] In order to attract the desired quantity and quality of employees at the base of the civil service hierarchy, Europeans were generally prepared to pay Africans wages above those a peasant might obtain from producing cash crops for export—and considerably above the income equivalent of a subsistence farmer or herder. At the same time, Europeans insisted that low-level civil service compensation not be raised far above African *per capita* income. If the reference point for setting European scales at the top of the hierarchy was to be Europe, the reference point for setting scales at the bottom was to be Africa—specifically, the quite limited alternative opportunities for employment and income available to the colonized population.

As a direct result of these policies, salaries at the top of the colonial bureaucratic hierarchy could only appear to employees at the base—to say nothing of the ordinary peasant or unskilled urban migrant—as phenomenally generous. In 1913 the governor-general of Nigeria earned L7,500 (including allowances) and the governor of much smaller Nyasaland L2,000. The governor-general of French West Africa earned the equivalent of L2,469, the governor-general of the Belgian Congo the equivalent of L2,058 (both figures including allowances).[36] In the 1930s the chief secretary in one of the larger British colonies earned L2,000-3,000, a provincial commissioner in British West Africa L1,200-1,600, and a member of the central secretariat L1,000-1,500.[37] On the African side, clerks in the British colonies during the interwar period might start at L30-50 and attain a maximum of L400, while an unskilled laborer employed by a central government agency might earn in the neighborhood of Ll5-20 a year. Estimating the income equivalent for the subsistence or partially subsistence farmers who constituted the vast bulk of the colonized African population is a hazardous business. This caveat having been noted, cash-equivalent incomes in most parts of rural Africa probably averaged below L15—and in the poorer areas below L10—during the interwar period.

European colonial decisionmakers thus laid the basis decades ago for the dramatic gap between maximum and minimum salaries *within* the bureaucracy that has been noted for the post-colonial era, as well as for the less dramatic but nonetheless substantial gap between the income a low-level government employee could earn and the income to which an ordinary peasant could reasonably aspire.

NATIONALISM AND BUREAUCRATIC SALARIES

African responses to the bureaucratic pay and recruitment policies of the colonial rulers varied considerably. At the risk of oversimplifying a complex topic, the most significant response prior to the Second World War was to seek available employment opportunities at the base of the bureaucracy, while the most significant postwar response was to attack the racist assumptions on which pay and recruitment policies at the top of the hierarchy were premised.

The early positive response was eminently rational in view of the comparative returns for effort expended in peasant agriculture and in administrative work. The peasant worked hard for very little return, under conditions of virtually complete dependence on weather patterns which themselves were highly undependable. By contrast, the European at the apex and the African at the base of the bureaucracy appeared to work at a more leisurely pace for a considerably higher material return. And they enjoyed the security of belonging to a large organization whose very purpose was—or so it seemed from the peasant's perspective—to protect and enhance the interests of its members. The peasant personified powerlessness, poverty, low status, and insecurity. The bureaucrat, by virtue of the resources he commanded and his links to the larger structures of government, exercised—or at least symbolized—power, wealth, status, and security. "Even in the most backward areas of the bush," observed Rene Dumont, "everyone has grasped the fact that the official with clean hands earns more and works much less."[38]

Given this contrast, it only made sense for the peasant to attempt to gain access to the bureaucracy. A short-run strategy might involve efforts to gain personal favors and exemptions from harsh regulations by becoming a client to patrons ensconced within the governmental structure. The longer-term strategy entailed sending one's ablest children to school. Formal education in a missionary or government-run school provided the skills of literacy, numeracy, and command of the official (European) language that in turn constituted the formal prerequisites for access to a government post. The further one's children advanced in school, moreover, the higher was the expected return on the investment in their education. Each additional certificate of educational achievement provided the minimum qualification for entering at the next rung up the official employment ladder—a ladder whose rungs, as we have seen, were set far apart in terms of the salaries and perks attached to them. Schooling enabled some members of the colonized population to make the transition from the local, pre-colonial standard of living to an imported, contemporary standard set by the European ruler with the ruler's interests in mind. It is no wonder that African peasants made extraordinary personal sacrifices to pay school fees for their children—or that African politicians in the postwar period found the promise to expand educational opportunities and to reduce school fees among the most emotionally powerful and popular of their appeals.[39]

If the reference group for African peasants was the African bureaucrats at the low end of the colonial hierarchy, the reference group for these low-level bureaucrats was the Europeans at the top of the hierarchy, individuals whose income and perquisites might be worth, in the extreme case, over one hundred times the material rewards at the bottom. At first the power inequalities and disparities in formal educational achievement between Africans and Europeans were so great that the enormous remuneration gap within the bureaucracy was widely perceived as a fact of life meriting little complaint because so little could be done about it. But the effects of the two world wars and the depression on Europe's grasp of global power—and on Europeans' hitherto unquestioned assumptions of their own superiority—profoundly changed the psychological relationship between colonizer and colonized. And as increasing numbers of Africans earned secondary school diplomas and eventually university degrees, the mere fact of the income gap—not to mention the reasons offered to justify it—became increasingly intolerable to them. Their certification of educational achievement having been won, Africans found the ascriptive reality of their race an additional barrier. This was a hurdle that was set by the colonizer and could not readily be overcome within the framework of the colonial order. The often implicit racist assumptions on which the colonial bureaucracy operated[40] could no longer be kept hidden from public scrutiny once Africans with the necessary formal qualifications began demanding entry to positions of real administrative power.

Not unlike the pre-revolutionary French bourgeoisie analyzed by deTocqueville, whose discontent with the status quo increased the more closely it came in objective terms to resemble the ruling aristocracy, so the educated African middle class found increasing cause to shift from politely airing specific grievances to angrily challenging the entire colonial system at precisely the moment when its members came to resemble the European rulers in educational attainments and in lifestyle and career aspirations.[41]

Among the most deeply felt grievances of nationalist movements throughout the African continent was the de facto if not de jure reservation of top government posts to Europeans, coupled with the Europeans' refusal in principle to offer all employees, regardless of race, equal salaries and benefits for equal work. The nationalist rallying cry was equality, operationally defined as *equality with Europeans* in access to top posts and in remuneration for a given level of responsibility. That nationalists focused so much of their attention on this matter is hardly surprising. It was an issue on which all Africans, despite their differences and rivalries in other respects, could agree. It was an issue that touched a deep emotional chord, for the refusal to grant equal pay for equal work served as an explicit operational indicator of the contempt in which the foreign colonizers held the people of color whom they ruled. And it was an issue that highlighted the moral contradictions of colonial rule. How, nationalists asked, could colonial regimes reconcile their loudly vaunted civilizing mission with such manifestly uncivilized policies and practices? How could European norms of individual achievement, equality, bureaucratic rationality, and representative democracy be squared with these restrictive European regulations?

The personal career interests of the nationalists were also at stake over this issue. Many activists in post-1945 African politics were themselves government employees or had built a power base organizing government workers in trade unions. For example, 160 of the 227 territorial assembly representatives elected in 1952 from French West Africa, and 66 of the 137 deputies in the 1960 (Belgian) Congo assembly were functionaries.[42] Guinea's Sekou Toure and Kenya's Tom Mboya, among others, first came to political prominence as organizers of civil service trade unions. Such leaders were fully aware that unprecedented opportunities for upward mobility would be available in the public sector of an independent state. This awareness conveniently coincided with and reinforced the nationalists' larger goals for the society as a whole, as well as their deeply held moral commitment to the dignity and autonomy of people of color everywhere.

As nationalist movements gained momentum in the post-1945 years, their leaders were able to press successfully for an end to the inequalities of the pre-war period. Africans elected to the French National Assembly, for instance, achieved one of their most significant political gains when the 1950 Deuxième Loi Lamine Gueye, named after a prominent Senegalese representative, formally declared equality in civil service recruitment and pay. The law went on to grant African functionaries family allowances similar to those in France. In the British territories each colony moved at its own pace toward affirmation and implementation of the same principles, the pace accelerating as Africans gained control of the territorial legislature and as the civil service's senior ranks were Africanized. Movement along these lines was much slower in the Belgian and Portuguese colonies; for precisely this reason the pace was greatly accelerated once these territories gained independence. Only in South Africa and to a lesser extent in Rhodesia was administrative reform effectively blocked by white-minority interests working through openly discriminatory policies to monopolize their own access to one of the more tangible benefits of state power.

African nationalists, in short, did not reject or even half-heartedly accept the top-level salary scales initially set by European colonialists with European conditions in mind. On the contrary, nationalists firmly *insisted* upon retention of these scales. Ironically, retention was justified on egalitarian grounds, even though its effect was to institutionalize within the independent polity the powerful inegalitarian legacy of European rule. The reference group for the nationalist leaders was still the colonialists who were departing, not the peasants and the urban poor who remained. "It does not seem to happen," Tanzania's President Julius Nyerere once noted sardonically, "that anyone compares himself with those at the bottom economic level."[43]

POST-COLONIAL STATE

At the time of political independence, the mutually reinforcing actions of politically opposed forces—European colonialism and African anticolonial nationalism—had produced a structure of remuneration for individual civil servants that possessed the unusual features noted earlier. That Africa was the last continental region to decolonize only accentuated the inegalitarian aspects of this structure, for bureaucratic remuneration within Europe (which non-European nationalists could employ as a reference point) grew rapidly in dollar-equivalent terms with each passing year. It remained for the political leaders of the new African states to greatly expand the functional scope and size of the state, in effect multiplying the already high unit cost of administering the public sector by a rapidly growing number of administrators and administrative units.

Several politically powerful domestic factors help to explain the expansion of the post-colonial state. In order to broaden their base of support during the final years of colonial rule, nationalist politicians had promised to outperform the colonial regime in providing such popular amenities as primary education, health clinics, potable water, electricity, roads, bridges, and agricultural credit. These were the kinds of "all else" services Ghana's Kwame Nkrumah doubtless had in mind when he urged his followers to "seek ye first the political kingdom, and all else shall be added unto you." With independence, the political kingdom was at hand. Now the people looked to their leaders to deliver on earlier promises.[44]

Complementing the effort to allocate more public goods to a greater number of people has been the desire to extract more resources from a largely rural population. Many African farmers and herders are relatively autonomous economic actors living close to the margin of subsistence. These people operate within a pre-capitalist or peasant mode of production that makes it easier for them than for rural producers in other developing regions to escape from the demands and enticements of the national and international market economy. "Capturing" this elusive peasantry is a task African leaders have felt is necessary, if only to finance ambitious national development plans from domestic sources to the greatest extent possible.[45] Expanding the bureaucratic apparatus to reach the rural populace and then to extract resources from its members has seemed the most—perhaps the only—feasible means to this end.

Not to be ignored by leaders struggling to consolidate an often tenuous hold on power were the demands for political patronage by party activists, camp followers, and other individuals linked to the leaders by kinship or regional ties. The country's poverty, the dearth of opportunities in the private sector for secure, high-paying employment, and the powerful mutual-support moral imperatives of what Goran Hyden has termed "clan politics" only accentuated the acute pressures on politicians to treat the public sector as the neopatrimonial sector.[46] And leaders as well as their followers "had all been in the rain together until yesterday," in the words of Nigerian novelist Chinua Achebe. The fortunate occupants of "the one shelter our former rulers left" could take advantage of unaccustomed security and income to "dry their clothes"—and perchance to acquire some attractive new ones as well.[47]

Ideological preferences played a role, but probably only a marginal one, in expanding the African public sector. Leaders who believed Africa's economic problems to be the result of the continent's incorporation into the world capitalist system, and who consequently leaned toward some form of socialist alternative, naturally looked to the state to assume more direct control of the productive and distributive "commanding heights" of the economy. But because the private sector in most African countries features to an unusual degree the developmental limitations noted at the outset of this essay, African non-socialists also found themselves turning to government ministries and parastatal bodies as the only relatively large-scale institutions under their control that could undertake needed economic initiatives. If African socialists turned to the state out of preference, non-socialists turned to it by default.[48]

INTERNATIONAL INFLUENCIES

The international environment in which newly independent African countries find themselves has contributed in several important ways to the high costs of the contemporary African public sector. European colonial rule in Third World countries served quite effectively to diffuse throughout the globe the structures and generally accepted functions of the modern nation-state. Establishment of a state apparatus within each colony domesticated, as it were, what the Europeans had brought with them and provided the "national" prize that the nationalist movement could then set out to capture. Upon attaining independence, the new states have been expected by the international community to behave like old states, with all the institutional manifestations of an official commitment to rapid, equitable economic growth at home and active diplomatic engagement abroad.[49] There are doubtless economies of scale in establishing and maintaining this governmental infrastructure, such that the larger a country's population the smaller the per capita cost of doing what is minimally acceptable internationally. In this respect the small populations of African countries relative to other developing regions impose an unusually heavy financial burden upon them. Thirty-one of the forty-one countries of continental sub-Saharan Africa have 1985 populations under 10 million; seven have less than a million inhabitants. (Not even included in this statistic are numerous island microstates that lie off the African coast.)

The remuneration standards of the international environment continue to provide a reference point for ambitious, well-educated Africans. What is different is that in the post-colonial period the frame of reference has itself become internationalized, shifting from the institutions of the former European metropole to corporations, consulting firms, and government agencies based in many foreign countries, and to multilateral or international organizations like the World Bank, the International Monetary Fund, and the numerous agencies of the United Nations. Salaries and perquisites for top African bureaucrats, which are extraordinarily high by rural African standards, are simultaneously quite modest by the standards of a far more affluent external world. The greater the gap between top-level African government salaries and those of outside organizations, the more likely the exodus of many of the region's most experienced and talented public servants to work for these organizations.[50] The harmful developmental consequences of such a "brain drain" must be cause for serious concern for African policymakers contemplating the obvious reform of seriously reducing compensation levels in their bureaucracy's upper echelons.

International agencies, national governments, corporations, and private nonprofit agencies based outside of Africa are not simply influential as external reference groups. They also penetrate the economies and polities of formally independent African countries. Non-African institutions provide technical assistance personnel to the region's governments—an estimated 80,000 foreigners made available through foreign aid programs.[51] And through their "policy dialogues" and "structural adjustment" proposals they exert a profound impact on the savings rates, balances of trade, external debt levels, and indeed the basic fiscal and monetary policies of African countries. Referring to Western Europe, David Cameron has shown that a key determinant of the rate of public sector expansion is a country's degree of openness to the international economy.[52] If anything, conclusions applicable to European countries apply even more strongly to Africa's small, underdeveloped, trade-oriented, porous, highly vulnerable economies. One reason the African state expands is to enable it to cope with powerful institutional forces in its international environment. By enlarging the scope and size of the state, African leaders hope to cope more effectively with a veritable host of governmental and private sector agencies that, although based in the outside world, are quite able and willing to exert considerable influence as *domestic* actors within the newly independent polity.

The poverty of Africa prevents its governments from successfully extracting from internal sources more than a fraction of the financial resources required for development. At the same time, the wealth of many "First World" countries and of the multilateral financial institutions under their control renders it both possible and sensible for African states to attempt to attract needed resources externally. In this respect, the growth of African government may be viewed as a response to external economic opportunities, as a way of increasing a poor country's international as well as its domestic extractive capability.[53] An African country needs its ablest and best-trained citizens to negotiate on behalf of its citizens the terms of a joint venture agreement with a foreign textile-manufacturing firm, an irrigation project with a bilateral aid agency, a structural adjustment loan from the World Bank, or a debt-rescheduling agreement with the International Monetary Fund. The most critical of these negotiations tend in fact to be with foreign governments and international public sector agencies. This is because very poor countries are more likely to depend on official sources for development assistance than on private-profit sources for large infusions of foreign capital.[54] The largely public character of resource flows between rich and very poor countries probably increases the size of the recipients' public sectors, for it is through the recipient government that these resources initially flow and to that government that they may ultimately be directed.[55]

IMPACT ON AFRICAN DEVELOPMENT

Having suggested the principal factors affecting the cost of the public sector in contemporary sub-Saharan Africa, we return to the question prompting our investigation. Do the expenses of maintaining the region's national governments, and the structure of public sector remuneration, have on balance a positive or negative effect on Africa's economic development? Any effort to answer this question can at best be highly speculative, because so many factors other than those discussed here have been and remain influential, and because assigning a monetary value to the consequences of particular public policies and bureaucratic behaviors is inevitably quite arbitrary. With these qualifications in mind, and employing ceteris paribus assumptions, I will proceed to speculate.

On the positive side, the steep upward curve of remuneration from rural peasant to low-level government employee to top-level bureaucrat has stimulated a high level of private as well as public saving for investment in formal education, which continues to provide the principal means by which individuals move up this curve. A rapid expansion of enrollment at all educational levels has thus been effected during the past two decades. This expansion in turn has helped African states to rely increasingly on their own citizens to carry out development tasks. The region is still experiencing serious shortages of skilled manpower, particularly in technical fields, and it is much more dependent than other developing regions on expensive imported technical assistance. But the manpower bottleneck might have been even more of an obstacle to self-reliant development had the educational system not expanded as rapidly as it has since the early years of independence.

In a number of African countries, the rapid growth of state employment has probably had positive effects on political integration by providing upward mobility opportunities for members of diverse ethnic, regional, and religious groups. Political integration may likewise have been facilitated by the intense pressures exerted on national leaders to allocate public funds to ethnic groups and geographic regions in rough proportion to population.[56] A more leisurely expansion of the public sector, or a greater share of GDP in the hands of private sector actors not as subject to pressures for ethno-regional proportionality, might have produced higher and more violent levels of domestic political conflict than have actually been experienced. In turn, the greater the level of conflict threatening the very existence of a polity, the smaller the likelihood that either its public or its private sectors can save and productively invest the capital required for rapid economic development. As is well known, African states tend to have high potential for such polity-threatening conflict, given the artificial and externally imposed character of their boundaries and the large number of geographically based ethnic groups living within these boundaries.

The retention of generous salaries and perks for top civil servants has presumably reduced the temptation these individuals face to leave for even higher-paying positions with organizations based outside the country. To the extent that Africa's ablest negotiators and managers remain in the employ of their governments, the region maintains its capacity to cope with—and to extract needed resources from—the international environment.

What of the negative side of the ledger? Here we return to the criticisms of government's economic role noted at the outset, briefly noting likely net effects of public sector expenditure patterns on (1) the resources available to the private sector for productive investment, (2) the character of public policy, and (3) the behavior of bureaucrats.

A high proportion of recurrent expenditure devoted to maintenance of the government apparatus—salaries, pensions, housing and travel allowances, car loans, and the like—leaves a small portion of an already-meager budget available for programs mainifestly benefiting citizens not employed by the state. The relationship between public sector growth and private sector prosperity comes close to a zero-sum game under conditions of great poverty and prolonged economic stagnation, for the government of a poor country finds itself less able or willing than the government of a rich country to recycle through the formal budgeting process to the private sector the resources earlier collected from that sector. In Ruth First's evocative words, the post-independence African state "seems to be swallowing its own tail."[57]

Once the expensive state is in place, political leaders find it extremely difficult—if not harmful to their careers and even dangerous to their lives—to institute reforms reducing the size or pay scales of the bureaucracy. The national bureaucracy can readily respond to such a challenge by transforming itself into a trade union, practicing go-slow tactics, or going out on strike. In theory, bureaucrats are the agents of government output. In practice, the larger and more privileged their ranks relative to the population they govern, the more they should be analyzed as powerful *input* agencies within a political system. The salary structure of African governments has helped transform these governments into powerful interest groups whose overriding interest is themselves. With the system reproducing itself in this manner, able young people face continuing strong incentives to eschew private sector entrepreneurial activity in favor of government employment. The prospects are thus reduced that an indigenous and autonomous bourgeoisie, dependent for its wealth on the production of new goods and services, will emerge.[58]

To the extent that "development" refers to distributional equity as well as GDP growth, African governments find themselves in an uncomfortably paradoxical situation. Many of them are formally committed to some form of socialism, in the sense that their leaders wish to utilize the public sector to reduce the enormous income and productivity inequalities between rural peasants and the foreign-controlled, export-oriented enclaves that occupy the private sector's "commanding heights." But the structure of public remuneration—together with the role the state plays in regulating if not directly controlling the national means of production, distribution, and exchange—virtually ensures that the top civil servants and leading politicians will themselves be the most prominent members of a "new class."[59] A relatively well-paid public sector elite, acting in the name of African egalitarian values, thus becomes a powerful force accentuating societal inequality. The paradox is that an active and powerful state may be a necessary condition for the transition to socialism, while the expenditure patterns apparently required to maintain such a state could become a sufficient condition for non-attainment of an egalitarian, socialist society.

The factors we have noted can influence in economically harmful ways the policies governments set. It is widely noted, for example, that many African currencies have been officially overvalued, with the result that exports become less competitive on the world market while the real cost of imports is lowered. Monetary policy thus contributes directly to a balance of payments crisis which in due course inevitably becomes a debt-repayment crisis.[60] One possible explanation for systematic currency overvaluations is that the top bureaucrats and political leaders who set policy on such matters have a direct interest in lowering the cost of the imported consumer goods that their high incomes enable them to purchase. A highly skewed structure of remuneration thus pushes the society away from production (in this case, for export) while enabling its "new class" to enjoy goods purchased from abroad at officially subsidized rates. Currency devaluation makes eminent sense as a counter to structural balance of payments deficits. But such a reform is difficult to implement when it directly threatens the interests of a political and bureaucratic elite whose lifestyle is so import-intensive.

Also widely noted is the tendency of governments to exploit the rural populace through a combination of policies: high direct and indirect taxes, parastatal structures that regulate the pricing, transport, and marketing of agricultural commodities to the point of stifling peasants' incentives to produce, and minimal support for increased peasant output or productivity.[61] As Robert Bates has persuasively argued, this pattern is linked to politicians' fears that their hold on power will be jeopardized if rurally generated economic surplus is not transferred to politically better-organized and more volatile urban constituencies. To employ Albert Hirschman's terms, the politician is more worried about the "voice" or protest option exercised by urban dwellers unhappy over high staple-food prices than about the "exit" option likely to be exercised by rural dwellers unhappy over low staple-food prices.[62] To Bates' political explanation for policies of rural neglect and impoverishment may be added a more bureaucratically oriented set of explanations. The more expensive the government apparatus sitting, as it were, atop the peasantry, the greater the need to extract even more from the already most marginal elements in society in order to pay for this apparatus. And the more rapidly the numbers of government employees grow, the greater the need to provide something for them to do. Parastatal bodies regulating or directly managing the functions of agricultural pricing, transport, and marketing are ideally suited to employ large numbers of would-be entrants to the bureaucratic labor force.

The agricultural policies just outlined make eminently rational sense when analyzed from both a political and bureaucratic short-term perspective. But they constitute, in effect, "rural dedevelopment" policies that lead to economic disaster over the medium and long term. The peasant's "exit" option in response to high levels of regulation and extraction actually consists of two suboptions: to withdraw from production for the market into self-reliant subsistence, or to withdraw from agriculture altogether and migrate to the city. The exercise of either or both of these suboptions by large numbers of peasants reduces the volume of domestically produced food and hence pushes food prices in a politically volatile upward direction. In such a situation, the plight of the rural food-producing population does not lighten the burdens of the urban food-consuming population but only compounds the urbanites' problems. The misery of the one group translates into the misery of the other. Finally the steeply rising remuneration curve within the African bureaucracy may encourage behavior by individual government employees that is harmful for national economic development. Individuals at each level of the hierarchy are acutely aware that employees at still higher levels enjoy considerably greater salaries and prequisites than they. Consequently, although civil servants (even those at the base) are objectively quite privileged members of a very poor society, subjectively they feel themselves underprivileged relative to the reference groups far above them. The result is profound and pervasive discontent with what appears to be one's meagre lot at all levels of the bureaucracy. (The highest-paid civil servant is no exception to this observation, feeling underpaid relative to the representatives of international agencies with whom he or she regularly interacts.) This sentiment contributes directly to low morale, absenteeism, poor job performance, an obsession with playing bureaucratic politics in order to win promotion, and corrupt practices in order to augment a salary one firmly believes to be grossly inadequate.

The extent of bureaucratic corruption has been well documented in several African countries.[63] Societal values obligating the government employees to satisfy the financial and employment demands of kin, ethnic, and hometown networks doubtless play an important role in this phenomenon. However, the pressures and temptations to earn more that are encouraged by retention of the colonial remuneration structure should not be ignored by analysts. In any event, the bureaucratic behaviors noted here are not likely to stimulate national development, even if this particular form of privatizing the public sector does generate personal gain.[64]

CONCLUSION

It seems reasonable to conclude that the economically negative consequences of bureaucratic growth in sub-Saharan Africa have been more significant than the positive ones. The French agronomist Rene Dumont was quite correct when he wrote in the 1960s that "the principal 'industry' (in Africa) at the moment is administration. . . . As presently conceived, administration will be the ruin of these countries."[65] Strong confirmation of this conclusion is the intriguing fact that political analysts with widely varying ideological perspectives tend to converge in their views of the African state. To be sure, the terms differ: the Left attacks the "bureaucratic bourgeoisie" and the "overdeveloped state," while conservatives are critical of the "overextended socialist state." And the world view from which the terms are derived differs: the Left perceives the African bureaucracy as the nonproductive *comprador* of an economically and morally bankrupt international capitalist ruling class, while the Right perceives it as the institutional expression of an economically and morally bankrupt fling with socialism.[66] Nonetheless, the two sides are far closer to consensus than they may believe themselves to be. Both find themselves alluding to the same phenomenon as an important cause of the region's ongoing economic crisis.

The policy implications of this conclusion are not, however, particularly clear. As we have seen, the causes of bureaucratic growth and of the distribution of rewards within the bureaucracy are deeply rooted in the policies of European colonial rulers *and* the demands of anticolonial nationalists *and* the political imperatives of post-colonial state-builders *and* the operations of the contemporary international system. Each of these forces was or is powerful in its own right. That all of them have converged to produce the characteristics we now term harmful for African development makes it extremely difficult to discern how reforms designed significantly to reduce the size and/or unit costs of the bureaucracy could be successfully implemented.

It is true that the severe economic crisis of the 1980s is forcing just such reforms on African states whether their rulers wish them or not. High rates of inflation have eroded the real purchasing power of the bureaucrats, particularly those at the top of the scale. Virtually empty state treasuries mean that many government employees—particularly those at the lower and middle ranks, including teachers in public schools—have gone unpaid for months at a time. As African states have increased their indebtedness to international financial institutions in order to keep trade and fiscal deficits within manageable proportions, the rulers of these states have had no option but to take seriously the critiques of public sector costs and inefficiencies mounted by structural reformists from these external institutions. Stark economic necessity has driven many states by the mid-1980s to reduce public sector employment levels, salary scales, and housing and transportation perquisites. But there are limits to the degree to which political leaders will dismantle the institutions that keep them in power and that, in fact, define the very existence of fragile political entities. And, of course, the economic crisis affects the private sector as well, increasing pressures on the state to serve as employer-of-last-resort for formerly self-employed individuals who can no longer support themselves and their kin.

Nor is it clear that a significant shift of resources and responsibilities from the public to the private sector will unleash the productive forces that advocates of "privatization" envisage. To be sure, dismantling government monopolies and regulatory agencies in certain arenas—notably the pricing and marketing of staple foods, and urban and riverine transportation systems—has the potential for generating an efficient and productive response within the African private sector. There is evidence that privatization measures recently undertaken in countries such as Ghana, Togo, Benin, Somalia, and Mali are proving economically sound.[67]

Still, the constraints on private sector growth remain severe, regardless of changes in public sector activity and policy envisaged in structural reform proposals. If anything, the combined effects of rapid demographic growth, ecological deterioration, and drought now confront the small-scale African peasantry with a more serious set of constraints on production than ever before in its history. National governments are not the peasants' only enemy. The natural environment, made less productive through the actions of human beings, is increasingly becoming another foe. The peasants' capacity to expand output by expanding acreage is severely limited under the new ecological regime, while their need for agricultural inputs to increase productivity is greatly increased, with government agencies the most likely instruments to provide many of these inputs for at least the poorest and most isolated of African farmers and herders.

Likewise, prospects are not favorable for an indigenous bourgeoisie that will take charge of medium- or large-scale productive enterprises. On the one hand, societal norms may operate to limit the geographical scope and capital-accumulating capacity of indigenous enterprise. On the other hand, competition from multinational corporations effectively in league with national political elites remains a serious constraint to the growth of indigenous capitalism.[68] To privatize an economy is not necessarily to place it in the hands of a country's own citizens; equally consistent with the concept is an increased role for expatriate private enterprise. To the extent that the privatization movement of the 1980s effectively means the takeover of nonviable parastatal operations by non-African entrepreneurs, such a trend hardly encourages the emergence of a productive indigenous bourgeoisie.[69]

Foreign-controlled enterprises in mining, industry, and agribusiness can help to relieve serious foreign exchange constraints and can provide technical and managerial training to African employees who may at some point wish to set up their own businesses. But the capacity and the will of foreign enclaves to reach out in transforming ways to the rural majority—or even to the large and growing "informal" artisan and petty-trading sector in the cities—are inevitably quite limited.

The African case may thus be one in which, tragically, neither the public or the private sector is well positioned to initiate and maintain the economic development the region's people desperately seek. The underdeveloped economy may indeed be kept in its place by the overdeveloped—or at least the overextended—state. At the same time the overdeveloped state may be kept in its place by the underdeveloped economy. Will the underdevelopment of the state by would-be reformers lead to the development of the region's economy? A positive response to this question is by no means a foregone conclusion. For just as we have seen with the case in favor of greater state activity, the persuasive argument that the private sector *must* stimulate needed growth provides absolutely no guarantee that it *will.*

NOTES

I would like to thank Gabriel Almond, Larry Diamond, Lewis Gann, Raymond Hopkins, Bruce Johnston, Irving Leonard Markovitz, Donald Rothchild, Dunstan Wai, and Tracey Webb for helpful criticisms of earlier drafts of this essay. Karen Fung provided valuable bibliographic assistance.

1. Gabriel Roth, *The Private Provision of Public Services in Developing Countries,* New York: Oxford University Press for the World Bank, 1987, p. 7.

2. For a balanced discussion of the advantages and disadvantages of government-initiated development activity, see Benjamin Cohen and Gustav Ranis, "The Second Postwar Structuring," in Gustav Ranis, ed., *Government and Economic Development,* New Haven: Yale University Press, 1971, pp. 431-469.

3. For the multiple goals of politicians, and the extraordinarily complex set of considerations affecting their policy decisions, see Warren Ilchman and Norman Uphoff, *The Political Economy of Change,* Berkeley: University of California Press, 1969, pp. 39-91.

4. Jürgen Kohl, "The Functional Structure of Public Expenditures: Long-Term Changes," in Charles Lewis Taylor, ed., *Why Governments Grow: Measuring Public Sector Size,* Beverly Hills: Sage, 1983, pp. 201-206. For the British case, the classic study is Alan A. Peacock and Jack Wiseman, *The Growth of Public Expenditure in the United Kingdom,* Princeton: Princeton University Press, 1961.

5. Frank Gould, "The Development of Public Expenditure in Western Industrialized Countries: A Comparative Analysis," *Public Finance* (The Hague), 38:1, 1983, pp. 38-69. See also David Cameron, "The Expansion of the Public Economy: A Comparative Analysis," *American Political Science Review,* 72:4, December 1978, pp. 1243-1261; and Morris Beck, *Government Spending: Trends and Issues,* New York: Praeger, pp. 122-123. OECD, Organization for Economic Cooperation and Development, comprising the economically advanced industrial market economies.

6. World Bank, *World Development Report, 1987,* New York: Oxford University Press, 1987, p. 247. Central government expenditure for twenty industrial market economies listed by the Bank was 22.9 percent of GNP in 1972, 29.1 percent in 1985.

7. See, for example, Richard Rose and Guy Peters, *Can Governments Go Bankrupt?,* New York: Basic Books, 1978; Roger A. Freeman, *The Growth of American Government,* Stanford, Calif.: Hoover Institution, 1975; James Buchanan and Gordon Tullock, "The Expanding Public Sector: Wagner Squared," *Public Choice,* 31, 1977, pp. 147-150.

8. Gould (note 5), p. 54.

9. Murray Weidenbaum, *The Modern Public Sector,* New York: Basic

Books, 1969, p. 4.

10. See Beck (note 5) for a critique of the critiques of rising government costs.

11. See, for example, Fred W. Riggs, *Administration in Developing Countries*, Boston: Houghton Mifflin, 1964; David J. Gould and José A. Amaro-Reyes, *The Effects of Corruption on Administrative Performance*, World Bank, Staff Working Paper 580, 1983. Country studies include Lucian Pye, *Politics, Personality, and Nation Building in Burma*, New Haven: Yale University Press, 1962; Robert M. Price, *Society and Bureaucracy in Contemporary Ghana*, Berkeley and Los Angeles: University of California Press, 1975; David J. Gould, *Bureaucratic Corruption and Underdevelopment in the Third World: The Case of Zaire*, New York: Pergamon, 1980.

12. Alan A. Tait and Peter S. Heller, *International Comparisons of Government Expenditure*, Washington, International Monetary Fund, Occasional Paper 10, 1982, Table 14, pp. 36-37. Of twenty-five African countries in this study, three had 1977 ratios between 26 percent and 30 percent, and seven were between 31 percent and 39 percent. The U.S. ratio, using the same criteria, was 23 percent.

13. Several reasons why Wagner's Law is invalid in this respect are suggested in this essay. See also Alexander Gerschenkron, *Economic Backwardness in Historical Perspective*, Cambridge: Harvard University Press, esp. pp. 5-30.

14. World Bank, *World Development Report, 1983*, Washington: Oxford University Press, 1983, Table 1, p. 148; *World Development Report, 1987*, pp. 202-203, 269.

15. World Bank, *Financing Adjustment with Growth in Sub-Saharan Africa, 1986-90*, Washington, D.C.: World Bank, April 1986, p. 9. An even more alarming estimate of a 4.1 percent annual per capita decline between 1980 and 1985 was given by African ministers in charge of economic development and planning at a 1985 meeting of the U.N. Economic Commission for Africa. Cited in Lester R. Brown and Edward C. Wolf, *Reversing Africa's Decline*, Washington: Worldwatch Institute, 1985, p. 8.

16. *Ibid.*, p. 9. For other overviews of the economic crisis, see OECD, *Development Cooperation, 1984 Review*, Paris: OECD, 1984, pp. 11-36; *Africa Report*, July/August, 1984; and Lloyd Timberlake, *Africa in Crisis*, Philadelphia: New Society Publications, 1986.

17. Figures estimated from data in World Bank, *World Development Report, 1987*, p. 213.

18. Republic of Kenya, *Report of the Commission of Enquiry* (Public Service Structure and Remuneration Commission), 1970-71, Nairobi, p. 29; Henry Bienen, *Kenya: The Politics of Participation and Control*, Princeton: Princeton University Press, 1974, p. 32; Republic of Kenya, *Report of the Civil Service Review Committee*, 1979-80, Nairobi, 1980, pp. 25-36.

19. Sheldon Gellar, *Senegal: An African Nation Between Islam and the West*, Boulder, Colo.: Westview Press, 1982, pp. 55-56.

20. Tony Killick, *Development Economics in Action: A Study of Economic Policies in Ghana*, New York: St. Martin's Press, 1978, pp. 217, 320-322.

21. Zambian and Nigerian figures from Goran Hyden, *No Shortcuts to Progress: African Development Management in Perspective*, Berkeley and Los Angeles: University of California Press, 1983, p. 97; Tanzanian figure from John R. Nellis, *Public Enterprise in Sub-Saharan Africa*, World Bank Discussion Paper 1, November 1986, p. 5. Also Sheridan Johns, "Para-Statal Bodies in

Zambia: Problems and Prospects," in Heide and Udo Simonis, eds., *Socioeconomic Development in Dual Economies: The Example of Zambia*, Munich: Weltforum Verlag, 1971, pp. 218-252; and overview by Nellis, cited in this note, and by L. Gray Cowan in "Africa Reconsiders Its Parastatals," *CSIS Africa Notes*, 33, Washington, September 4, 1983.

22. Nellis (note 21), p. 5.

23. Estimates for 1960 derived from K.C. Doctor and H. Gallis, "Size and Characteristics of Wage Employment in Africa: Some Statistical Estimates," *International Labor Review*, 93, 1966, pp. 163, 166-167, 170, for six countries where "general" and ten countries where "public sector" employment information was available. See also P. Robson and D. A. Lury, eds., *The Economies of Africa*, Evanston, Ill.: Northwestern University Press, 1969, p. 60. Data for 1980 derived from Peter S. Heller and Alan A. Tait, *Government Employment and Pay: Some International Comparisons*, Washington, International Monetary Fund, Occasional Paper 24, 1983, based on estimates from sixteen countries.

24. Estimates based on data in Appendix to Martin Godfrey, "The International Market in Skills and the Transmission of Inequality," *Development and Change*, 6:4, October 1975, p. 23. Godfrey's figures are for salaries and do not include perquisites.

25. In the United States as of 1980, top political appointees to federal administrative posts earned slightly above $60,000, plus awards for performance. Robert W. Hartman, *Pay and Pensions of Federal Workers*, Washington: Brookings Institution, 1983.

26. Cited in Charles Elliott, *Patterns of Poverty in the Third World*, New York: Praeger, 1975, pp. 184-185.

27. Godfrey (note 24), p. 23.

28. Heller and Tait (note 23), pp. 23, 59.

29. Charles Jeffries, *The Colonial Empire and Its Civil Service*, London: Cambridge University Press, 1938; Henrika Kuklick, *The Imperial Bureaucracy: The Colonial Administrative Service in the Gold Coast, 1920-1939*, Stanford, Calif.: Hoover Institution Press, 1979, Chap. 1.

30. Jeffries (note 29).

31. *Ibid.*, pp. 84-86; also 105-127 and 138-142.

32. Lord Hailey, *An African Survey, Revised, 1956*, London: Oxford University Press, 1957, pp. 373-374.

33. Virginia Thompson and Richard Adloff, *French West Africa*, Stanford: Stanford University Press, 1957, pp. 193-194.

34. This is acknowledged in Republic of Kenya, *Report of The Commission of Enquiry* (note 18), p. 47; and in Gold Coast, *Report of the Commission on the Civil Service of the Gold Coast, 1950-51*, Accra, 1951, p. 62.

35. In French West Africa, for example, about 37,000 of the 42,000 civil servants as of 1954 were African. Thompson and Adloff (note 33), p. 194. On the crucial intermediary role played by Africans in the British colonies, see Lewis Gann and Peter Duignan, *The Rulers of British Africa, 1870-1914*, Stanford: Stanford University Press, 1978.

36. Gann and Duignan (note 35), Table 13, p. 159.

37. Jeffries (note 29), pp. 141-42.

38. Rene Dumont, *False Start in Africa*, New York: Praeger, second edition, revised, 1969, p. 88.

39. For examples from Southern Nigeria, see David B. Abernethy, *The Political Dilemma of Popular Education: An African Case*, Stanford: Stanford

University Press, 1969.

40. These assumptions could also be quite explicit. Until 1942 candidates for the British Colonial Administrative Service were required to be "of pure European descent." Richard Symonds, *The British and Their Successors: A Study in the Development of the Government Services in the New States*, London: Faber and Faber, 1966, p. 128.

41. For the effects of different amounts of formal education on political attitudes in a colonial situation, see Gustav Jahoda, *White Man*, London: Oxford University Press, 1961. An early study of lifestyle and lifestyle aspirations is Hugh H. Smythe and Mabel M. Smythe, *The New Nigerian Elite*, Stanford: Stanford University Press, 1960.

42. Thompson and Adloff (note 33), p. 63. Edouard Bustin, "The Congo," in Gwendolyn Carter, ed., *Five African States: Responses to Diversity*, Ithaca: Cornell University Press, p. 108.

43. Julius Nyerere, *Freedom and Unity*, London: Oxford University Press, 1968, p. 17. In the same essay, written in 1966, Nyerere was frank to point out that "the wage differentials in Tanzania are now out of proportion to any conceivable concept of human equality." *Ibid.*, p. 16.

44. For the popular appeal of social and economic amenities, see Donald Rothchild, "Collective Demands for Improved Distributions," in Rothchild and Victor Olorunsula, eds., *State Versus Ethnic Claims: African Policy Dilemmas*, Boulder, Colo.: Westview Press, 1983, pp. 172-198.

45. This idea is elaborated in Hyden, *No Shortcuts to Progress* (note 21), and in his *Beyond Ujamaa in Tanzania*, Berkeley and Los Angeles: University of California Press, 1980.

46. Jean-Claude Willame, *Patrimonialism and Political Change in the Congo*, Stanford: Stanford University Press, 1972; Hyden (note 21).

47. Chinua Achebe, *A Man of the People*, Garden City, N.Y.: Doubleday, 1967, p. 34.

48. For a general discussion of the role of ideology in setting and implementing public policy, see Crawford Young, *Ideology and Development in Africa*, New Haven: Yale University Press, 1982.

49. John Nettl and Roland Robertson, *International Systems and the Modernization of Societies*, London: Faber and Faber, 1968; Bertrand Badie and Pierre Birnbaum, *The Sociology of the State*, Chicago: University of Chicago, 1983, pp. 97-101.

50. This problem has been particularly acute in Sudan and Somalia, because of the high salaries oil-producing countries in the neighboring Middle East have been able to offer experienced managers and technicians.

51. World Bank, *World Development Report, 1983*, p. 112. As Rene Dumont and Marie-France Mottin note of Zambia, foreign employees of embassies or international organizations who work in the country "enjoy an inordinately lavish lifestyle that exacerbates the envy and the longing for luxury experienced by the Africans who mix with them, or merely watch them." Dumont and Mottin, *Stranglehold on Africa*, London: Andre Deutsch, 1983, p. 74.

52. Cameron (note 5).

53. See Gabriel Almond and G. Bingham Powell, *Comparative Politics: System, Process and Policy*, Boston: Little, Brown, second edition, 1978, pp. 289-298, for the concepts of extractive capability and performance, and pp. 315-316 for the international dimension of these concepts.

54. With 11 percent of the population of the world's developing

countries, sub-Saharan Africa received 30 percent of official development assistance (ODA) from all sources in 1982/83. In 1981/82, ODA accounted for 56 percent of the region's net external financial receipts. Officially supported nonconcessional flows accounted for 19 percent, private nonconcessional flows for only 25 percent (of which direct investment was 14 percent). OECD (note 16), pp. 74, 203.

55. For conservatives critical of government expansion, this aspect of foreign aid is cited as one of aid's more negative consequences. See P. T. Bauer, *Reality and Rhetoric: Studies in the Economics of Development*, Cambridge: Harvard University press, 1984, pp. 38-62.

56. Donald Rothchild, "Middle Africa: Hegemonial Exchange and Resource Allocation," in Alexander J. Groth and Larry L. Wade, eds., *Comparative Resource Allocation*, Beverly Hills: Sage, 1984, pp. 151-180.

57. Ruth First, *Power in Africa*, Harmondsworth: Penguin Books, 1971, p. 108.

58. In this respect see Abner Cohen's analysis of Sierra Leone Creoles in *The Politics of Elite Culture*, Berkeley and Los Angeles: University of California Press, 1981, pp. 39-59.

59. Milovan Djilas's phrase refers to trends in supposedly classless postwar Yugoslavia. Djilas, *The New Class*, New York: Praeger, 1957. For varying interpretations of the process of class formation in Africa see Issa Shivji, *Class Struggles in Tanzania*, New York: Monthly Review Press, 1976; Richard Sklar, "The Nature of Class Domination in Africa," *Journal of Modern African Studies*, 18:4, 1979, pp. 531-552; Giovanni Arrighi and John S. Saul, *Essays on the Political Economy of Africa*, New York: Monthly Review Press, 1973; and articles in the *Review of African Political Economy*.

60. World Bank, *Accelerated Development in Sub-Saharan Africa: An Agenda for Action*, Washington: World Bank, 1981, pp. 24-31.

61. Robert H. Bates, *Markets and States in Tropical Africa*, Berkeley and Los Angeles: University of California Press, 1981; Keith Hart, *The Political Economy of West African Agriculture*, Cambridge: Cambridge University Press, 1982, pp. 83-105; World Bank, *Accelerated Development* (note 60); Donal Cruise O'Brien, "Co-operators and Bureaucrats: Class Formation in a Senegalese Peasant Society," *Africa*, 61:4, October 1971, pp. 263-278; David B. Jones, "State Structures in New Nations: the Case of Primary Agricultural Marketing in Africa," *Journal of Modern African Studies*, 20:4, December 1982, pp. 553-569.

62. Albert Hirschman, *Exit Voice, and Loyalty: Responses to Decline in Firms, Organizations, and States*, Cambridge: Harvard University Press, 1970.

63. Gould (note 11) for Zaire; Larry Diamond, "Nigeria in Search of Democracy," *Foreign Affairs*, Spring 1984, pp. 905-927; Robert Williams, *Political Corruption in Africa*, Aldershot: Gower Publishing Co., 1987.

64. Gould and Amaro-Reyes (note 11). A particularly destructive result of corruption—and of the effort to cover it up through arson—was the 1983 fire that destroyed much of the thirty-seven-story Nigerian External Telecommunication building in Lagos.

65. Dumont (note 38), p. 78.

66. Criticism from the Left may be found in the works of Frantz Fanon, Hamza Alavi, Issa Shivji (e.g., note 59), Mahmoud Mamdani, Colin Leys, Lionel Cliffe; and in the pages of the *African Review of Political Economy*. Criticism from relatively conservative quarters is to be found in the works of P.T. Bauer (e.g., note 55), the World Bank's *Accelerated Development* (note 60), and the Bank's *World Development Report, 1983*, which focused on development

management issues.

67. Elliot Berg, "The Potentials of the Private Sector in Africa," *Washington Quarterly*, 8:4, Fall 1985, pp. 73-83; L. Gray Cowan, "Benin Joins the Pragmatists," *CSIS Africa Notes*, February 28, 1986; Nellis (note 21); James Brooke, "In Africa, a Rush to Privatize," *New York Times*, July 30, 1987.

68. On societal norms and pressures see Peter Marris and Anthony Somerset, *African Businessmen*, Nairobi: East African Publishing House, 1971. On competition from multinational corporations see Steven Langdon, *Multinational Corporations in the Political Economy of Kenya*, London: Macmillan, 1981.

69. Brooke (note 67) quotes a Western diplomat based in Africa as saying: "Privatization equals foreign management."

CHAPTER 10

Structural Adjustment in the Longer Run: Some Uncomfortable Questions

Charles Elliott

One of the interesting features of the academic and agency response to the crisis of African development in this decade is that there is as near unanimity on the causes of the problem as one will ever encounter in disciplines beset by paradigmatic debate. Naturally there are idiosyncratic variations, but the basic theme is clear. It can be put shortly but crudely like this. Africa's problems arose from a combination of two basic factors: internal mismanagement in general and of prices in particular (most notably agricultural prices and the prices of foreign exchange); and a series of external shocks, some of them human-made (such as the oil price revolution) and some natural (such as the climatic shift that produced the series of droughts in the early years of this decade). The argument is that the latter had the effect of sharpening the effects of the former, and it is only when the former problems are addressed that Africa will be able to regain the road to "economic prosperity" (the elevating phrase repeated in the World Bank paper, Chapter 2, in this volume).

Most analyses put the problems of agricultural pricing and exchange rates in the wider context of the post-oil shock recession in the Organization for Economic Cooperation and Development (OECD) countries and the effect of that recession on the prices of most African commodity exports. That, however, is seen as the context within which the key operational variables are set. Particularly in the analyses of the World Bank and the International Monetary Fund (IMF), those operational variables are identified as internal prices, exchange rates, non-price barriers to the effective working of market forces; e.g., parastatals and marketing boards. In other words, the operational variables are located within the African countries themselves and the analysis is presented in a way that makes that an inevitable conclusion.

Lest I be misunderstood—which I seem to have been fairly comprehensively at the conference at which this paper was originally presented. Let me say now what I shall certainly have to repeat later: *I do not disagree with that analysis as far as it goes.* With its excessively short-term horizon, it does not, however, go far enough, with the result that the prescriptions based on it may in some instances be unhelpful and in the extreme case dangerous or damaging.

In terms of theory, my major complaint about what I shall hereafter call the orthodox view is both its remarkable ahistoricity and its insensitivity to the deeper social forces that led African countries to adopt a variant of the Galbraith/Kindelberger disequilibrium system as a means of survival.[1] It is my contention that we have to understand the social forces at work within a sociohistorical context if we are to be delivered from development fetishness.

THE POLITICS OF DISEQUILIBRIUM

This is not the place to review the literature on class and state in Africa. All that can be done is to highlight a number of significant background issues, warning the reader that each is part of a wider and deeply fought debate.

1. Most observers are struck by the fact that the nature of the state in sub-Saharan Africa is evolving rapidly—and probably along different paths in different countries. We are thus dealing with very different sets of social and political forces: compare and contrast Kenya and Tanzania; Botswana and Zimbabwe; Zaire and Ivory Coast, for example. "Structural adjustment" should take account of those differences, not only in economic terms but in social and political terms.

2. The social formations within any one state are changing fast by historical standards—see, for example, the growth of wage-labor 1940-1980;[2] the development of a "bureaucratic bourgeoisie";[3] the relations between that bourgeoisie and international capital on one side and domestic entrepreneurship on the other;[4] the growth in the political power of the military, especially in central and southern Africa; and the development of protoclasses in the rural areas.[5] The political effects of this rapid change include the search for ways of governing and protecting power and influence in an unstable, unpredictable, and constantly changing environment. It is not only that any one regime is likely to feel insecure under certain circumstances. It is that the political map is constantly being redrawn. Under such conditions, accomodation and compromise are not only culturally preferable—they

may be politically mandatory.

3. This is reinforced by reflections on the transitoriness of political alliances that power blocs can engineer in the conditions described above. Whatever "autonomy" the state may acquire from dominant interests,[6] the state is not ontologically separable from the social groups that it comprises. Those social groups ally and disaffiliate in a bewildering array of relationships, only some of which can be analyzed in economic terms.[7] Consider, for example, the relation of the United National Independence Party (UNIP) with the Zambian Miners Union (ZMU) and contrast it with shifts in the relative strengths of north/south and east/west alliances within the major language groups in Zambia. The need to build and repair alliances both within and outside "class" relations puts a high premium on various forms of patron-client relationships, and therefore on the development of a wide array of patronage forms. This is not necessarily to imply an unduly functionalist view of the state, but it is to imply that access to and maintenance of political power is related to, and may at the margin be determined by, access to patronage.

4. The same general comments can be made with respect to social control. Groups, classes, organizations, and institutions have to be "controlled" in the sense of the acquisition and maintenance of their adherence to a fairly flexible consensus. A variety of means of achieving this is being developed: emphasis on external threats, "national developmentalism," nationalism, personalism, or appeals to a particular (often national) ideology are all too familiar. Social control is also exercised, however, through variants of patronage, from generous wage settlements to privileged access to foreign exchange to location of specific investments. This form of political activity is an important form of social control and therefore has its own dynamic that may or may not be consistent with economistic efficiency algorithms—and may or may not benefit international capital.

5. Many of the features above (e.g., the formation of patron-client relations, "national developmentalism," and ethnic alliances) favor a form of bureaucratic organization that is geographically extensive and in which administrative and party functions are interwoven. Two important implications follow: constant pressure on public expenditure that is not readily reducible to economic calculus, and a political sensitivity to a wide range of social groups whose own economic base of power may be quite modest.

6. None of this is to deny a degree of autonomy to the state; it is, however, to suggest that there are limits to the way in which "the public interest" can be defined and defended. Indeed the nature of politics in Africa is a constantly shifting interaction between the

autonomy of the state and arrays of sectoral interests—that is, between a purist liberal politics and a widely functional one. My argument is that African economies have a tendency to disequilibrium that results from the nature of political processes in African society. To attempt to squeeze disequilibria out of the economies of Africa by operating on domestic economic variables alone is therefore misguided. One needs to address both domestic political processes and the international environment in which African economies are set. This paper is a modest contribution to sketching in those two wider dimensions that the Bank and the Fund sometimes ignore. (They can be forgiven for saying little of the former in public; they should not be forgiven for their confusions on the latter).

The presence of these features makes the maintenance of an equilibrial system difficult, for an equilibrial system imposes heavy *political* demands that a political culture with these six features cannot readily meet. Some of those demands are: an efficient tax base that is responsive to changes in real incomes of different groups and formations in society; a system of public finance that will control liquidity in accordance with the demands of the real economy, even if savings behavior requires it to do so at very high rates of interest; a system of public expenditure decisionmaking that can adjust rapidly to changes in revenues (and/or the governments' capacity to borrow at home or abroad); a readiness to raise the cost or reduce the availability of imports and/or subsidize exports in a way that maintains overseas payments in balance; and a readiness to increase savings in the public sector if savings in the private sector prove deficient in terms of either domestic or foreign balances.

The argument is not that policies are not available to ensure equilibrium. Nor is it that politicians and civil servants are somehow deficient because they do not put those policies into effect. Rather the argument is that there is a fundamental asymmetry between the way the political system actually operates and the way economic decisionmaking would have to operate if the demanding conditions of equilibrium—i.e., noninflationary balances on internal and external account—were to be achieved. Some simple illustrations will clarify this point.

In most African countries, the tax base is narrow, inefficient, and inequitable. It is heavily loaded on "invisible" taxes such as export crops—i.e., the incidence of tax is correlated closely with political influence. The result has been that windfall profits have been heavily taxed, but the high rates of tax have stayed in place when the windfall has disappeared—a lag that would have been inconceivable among better-organized groups. Capital, property, and land taxes remain rare despite the powerful arguments that can be made for them from the standpoint of economic efficiency. Although tax as a proportion of income paid by the salariat has risen sharply in many African countries in the last seven years, *effective* rates of corporaton tax remain low.

When we move to public expenditure, it is no surprise to find that the political demands of accomodation, patronage, regional jealousies, and ministerial pecking orders make it hard to keep expenditure levels in line with revenues in "normal" times and, given the ease with which deficits can be "financed" by the Central Bank, almost impossible when revenues collapse as a result of falling commodity prices or levels of inflation that make government borrowing attractive within acceptable (i.e., politically acceptable) interest rates.

With high average propensities to import, the urban middle (and perhaps some of the working) classes make common cause with the military and much of the corporate sector to resist measures that will constrain imports either directly or through raising their price. That is a formidable alliance of political influence, made the more so by the fact that many politicians have direct personal and/or family linkages with at least two of those groups.

This is not to imply corruption—though sometimes the way in which political forces impact on economic behavior may come close to it. It is well known in IMF circles, for example, that foreign exchange surrender obligations are persistently ignored by politically powerful exporters, whether publicly or privately owned. It is not coincidental that the one governor of the Central Bank of Sierra Leone who tried to impose those obligations on the lucrative diamond industry was removed. The beneficiaries were not only necessarily enriching themselves; their ministries had become part of the system that ensured that they had privileged if wholly unofficial access to foreign exchange. It was too rewarding an alliance to be allowed to be disturbed.

More fundamentally, the high rates of inflation that have come to characterize many sub-Saharan African economies can themselves be seen to have a political origin: that is, they betoken a failure for a national consensus to emerge about the distribution of income, or, to put the same thing another way, patronage and social control mechanisms prove inadequate or inconsistent in forming and maintaining such a consensus. Indeed, they may well operate in such a way—e.g., doubling the size of the Gambian civil service 1980-1985 as a direct response to rising unemployment—as to increase inflation. In this sense, manipulating the internal economic variables identified above may be irrelevant or worse.

The argument is, then, that the roots of disequilibrium do not lie in the particular economic events of 1981-1985, nor in the technical or moral inadequacy of politicians and civil servants. The former throw into sharper relief the effects of a fundamental mismatch between the way in which politics is done and the demands—demands so fierce that neither the United States nor the United Kingdom can currently meet them—of orthodox economic management. For orthodoxy is never easy for politicians; when real GNP is contracting rapidly it is nearly impossible for African politicians.

We get a good post facto view of this when we look at the great difficulty African countries have had in applying one of the key parts of the Bank/Fund strategy of structural adjustment, namely devaluation. Ajit Singh has examined the theoretical objections to devaluation for a country such as Tanzania.[8] Those objections are important, but more significant for this argument is the fact that so many African countries have actually failed to improve the real exchange rate by devaluation (see Table 10.1). And if real exchange rates have not improved, it is highly unlikely that the *balance* of trade will improve at all.

Behind this frustrated devaluation lies a mix of a number of political/economic interactions. First, the government may not pursue a suitable monetary policy after devaluation because to do so would force interest rates so high that it would antagonize all borrowers (urban and rural) and require further heavy cuts in public expenditure at a time when the real incomes of many urban groups is already falling—by 50 percent during 1980-1984 in Tanzania and 40 percent over the same period in Ghana. Second, the government may be required to compensate losses—e.g., to urban salariat—and do so in a way that is inflationary (e.g., raise civil servants' salaries without matching tax increases as in Ghana in early 1986). Third, private sector employees may demand the restoration of their real incomes and, given the highly monopolistic/oligopolistic structure of the private sector, higher costs are easily passed on by price-makers. Government is powerless to stop the resultant inflation except by monetary policy as above. Fourth, wage goods may be in short supply because of the import intensity of local manufacturing, with the result that prices rise in response to increased money demand from exports. Government, again, can only respond by a politically unacceptable restrictive monetary policy. It is thus no surprise to find that attempts to raise agricultural production prices in real terms have been almost as frustrated as attempts to change the real exchange rate (see Table 10.2).

What we are analyzing here is, it is important to emphasize, less a failure of economic management and more a recognition of the perception of political risks that accompany economic policies required by orthodox economic management. Given the nature of the political

Table 10.1 Changes in Real Effective Exchange Rates in Sub-Saharan Africa, 1980-1983[a]

Percentage change, 1980-1983	Country
Appreciation	
20 percent and above	Burundi (40), Liberia (27), Mauritania (34), Nigeria (38), Rwanda (41), Sierra Leone (53), Tanzania (77), Chad (22), Ethiopia (20)
0 to 19 percent	Madagascar (15), Zimbabwe (14), Central African Republic (0.4), Congo (7), Niger (2), Somalia (6), Zambia (3).
Depreciation	
0 to -19 percent	Cameroon (-2), The Gambia (-5), Malawi (-1), Mauritius (-6), Senegal (-9), Sudan (-6), Togo (-3), Botswana (-3), Kenya (-11), Mali (-12), Burkina Faso (-14).
-20 percent and below	Benin (-24), Ivory Coast (-20), Zaire (-20), Ghana (-37), Uganda (-78).

Source: World Bank. *Toward Sustained Development in Sub-Saharan Africa: A Joint Program of Action.* Washington, D.C., 1984.

[a]The real effective exchange rate is defined as the import-weighted exchange rate adjusted by the ratio of the domestic consumer price index to the import-weighted combination of consumer price indexes of the trading partners. Figures in parentheses are the percentage changes in real effective exchange rates. Minus signs denote depreciations.

system I have outlined, that perception almost inevitably (and there *are* some exceptions of which Malawi is interestingly and perhaps revealingly the most notable) means that economic orthodoxy is sacrificed for political reality—or perceptions of it—not every time (see Nigeria's courageous monetary policy in 1985/86) but often enough to tilt the system permanently and irresistibly towards disequilibrium.

THE PROBLEM OF MANAGING DISEQUILIBRIUM

If there is, as it were, a permanent tendency towards disequilibrium, two questions become central. First, can disequilibrium be "managed" in a way that does not sacrifice too much growth or equity? That is, if

Table 10.2 Trends in Producer Prices and Yields, 1980–1985

	Nominal producer price change (%)	Real producer price change (%)[a]
Ivory Coast		
Rice	60	22
Maize	0	-26
Nigeria		
Rice	113	-17
Millet	127	-12
Maize	150	-3
Senegal		
Rice	105	17
Kenya		
Maize	94	4
Tanzania		
Maize	420	43
Zambia		
Maize	142	6
Zimbabwe		
Maize	112	3

Source: U.S. Department of Agriculture.

[a] Real price calculated as nominal producer price in local currency, divided by the consumer price index.

we take the political culture as given, what economic devices can be employed to minimize the economic costs of that culture? Second, if we reject the givenness of the political culture, is there evidence that it can change in ways that make financial orthodoxy more attainable? Or is it Africa's grim fate to have to suffer a historical period in which politics and economics are in so fundamental a conflict that unmanageable disequilibrium will be relieved, if that is the word, by periods of extremely high-cost (in social and human terms), externally imposed attempts to achieve equilibrium—attempts that may be successful in the ultra short term but that will collapse in the longer term?

First, then, we need to ask what are the conditions required to enable the disequilibrium system to work without getting so far out of control that adjustment is forced upon the country concerned either by hyperinflation (the power of which to reimpose orthodox discipline is much overrated, as reflection on the historical experience of Brazil and Chile will demonstrate) or a chronic balance of payments deficit that makes frequent and large devaluations inevitable (which is not the same necessarily as the reestablishment of an equilibrial exchange rate: see Brazil and Chile again). In other words, in a suboptimal world and given the fundamental asymmetry mentioned in the last section, what conditions have to be met to allow the political culture of most African countries to coexist with a disequilibrial economic system that will simultaneously avoid the kind of chronic imbalances that usually are associated with both inefficient and inequitable resource allocations in the longer run?

Four features suggest themselves as necessary preconditions of the long-run quasi-stability of the disequilibrium system. The first, and arguably the most important, is the attainment of some level of economic growth that will supply new resources of both foreign exchange and tax revenue to enable the patronage/social control mechanisms to be financed. The critical questions can then be put like this: what is the minimal level of growth that will enable the political culture to survive and operate without implosion or explosion and what is the optimal *nature* of that growth in terms of sectoral distribution, distribution among different social groups and formations, product distribution, and import intensity? Few people, either in traditional policymaking forums or in academia, see those issues as worthy of address because the current assumption is that financial orthodoxy can be reestablished and, having been so, will be maintained in a way that will produce economic growth. And yet I would argue that the notion of a politically critical threshold of growth and an optimal nature or composition of that growth are questions that are central to an approach to the economic development of Africa in the long run.

Let us hypothesize some answers to those two questions. How would we define a critical threshold of growth? It is surely that rate of growth that delivers an adequate increment of resources that will just enable necessary social control and patronage obligations to be met without putting unmanageable strain on political relationships or economic balances. That does not necessarily mean the resources that are necessary to buy off a coup; that is far too crude a formulation. It is rather the increment of resources that enable an operable consensus to be maintained—on, for example, the real distribution of income —which allows the economic and social processes that are defined by that consensus to continue at an acceptable rate. (That formulation neither predicates nor excludes changes of leadership and/or regime, either legitimately or illegitimately.) There are reasons for believing that this threshold level of growth is high and rising. Demographic, military, aspirational, technological, and communications changes that are only very loosely related to conventional economic growth rates have created, and are likely to continue to create, demands upon resources that can only be met, even within disequilibrium, by rates of growth that are considerably higher than sub-Saharan Africa has achieved at any time since the late 1960s. On this account it is no surprise to find that origins of the disequilibrium system can be found in the late 1960s and early 1970s, i.e., *before* the first oil shock, the international recession, and the associated collapse of commodity prices.

This brings us to the heart of the African paradox. Both the disequilibrium system and sustainable financial orthodoxy require higher rates of growth, something of the region of 5-10 percent per year (and the latter requires higher rates than the former almost by definition). Yet, current orthodoxy thinking on "African adjustment" includes no strategy that makes these higher rates of growth attainable. In that sense, and for reasons that we shall come to presently, I believe there is an internal inconsistency of titanic proportions at the heart of current orthodox thinking. Unless much higher rates of growth than are currently considered attainable in Bank/Fund circles are achieved, the political culture will, all things being equal, ensure that the economy slips back to an unmanageable disequilibrium system with all that implies in human, social, and political terms.

A second necessary condition of manageable disequilibrium is that creative use must be made of whatever additional resources are achieved through the higher rates of growth discussed in the preceding paragraph. I use "creative" in two senses. First, the surplus has to be used in a way that acknowledges the realities of the political culture. In other words, it will have to be used in large part for patronage and/or social control purposes. However, what is required within this algorithm is that the surplus be used to rebuild an enlarging consensus rather than to increase the share of those whose support is already assured. This is in fact a very demanding criterion; it requires fine political judgment, the capacity to resist strong pressures from close allies, and the wisdom to use resources deliberately to extend consensus rather than reward the faithful—all conditions inconsistent with the political culture I described in the opening pages.

There is also required, however, an economic creativity. Additional resources have to be used in a way that increases the likelihood of achieving the high rates of growth that I have posited. Again, note the conflicting objectives and the essential paradox. There can be no guarantee that those groups whose consensus has to be assured are those groups that will in fact use additional resources effectively—as the rural credit boom in Zambia 1965-1972 demonstrated so tragically. Nor can there be any guarantee that those from whom resources are removed or to whom resources are denied would not be more economically efficient in using them—see the "kulak" debate in Tanzania in the late 1960s or the history of agricultural marketing in Senegal.

The political/economic trade-off is familiar. All but the most repressive states face it constantly. What is particular in the African context is that with growth so hard to achieve, given the international economic and political environment to which we shall have to revert, the penalties for getting the trade-off wrong are extraordinarily high. At its extreme it means either political breakdown (as in Uganda, Sudan, and Ethiopia—or in a rather different sense, Nigeria), or economic breakdown (as in Zambia). It surely has to be an open question whether the short-run reimposition of financial orthodoxy is capable of managing these trade-offs in a way that optimizes the long-run trajectories of the countries concerned.

The third condition of the disequilibrium system can be mentioned more briefly. By definition, a disequilibrium system implies a more or less chronic imbalance on the internal and external account. That imbalance has to be funded. The funding of the internal deficit has to be achieved in part by real savings or it might quickly become inflationary at a gathering pace, i.e., become unmanageable. That, however, implies substantial retrenchment in public expenditure; or a degree of compulsion; or a rate of interest that is so high that it will drive out of competition for investible resources all but the very highest yielding projects; or, as in Nigeria in 1985/86, a combination of these. None of this is easily compatible with the high rates of economic growth that are required to maintain the disequilibrium system within manageable proportions.

On the foreign exchange side the difficulties are even greater. If the balance of payments deficit is chronic and not merely managed by variants of exchange rationing, the capital account will become even more demanding at a time when the internal disequilibrium represents an increasing threat to those official or commercial investors who might otherwise have funded the balance of payments deficit. This is another reason for believing that for a disequilibrium system to be sustainable, high rates of growth are necessary. High rates of growth generate opportunities that foreign investors, both short- and long-run, will find sufficiently attractive to discount at least a proportion of the risk implied by the internal imbalance.

On this account the management of a permanent disequilibrium system is extraordinarily difficult, as those who have tried it in Latin America could readily attest. Yet I have argued that the realities of African politics make the maintenance of financial orthodoxy no less demanding within the prevailing political culture. Politics makes for disequilibrium. Economics makes disequilibrium difficult to manage, but the management of disequilibrium is made a great deal easier by the attainment of high levels of economic growth.

It will rightly be objected at this point that our analysis is too static.

We need to ask where are the external sources of growth that are capable of lifting African economies on to growth paths that make their own politics less of a threat to that growth.

Orthodox thinking on this (and this may be essentially World Bank thinking) seems to have gone through three phases. The first, much advocated in the 1960s and early 1970s, was that African countries should concentrate on their area of comparative advantage, namely the production of export crops. That was well reflected not only by the pattern of Bank lending in Africa, but also by the policies pursued by many bilateral donors. By roughly the mid-1970s the terms of trade debate and the internal inconsistency of encouraging all developing countries to develop the same rather narrow range of export crops had combined to demonstrate the falsity of that position. It is not, however, dead. Thus, Bank advice to Ivory Coast: "The process of resource allocation should reflect the relative comparative advantage of various crops. Thus cocoa, coffee, rubber and oil palm are Ivory Coast's most attractive development options [sic]."[9]

The next position was to argue that developing countries in general, and African countries in particular, should concentrate on agro-processing. Raising local value added became popular and was again reflected in the pattern of Bank lending exemplified by wood-processing industries in Ghana, textile industries in many cotton growing countries and oil-seed crushing industries for both domestic consumption and export in Nigeria, Senegal, and Ivory Coast. As import substitution this had modest success; indeed in some countries, for example oil seeds in Zambia, it had striking success. But in terms of increasing the value of exports, successes are harder to find, and for two obvious reasons: protectionism in the north (which dealt Ghanaian plywood imports a severe blow) and extreme competition among producers in the south, as palm oil producers can most vividly attest.[10]

We now hear a different strategy. It is beginning to be accepted, it seems, that export-oriented agriculture has irremediable problems associated with it in the absence of a comprehensive solution to the commodity problem—a prospect that seems further from the political realities of the north than at any time since 1970. It is also accepted, it seems, that the rise of the newly industrialized countries has made the entry of the late starters into the export-oriented manufacturing industry dificult to the point of impossible, particularly given the peculiar constraints on exported manufacture from sub-Saharan Africa. The cupboard is beginning to look a little bare. The latest orthodoxy however, is that African growth can be achieved by cooperation in industrialization based on regional markets and the greater range of substitutive possibilities offered by the economies of scale based upon such a market.

If space permitted, it would be an interesting exercise to apply the same kind of analysis of political and social formations in sub-Saharan Africa at the regional level as I have sketched so roughly for national politics. With one exception, the conclusion would, I suggest, be roughly the same: namely, that whatever the economic case that can be made (and it is at least open to question whether it is as strong as some Bank representatives currently suggest) the political realities are that the intensity of competition for scarce resources, which in turn is associated with the political culture I have described, makes it impossible to conceive of regional cooperation in any form with which we are familiar. The exception is the Southern African Development Coordination Conference (SADCC). It is not inconceiveable that under external political threat, the domestic political constraints on regional cooperation may be broken. Certainly that is a view among senior African technocrats. "The South African threat *makes* our politicians take decisions that in other circumstances they would avoid," the chairman of a leading commercial bank in Zimbabwe told me. South African aggression certainly generates a political dynamic that could enable SADCC to survive the kind of tensions that tripped up the East African Common Market and which has so far played a major (though arguably not definitive) role in disabling the Economic Community of West African States (ECOWAS). It is, however, an open question whether the politics of SADCC will hasten regional cooperation in the *manufacturing* industry on a scale that is required to lift the growth rates of the cooperating countries to the levels required. At the moment, the indications are that cooperation on defense, transport, communications, and power will be much easier to achieve. That is not insignificant, but it is nearly irrelevant to the "engine of growth" issue.

It is therefore hard to maintain much optimism that structural adjustment will enable Africa to achieve a rate of growth that, within the existing political culture, enables financial orthodoxy to be sustained. In other words, in the absence of the solution to the commodity problem—whether that solution be found by the international community or imposed spontaneously—rates of growth achievable by African countries are likely to be so low as to make extremely improbable a return to levels of economic growth that make either financial orthodoxy sustainable or disequilibrium manageable.

There is an objection to this line of argument: the process of adjustment itself involves a learning experience for individuals and political systems and therefore changes the pattern of response of those systems to the kind of stimuli that in the past have produced disequilibria. That view must be taken seriously; it is based on the experience of Bank and Fund personnel, negotiating structural adjustment loans in a large number of countries and seeing politicians grasping nettles that for too long have remained either unidentified or ungrasped. One had only to look at the process of negotiation in, for example, Tanzania and Nigeria to see both the resistance of the political system to orthodox conditionality and at the same time the flexibility of the political system to accomodate the political and social shocks associated with reform. Indeed, there is a paradox here. Often, the longer negotiations are delayed and the more public the disagreement between the Bank/Fund team and the host government, the easier it subsequently turns out for the host government to take the unpopular steps being demanded by the Bank and/or Fund. This reinforces the claim of the Bank and Fund that the process of negotiating a structural adjustment loan (SAL) or second tranche Fund loan is itself an educative experience, not only for the politicians and administrators directly involved, but for a wider public, including some of the key interest groups that I identified earlier—a process taken to its logical conclusion in Nigeria. On this account, then, it is argued that conditionality changes political culture.

Much of that line of argument may be admitted without meeting the major source of unease that prompts the writing of this paper. A government may indeed "get away with" a particular set of policy reforms and if it can distance itself significantly from those reforms by the kind of public disagreement and disassociations that the government of Tanzania has developed as an art form, it may be able to get away with them to a greater degree and over a longer period than seemed probable at the start of the negotiations. The significant question so underaddressed in the current literature, is whether the implementation of a given set of policy reforms in the name of structural adjustment actually shifts the political substrata in a way that removes the pressures that hitherto have made the adoption of a disequilibrium system almost unavoidable. On the face of it there seems no reason why this should be so, and the Zambian experience in 1986 suggests that, despite much public discussion and preparation, people's capacity for adjustment is finite: and so is government's.

True, structural adjustment may change income distribution, but whether it will make it more progressive or more regressive is very much an open question depending heavily on what happens to food prices, the supply of wage goods and other tradeables, and the numeric, social, and geographical distribution of food sellers and food purchasers.[11] It may also change the pattern of expectations. Arguably that could have major long-term implications for political behavior and even the way in which power is mediated. That apart, it is hard to see how structural adjustment will change the more fundamental determinants of political culture that I tried to describe earlier in this paper, i.e., social formations, systems of patronage, and systems of social control. It is inadequate in my view to argue that the policy reforms currently in vogue will "persuade" the key political and social actors to change the way in which they use political networks, the demands that they make on those networks, the way in which they protect or reinforce their own positions vis-à-vis critical client groups, or the way in which they defend their own positions when challenged. Notice, for example, the government of Zambia retreated in the face of riots in the Copperbelt in 1986.

The argument that the emergence of a technocratic civil service will insulate the economic system from these pressures seems to me to be wrong both in concept and in fact. It is wrong in concept because it assumes that the civil service in African countries is ontologically separate from the political processes I have described. It is wrong in fact because it assumes that such a technocratic civil service is in being or at least on the horizon. I see little evidence of that. If anything, the limited field research I have been able to do in the preparation of this paper suggests that the civil service is more politicized in the sense of being coopted into the processes of patronage and social control than it was ten years ago. (Nor do I necessarily regard that as a retrograde step.)

If we have to enclose the "learning from experience hypothesis" in quotation marks (which is not the same as rejecting it outright), two other hypotheses could be advanced in favor of the new orthodoxy. The first is that governments and the ruling groups around them will find other forms of social control that will have a reduced tendency to push the economy into a trajectory of disequilibrium. It is hard, however, to think of what other forms of social control are available to African politicians other than repression in one form or another. In the very long term, of course, education and political reculturation may provide other forms than the two rather crude methods currently on offer—repression or various forms of bribery. That is, however, a long way down the track, and most of the structural adjustment policies currently in place put it even farther down the track by limiting access to education.

The most attractive hypothesis—one that is an extension of Bank orthodoxy—is that African countries will experience a sudden burst of economic growth as a result of the economic reforms currently proposed and that the additional resources thus made available will allow a residual form of the politics of control to be practiced that will be neither inflationary nor worrisomely growth inhibitive. Indeed the Bank puts so much emphasis on structural adjustment as the way to resume growth that we have to assume that this hypothesis is to be run in tandem with the learning from experience hypothesis. Does it hold up to critical examination?

There, it seems to me, we stumble across a key inconsistency in the whole Bank strategy. I take it that, however unlikely, it is not inconceivable that sufficiently vigorous devaluation will bring external payments into surplus in an individual African country. There is some evidence that this was achieved in Ghana, at least temporarily. Nor is it inconceivable that, having acquired such an advantage, an individual country is able to use the extra resources in a way that is genuinely growth promotive and therefore makes possible the accomodation of the political pressures I have described. There are a number of reasons for doubting whether reality is quite as simple as that, but let us leave those on one side. The key point is that what is true of one country is not true of all countries. We may well have to enlarge the canvas from sub-Saharan Africa to include competitive producers of exports, e.g., Malaysia and the Philippines for edible oils, the Latin American countries for coffee, India and Bangladesh for tea, Bangladesh and Phillipines for hard fibers, and Brazil for cocoa. Once the canvas is thus enlarged, we see that we are faced with a simple fallacy of composition. Significant devaluations for each of these countries will not produce an improvement in the external terms of trade unless one assumes against all the evidence a highly price-elastic demand for agricultural commodity exports.

The implications are fundamental. If, in a large group of countries, devaluation does not significantly improve the real exchange rate in the longer run, and agricultural prices in real terms do not much improve, it is extremely hard to see what is going to be the engine of growth that will generate rates of economic expansion above the threshold required to accommodate the political pressures that lead to disequilibrium.

It may be argued that declining net barter terms of trade are not decisive if export volumes can be increased.[12] Certainly it is true that African shares in major world markets have been falling, suggesting a problem more located in the supply side than the demand side (see Table 10.3).

The question remains: If devaluation and relative real price changes are frustrated through the failure to reach consensus on income distribution and through political manipulation of key variables that make that consensus unreachable, where will incentives to

Table 10.3 Sub-Saharan African Exports as a Percentage of Total World Exports: Selected Commodities, 1961-1963; 1968-1971; 1980-1982

	1961-1963	1968-1971	1980-1982
Groundnut oil	53.8	57.6	27.8
Groundnuts	85.5	69.1	18.0
Palm oil	55.0	16.4	3.0
Cotton	10.8	15.5	9.2
Tobacco	12.1	8.2	11.8
Cocoa	79.9	75.9	69.3
Coffee	25.6	29.3	25.9
Tea	8.7	14.4	9.3

Source: World Bank: *Toward Sustained Development in Sub-Saharan Africa: A Joint Program of Action.* Washington, D.C., 1984.

increase volume come from?

Two points need to be made. First, as Wheeler has shown, insofar as the inadequacy of African economic performance has stemmed from weak commodity prices, international action to raise those prices in real terms is an essential condition of African recovery.[13] No one country can do it alone; and all developing countries, trying to compensate for weak prices by expanding volumes, cannot do it together.

Second, conflicting and ambiguous as it is, the evidence suggests that price reform alone is not enough.[14] Infrastructural improvement, rural credit, efficient marketing of inputs, outputs, and wage goods (which implies the efficient local manufacture of the latter in adequate quantities) and, in many sub-Saharan countries, a solution to the rural labor shortage are all required.

Yet, such a list is full of political agendas of a startling complexity and scale, for it is a coded demand for a quite different set of political relationships than that which now exists. It means not only that rural groups have to acquire more political clout, but that other (largely middle-income urban or military) groups have to be ready to see that clout used.

There is thus a depressing quasi-parallelism between the commodity issue as normally understood; and the supply-of-commodities issue as sketched here. Both require significant redistributions of political power of which there is not at present, to this observer, any sign whatever. A chronic tendency to economic disequilibrium seems inevitable.

CONCLUSION

It would be in the tradition of the genre to which this paper belongs to conclude by pulling a policy rabbit out of the hat. It is legitimate to ask what may then be done and many will regard it as illegitimate to reply probably nothing. Or maybe nothing else. The scenario I have tried to sketch sees the current phase of policy reform having limited success in restoring or at least moving economies somewhat towards internal and external balance in the short-term. Such movement will not be politically sustainable without substantial further reinforcement. That reinforcement will have to come from further highly conditional tranches of lending and grant aid at a time when short-term loans made available as part of the current round of structural adjustment are being repaid. The search for structural adjustment in the sense of political processes that encourage and enable decisions that favor the reestablishment of equilibrium to be taken is a goal that still looks a long way off.

That is not to deny, however, that some countries will achieve it more quickly than others, just as some with particularly favorable natural endowments, such as Botswana or possibly Ivory Coast, will be able to reestablish growth rates above the threshold that makes the process of accomodation so much easier. Nor is it to deny that some countries that looked very unlikely—perhaps Tanzania and conceivably Zambia—will move more quickly in this direction than countries such as Kenya and Zimbabwe which have been favored by foreign investors in the past. The processes of political maturation and the development of a political culture that can accomodate pressures within manageable economic parameters are both oddly unpredictable and anyway probably unstable—which makes a study of it the more important and the continuing neglect by both economists and political scientists the more regrettable.

NOTES

1. C. P. Kindleberger, "Liberal Policies vs. Controls in the Foreign Trade of Developing Countries," AID Discussion Paper No. 14, Washington, D.C.: Agency for International Development, April 1967.

2. A point much stressed (some would say overstressed) by John Sender and Sheila Smith in *The Development of Capitalism in Africa,* London: Methuen, 1986.

3. Issa Shivji, *Class Struggles in Tanzania,* New York: Monthly Review Press, 1976

4. Relations with international capital are extensively covered in the literature. See M. Blomstrom and B. Hettne, *Development Theory in*

Transition: The Dependency Debate and Beyond, London: Zed, 1984. For the implications of relations with entrepreneurship for the nature of the state, see R. Sklar, *Corporate Power in an African State: The Political Impact of Multinational Mining Companies in Zambia,* Berkeley and Los Angeles: University of California Press, 1975.

5. G. Kitching, *Class and Economic Change in Kenya: The Making of an African Petite Bourgeoisie, 1905-70,* London: Yale University Press, 1986. But note Kitching's terminal date.

6. Colin Leys, "Capital Accumulation, Class Formation and Dependency The Significance of the Kenyan Case," *The Socialist Register 1978,* London, 1979.

7. See R. Sandbrook, *The Politics of Basic Needs: Urban Aspects of Assaulting Poverty in Africa,* London: Heinemann, 1982, esp. chapter 6.

8. Ajit Singh, "The IMF-World Bank Policy Programme in Africa: A Commentary," in Peter Lawrence, ed., *World Recession and the Food Crisis in Africa,* London: James Currey, 1986.

9. World Bank Report No. 6051-IVC:121, quoted in T. Addison and L. Demery, "Poverty Alleviation and Structural Adjustment," Overseas Development Institute, forthcoming. Mimeo.

10. See Addision and Demery, note 9.

11. See Sender and Smith, note 2.

12. See Sender and Smith, note 2.

13. D. Wheeler, "Sources of Stagnation in Sub-Saharan Africa," *World Development* 12:1, January 1984.

14. See M. E. Bond, "Agricultural Responses to Prices in Sub-Saharan African Countries," *IMF Staff Papers* 30:4; and K. M. Cleaver, *The Impact of Price and Exchange Rate Policies on Agriculture in Sub-Saharan Africa,* World Bank, Staff Working Paper 728, 1985.

Index

Achebe, Chinua, 199
Africa, sub-Saharan; agriculture in. *See* Agriculture; aid in vs. South Africa, 137; and balance of payments, 36, 204, 218, 222; bourgeoisie in, 204, 208, 216; colonial bureaucracies in, 191–196; corruption in, 181, 206, 213(n64); coups in, 164; crisis in, 20–24, 91–92, 111(n1), 133–134, 135, 207, 215; debt in, 6, 9, 91, 133, 140, 207; and dependency theory, 167–168; devaluation in, 92, 143, 204, 220, 222, 230; droughts in, 22, 23, 31, 136, 188, 208, 215; educational achievement in, 195–196, 212; entrepreneurs in, 175, 178(n27); environmental protection in, 33–34; exchange rates in, 36, 220, 221(table), 230; exports of, 231(table); and external shocks, 21, 135, 215; famine in, 31, 53, 136; food prices in, 117, 118, 144, 228; food production, per capita, 5, 21, 186; foreign-controlled enterprises in, 208; foreigners in, 201; GDP in, 91, 187(table 9.1); imports of, 219; income, per capita, 21, 133, 186, 194; industrialization in, 34–40, 226–227; labor unrest in, 139; mining in, 21, 37, 116, 208; nationalism in, 185, 196–198; negative growth rates in, 186; overvaluation in, 116, 204; peasantry in, 111, 195, 199, 205, 208; policy reforms in. *See* Reforms, policy; political instability in, 50, 93, 96 (*see also* Disequilibrium, economic, and political processes); population growth in, 23, 91, 135, 188; populations of, 200; protectionism in, 226; public sector in. *See* Public sector; racism in, 195, 196; regional cooperation in, 226–227; repression in, 229; shares in world markets, 230, 231(table); socialism in, 118–119, 165–166, 199, 204; standard of living in, 21; state's role in, 138–139, 168–171 (*see also* Public sector, State(s)); taxation in, 218–219 (*see also* Agriculture, taxation on); trade unions in, 197; transportation in, 22–23, 24; urban elite vs. rural poor in, 115, 205. *See also* *individual countries*
African Development Bank, 44–45, 49, 134
Africa's Priority Program for Economic Recovery, 1986–1990, 134
Agricultural Development Project (Zambia), 79–84
Agriculture; and agribusiness, 208; commercialization of, 105–107, 226 (*see also* Export-oriented strategy); and exchange rates, 215; food vs. export crops, 119; government intervention in, 121–122, 129–130; and grains, 127, 135, 139, 144, 148, 151; and industry, 32–33,

34–35; and local cereals, 144; and peasant farming, 116; policy failure in, 22; and political environment, 31; and price controls, 35, 118–119; and price incentives, 22, 131(n5); and reforms, 91–92 (*see also* Reforms, policy); research in, 31, 33–34, 128; role in development, 97–99 (*see also* Export-oriented strategy); taxation on, 119, 125–127, 146; and World Bank, 30–34, 56, 215 (*see also* World Bank)
AMC. *See* Ethiopia, Agricultural Marketing Cooperation
Amin, Samir, 167
Argentina, 143

Bangladesh, 150
Bank Group. *See* World Bank
Bates, Robert, 205
Belgian Congo, 194, 197
Belgium, 45
Benin, 207, 221(table)
Berg Report, 1, 7–8, 98, 112(n4)
Botswana, 216, 221(table), 232
Brazil, 172, 222
British Colonial Service, 192
British West Africa, 192–193, 194
Buchanan, James, 160, 176(n3)

Caisse Centrale, 44–45
Cameron, David, 201
Canada, 67
Capitalism, 167, 199
Cardoso, F.H., 100
CGIAR. *See* Consultative Group on International Agricultural Research
Chad, 140, 221(table)
Chile, 222
CILSS. *See* Comté Interétats de Lutte Contra la Sécheresse
Civil service. *See* Public sector
Club du Sahel, 141
Coefficient of nominal protection, 119
Colonialism, 99–100, 185, 191–196
Comité Interétats de Lutte Contra la Sécheresse (CILSS), 141
Conable, Barber, 14, 51
Consultative Group on International Agricultural Research (CGIAR), 33–34, 141
Coopération Economique, 44–45
Corruption, 181, 206
Counterpart funds. *See* Food aid, for revenue generation

Dependency theory, 99–101, 108, 112(n5), 167–168, 169
Deuxième Loi Lamine Gueye, 197
Disequilibrium, economic; and deficit funding, 225; and economic growth threshold, 223–224, 225, 227, 232; management of, 221–231; and political processes, 218, 220–221, 222, 224–225, 231; and repression, 229; roots of, 219–220
Dos Santos, T., 100
Drought, 22, 23, 31, 136, 188, 208, 215
Dumont, Rene, 195, 206, 212(n51)

EAC. *See* East African Community
East African Common Market, 227
East African Community (EAC), 58
Economic Community of West African States (ECOWAS), 227
ECOWAS. *See* Economic Community of West African States
EEC. *See* European Economic Community
Egypt, 143, 146, 147, 150
EPADP. *See* Zambia, Eastern Province Agricultural Development Project
ERP. *See* Tanzania, Economic Recovery Program
Ethiopia, 24, 31, 33, 140, 144, 150, 154, 221(table), 225; Agricultural Marketing Cooperation (AMC), 139
European Development Fund, 45
European Economic Commission, 152
European Economic Community (EEC), 5
Export-oriented strategy, 95–96, 98,

226; abuses of, 108; and dependency theory, 99–101; and export promotion view, 101–102; political requirements for, 103–104, 107

Faletto, E., 100
Famine, 31, 53, 136
Financial sector, 39
Food aid, 133–135; and conditionality requirements, 149–150; consumption vs. sale of, 142–143; donors of, 152; emergency, 136, 139–140, 152, 153; growth of, 137–138; increases in, 186; in Kenya, 145; in Mali, 145, 152; negative attitudes toward, 152–153; and nutrition programs, 142, 143; overhead costs of, 150–151, 153–154; vs. policy-based lending, 137, 147–153; as political asset, 147; and the poor, 143–144; and project failure, 141–142; recommended changes, 153–154; for revenue generation, 142–143, 146–147, 153; and subsidies, 141, 148–149; in Tanzania, 152–153; and variable food needs, 151–152; and World Bank, 134; in Zambia, 152
Foreign aid, 6; and aid fatigue, 42; and dependency theory, 167; and donor coordination, 140–141; emergency, 139–140; and European civil servants, 193; growth of, 137–138; and policy reform, 172–173; and technical assistance, 201; and World Bank, 43–46
France, 139, 197
French West Africa, 193, 194, 197, 211(n35)

Gambia, 21, 219, 221(table)
Ghana, 6, 36, 116, 140, 153, 189, 207, 220, 221(table), 226, 230
Gould, Frank, 182
Great Britain, 67, 182, 220
Grenada, 147, 150
Guatemala, 190
Guinea, 36, 94, 139, 140, 149, 165
Gunder, Frank A., 100

Huntington, Samuel, 165
Hyden, Goran, 171

IBRD. *See* International Bank for Reconstruction and Development
ICRISAT. *See* International Crops Research Institute for the Semi-Arid Tropics
IDA. *See* International Development Association
Ideology and Development in Africa (Young), 166
IFC. *See* International Finance Corporation
IMF. *See* International Monetary Fund
Import substitution, 35, 36
India, 29, 129
Industrial Sector Adjustment Operations (ISALs), 38
Inflation, 57, 64, 65, 70, 207, 219, 220, 222
Integrated Rural Development Programme (IRDP), 77, 85
International Bank for Reconstruction and Development (IBRD), 24, 51(n1)
International Crops Research Institute for the Semi-Arid Tropics (ICRISAT), 34
International Development Association (IDA), 24, 46, 47, 49, 51(n1), 73–74, 74(table), 137, 139–140
International Finance Corporation (IFC), 49
International Fund for Agricultural Development, 45
International Labor Organization, 57
International Monetary Fund (IMF), 3, 215, 218; conditionality programs, 6; and export-oriented strategy, 101–102; and Kenya, 28; short-term assistance of, 136–137; stabilization programs of, 27, 29, 54–55; standby arrangements of, 28, 54, 60–61, 67, 68; Structural Adjustment Facility (SAF), 29; and Tanzania, 60–61, 67, 68, 69; and

World Bank, 29, 46, 49–50, 56, 137
IRDP. *See* Integrated Rural Development Programme
ISALs. *See* Industrial Sector Adjustment Operations
Italy, 45
Ivory Coast, 36, 165, 216, 221(table), 222(table), 226, 232

Jackson, Robert, 169–170

Kenya, 232; civil service of, 188–189, 190; and emergency aid, 150; exchange rates in, 221(table); export strategies of, 94; food aid in, 145; market controls in, 129; National Cereals and Produce Board (NCPB), 145; producer prices and yields in, 222(table); SAL programs in, 27–28, 126, 137; and Tanzania, 57, 216; Treasury in, 126; variable food needs of, 129, 151
Kenya Tea Development Authority, 33
Khartoum, 144
Korea, 172

Lagos Plan of Action, 152, 168
Latin America, 99–100, 105, 107, 110, 140, 187(tables), 190, 191(table), 225
Lele, Uma, 57
Liberia, 6, 144, 221(table)

Madagascar, 36, 149, 150, 221(table)
Maize, 144, 146, 149, 222(table)
Malawi, 189, 221, 221(table); SAL programs in, 28, 112(n8)
Mali, 140, 145, 149, 150, 152, 221(table)
Marobouts, 138
Marxists, 160, 169
Mauritius, 36, 140, 221(table)
Mboya, Tom, 197
Mellor, John, 98, 111–112(n3)
MIGA. *See* Multilateral Investment Guarantee Agency
Modernization theory, 161, 163–165, 167

Morocco, 144, 145
Mozambique, 31, 140, 150
Multilateral Investment Guarantee Agency (MIGA), 46, 48–49, 51(n1)

Nationalism, 185, 196–198
Nationalization, 41, 167–168
National liberation movements, 107
NCDP. *See* Zambia, National Commission for Development Planning
NCPB. *See* Kenya, National Cereals and Produce Board
Nellis, John, 189
Neoclassical theory, 105, 161
NESP. *See* Tanzania, National Economic Survival Program
Netherlands, 45, 67
Niemary, 144
Niger, 140, 144, 151, 221(table)
Nigeria, 36, 116, 117–118, 135, 146, 164, 189, 194, 221(table), 222(table), 225, 226, 228
Nkrumah, Kwame, 189, 198
NORAD. *See* Norwegian Overseas Aid
Norwegian Overseas Aid (NORAD), 77–78, 86(n4)
Nyasaland, 194
Nyerere, Julius, 60, 198, 212(n43)

OAU. *See* Organization of African Unity
ODA. *See* Official development assistance
OECD. *See* Organization for Economic Cooperation and Development
Official development assistance (ODA), 133, 137, 213(n54)
Oil exporting countries, 190, 191(table)
Oil price increases, 5, 6, 21, 36, 57, 135
Organization for Economic Cooperation and Development (OECD), 134, 137, 182, 215
Organization of African Unity (OAU), 2, 23, 136, 168

Pacific Basin countries, 102
Paris Consultative Group, 69
Patronage, 199, 217, 219, 223, 224, 229
People's Republic of China, 29
Personal Rule in Black Africa (Rosberg and Jackson), 169–170
Physiocrats, 129, 130
Please, Stanley, 110
Political economy, 129, 160; economistic school of, 162–163; and interest groups, 162; and models of political development, 163–164; and modernization theorists, 161, 163–165; and policy reforms, 161, 165, 173–174, 175
Political origins thesis, 115–116, 117–119, 120, 130–131
Private Provision of Public Services in Developing Countries, The (Roth), 180–181
Privatization, 41, 42, 55, 92, 174, 186, 207–208
"Program of Action for African Recovery and Development 1986–90," 48
Program of Action for African Economic Recovery, 24
Public sector; and bureaucratic politics, 181; costs of, 199–201, 207, 219; and economic development, 181–182, 202–206, 208–209; elite of, 204; employees of, 188–189, 202; expansion of, 198–199, 201, 207; and gross domestic product, 182, 183–184, 187(table 9.3), 188; and ideology, 199; Left vs. Right perceptions of, 206–207; and nationalists, 198; and patronage, 199, 217, 219, 223, 224, 229; personnel salaries and benefits of, 183, 184, 189–190, 190(table), 191 (table), 200, 203–204; vs. private sector, 180–181, 203, 207–209; and public consumption growth, 187 (table 9.2), 188, 189; and upward mobility, 202; in Western capitalist countries, 182–183. *See also* State(s)
Pye, Lucien, 163

Reagan, Ronald, 182
Recession, 5, 7
Reforms, policy, 47, 91–93, 136, 171–172, 175, 232; and agriculture, 91–92, 95–97, 128–129; and alienation of small land holdings, 96–97, 106–107; and communication, 121–123; and cultural factors, 171; and democratization, 174; and dependency theory, 168; and donors, 94, 108–111, 126–128, 145, 175; and economic research, 123; enforcement of, 124; and export-oriented strategy. *See* Export-oriented strategy; and food policies, 117–119, 124–125, 144–145; and food relief, 127–128 (*see also* Food aid); and foreign aid, 172–173; and foreign exchange, 104; and ideology, 166; and patrimonial state, 170 (*see also* Patronage); and peasantry, 111; and political economy, 161, 173–174, 175; political requisites for, 93, 94, 103–104, 110, 122–123, 171, 228–229, 231; and private sector, 174–175; and pro-reform coalitions, 109, 110; in public sector, 40, 41–42 (*see also* Public sector); sustainability of, 144, 173, 174–175; and tax reform, 125–127; and United States, 92; and World Bank, 25, 172, 175–176
Rhodesia, 197
Rice, 144, 149–150, 151, 222(table)
Rosberg, Carl, 169–170
Roth, Gabriel, 180–181
Ruggie, J.R., 101, 102, 103, 105, 107
Rwanda, 147, 150, 221(table)

Sadat, Anwar, 147
SADCC. *See* Southern African Development Coordination Conference
SAF. *See* International Monetary Fund, Structural Adjustment Facility
SALs. *See* Structural adjustment loans
SAP. *See* World Bank, structural adjustment program(s)

240   INDEX

Saudi Fund, 45
SDAP. *See* Zambia, Southern Province Agricultural Development Project
Senegal, 116, 138, 139, 140, 150, 189, 190, 221(table), 222(table), 224, 226
SFA. *See* World Bank, Special Facility for sub-Saharan Africa
SIDA. *See* Swedish International Development Agency
Sierra Leone, 219, 221(table)
Singh, Ajit, 220
Social control, 217, 223, 224, 229
Socialism, 118–119, 165–166, 199, 204
Somaliland, 192–193, 207
South Africa, 197, 227
Southern African Development Coordination Conference (SADCC), 141, 227
SPAAR. *See* Special Program of African Agricultural Research
Special Program of African Agricultural Research (SPAAR), 34
Sri Lanka, 143
State(s), 216; as autonomous, 161, 169, 217–128; and dependency theory, 167; patrimonial, 170, 199; post-colonial, 198–199; private vs. public sectors in, 180–181, 203, 207–209; role of, 168–171; as welfare maximizer, 161. *See also* Public sector
Structural adjustment loans (SALs), 26–30, 55, 106, 112(n7, 8), 149; and agriculture, 56; and food aid, 153; vs. IMF stability programs, 27; in Kenya, 27–28, 126, 137; in Malawi, 28; preconditions for, 29, 56, 109; vs. project and sector loans, 28–29; in Tanzania, 62 (*see also* Tanzania, structural adjustment program in); in Uganda, 126. *See also* World Bank
Sudan, 24, 31, 33, 140, 141, 144, 221(table), 225
Swaziland, 190
Swedish International Development Agency (SIDA), 77–78

T&V. *See* Training and Visit extension
Tanhanyika, 189
Tanzania, 6, 139, 140, 165, 232; balance of payments of, 58–59; Bank of Tanzania, 68; capital flight from, 66–67; cereals board in, 152–153; cooperatives in, 69, 70; crisis in, 56–60; deficits in, 59, 64; devaluation in, 61, 63, 64, 68, 220; Economic Recovery Program (ERP), 68–70; and exchange rate adjustments, 67, 68, 221(table); and external shocks, 57–58; food aid in, 152–153; GDP, per capita, 56; and IMF, 60–61, 67, 69; import structure in, 65–66, 67; income in, 220; industrial sector in, 69–70; inflation in, 57, 64, 65, 70; and Kenya, 57, 216; kulak debate in, 224; National Bank of Commerce, 59; National Economic Survival Program (NESP), 61; overvaluation in, 64–65; parallel market in, 59, 65; parastatal organizations in, 70, 189; and policy lessons, 65–67; policy reforms in, 228; prices in, 65, 66, 70; producer prices and yields in, 222(table); structural adjustment program in, 62, 63–65, 68; and Uganda war, 57, 58, 59, 60; wheat sales of, 149; and World Bank, 61–63, 68, 70
Thatcher, Margaret, 182
Togo, 140, 207, 221(table)
Toure, Sekou, 197
Training and Visit extension (T&V), 33, 79–80, 81(table), 82(table)

Uganda, 31, 33, 57, 126, 189–190, 221(table), 225
UN. *See* United Nations
UNDP. *See* United Nations Development Program
UNIP. *See* United National Independence Party
United Kingdom. *See* Great Britain
United National Independence Party (UNIP), 217

United Nations (UN); Decade for Women, 78; General Assembly, 48, 120; Special Session on Africa, 2, 24, 136, 141; 13th Special Session of, 134
United Nations Development Program (UNDP), 42, 141
United States, 92–93, 172, 220; Commodity Import Program, 146; Food for Progress program, 149; government expenditures, 182–183; government salaries, 189, 211(n25); and Kenya, 145; wheat food aid to Egypt, 146, 147
United States Agency for International Development (USAID), 128
USAID. *See* United States Agency for International Development

Wagner, Adolf, 181, 183
Weidenbaum, Murray, 182
WFP. *See* World Food Program
Wheat, 144, 146, 147, 149, 151
World Bank, 3, 24, 25, 218, 229–230; African Development Fund, 147; and agriculture, 30–34, 56, 215; and aid coordination, 46, 48, 141; and co-financing, 43–46, 48; and devaluation, 143; and environmental protection, 33–34; and export-oriented strategy, 101–102, 226; and food aid, 134; and foreign aid, 43–46; and foreign fund management, 45; and IMF, 29, 46, 49–50, 56, 137; and industrial development, 37–40; and institution building, 40–42; and Ivory Coast, 226; Joint Program of Action for sub-Saharan Africa, 26; and Kenya, 126, 137; lending of, 24–30, 137 (*see also* Structural adjustment loans); and medium-term development, 48; medium-term policy framework papers, 30; and mining, 37; objectives and functions of, 19–20, 51; and policy reforms, 25, 172, 175–176; and private sector, 46; and privatization, 55; and public sector reforms, 41–42; reports on Africa, 1, 7–9, 98, 101, 112(n4); and Senegal, 139; Special Facility for sub-Saharan Africa (SFA), 46, 47; structural adjustment loans. *See* Structural adjustment loans; structural adjustment program(s) (SAP), 62–63; and Tanzania, 61–63, 68, 70; and trade liberalization, 55; and Uganda, 126; and Zambia, 32, 78
World Development Report (1986), 49, 134
World Food Program (WFP), 134, 141, 147, 150
Worldwatch Institute, 23

Young, Crawford, 166

Zaire, 6, 22, 36, 140, 216, 221(table)
Zambia, 6, 36, 232; Agricultural Development Project, 73–74, 78–84; agriculture in, 31–32, 73; Eastern Province Agricultural Development Project (EPADP), 80–82; economic breakdown in, 225, 228; exchange rates in, 221 (table); food aid in, 152; food subsidies in, 138; foreign employees in, 212(n51); hoe cultivators in, 80; and IDA, 73–74, 74(table); and import substitution, 226; Lima project in, 77; National Commission for Development Planning (NCDP), 78; National Development Plans of, 78; parastatal bodies in, 189; political alliances in, 217; polygyny in, 77; producer prices and yields in, 222(table); riots in, 229; rural credit boom in, 224; Southern Province Agricultural Development Project (SPADP), 82–84; T&V extension in, 79–80, 81(table), 82(table), 84–85; women in, 75–78, 81, 83, 84–85, 86(n2)
Zambian Miners Union (ZMU), 217
Zimbabwe, 33, 216, 221(table), 232
ZMU. *See* Zambian Miners Union

About the Book

Among the most prominent of the solutions proposed to counter the economic stagnation and political weaknesses afflicting much of sub-Saharan Africa have been the suggested policies of the World Bank. This book begins with the views of the World Bank on some of the problems facing Africa and some of the options for change. The authors then look at donor policy, describe the challenges facing outside agencies, assess the experiences of particular African countries with World Bank programs and with adjustment policies, and pose some broad political and economic questions that are at risk of being overlooked in the search for immediate cures to Africa's development dilemmas.

The book provides a link between the specific policy questions facing the World Bank and Western donors and the underlying political-economic realities that affect African states and national economies. It raises a difficult and uneasy question: If the approaches of the World Bank are not effective, what alternatives remain?